THE SAHEL FACING THE FUTURE

INCREASING DEPENDENCE OR STRUCTURAL TRANSFORMATION

FUTURES STUDY OF THE SAHEL COUNTRIES 1985-2010

ORGANISATION FOR ECONOMIC CO-OPERATION AND DEVELOPMENT

Pursuant to article 1 of the Convention signed in Paris on 14th December, 1960, and which came into force on 30th September, 1961, the Organisation for Economic Co-operation and Development (OECD) shall promote policies designed:

- to achieve the highest sustainable economic growth and employment and a rising standard of living in Member countries, while maintaining financial stability, and thus to contribute to the development of the world economy;
- to contribute to sound economic expansion in Member as well as non-member countries in the process of economic development; and
- to contribute to the expansion of world trade on a multilateral, non-discriminatory basis in accordance with international obligations.

The original Member countries of the OECD are Austria, Belgium, Canada, Denmark, France, the Federal Republic of Germany, Greece, Iceland, Ireland, Italy, Luxembourg, the Netherlands, Norway, Portugal, Spain, Sweden, Switzerland, Turkey, the United Kingdom and the United States. The following countries acceded subsequently through accession at the dates hereafter: Japan (28th April, 1964), Finland (28th January, 1969), Australia (7th June, 1971) and New Zealand (29th May, 1973).

The Socialist Federal Republic of Yugoslavia takes part in some of the work of the OECD (agreement of 28th October, 1961).

Publié en français sous le titre:
LE SAHEL FACE AUX FUTURS

© OECD, 1988
Application for permission to reproduce or translate all or part of this publication should be made to:
Head of Publications Service, OECD
2, rue André-Pascal, 75775 PARIS CEDEX 16, France.

In political circles in Africa, and more particularly in the Sahel, it is widely recognized that the scope and gravity of today's problems are such that decision-makers are obliged to devote most of their energy to dealing with the present-day situation. Underdevelopment is a permanent crisis, and in most cases it is so serious that medium- and long-term policies are practically impossible to implement. Further, the compromise between short-term interests and the interests of future generations is eminently difficult to reach. It is through these perilous straits that Sahelian leaders are currently navigating the ark of development.

It is of course an extremely arduous task to implement a well structured, durable agricultural policy in the Sahel when there is no way of guaranteeing immediate food security for the region's population. Similarly, galloping desertification is forcing us to take steps to limit the consumption of wood, and yet the widespread use of replacement fuels is still a distant objective.

These contradictions have led to a situation where our partners in the North are launching training, research or investment programs covering several decades, while we in the South have no choice but to concentrate on the day-to-day realities of life.

There was thus a clear need to make a thorough investigation of what the future holds in store for the countries of the Sahel, and it was on this basis that the Futures Study was undertaken. The study in no way claims to have discovered the hidden secrets of the future, but we do consider that a prospective approach - which relies neither on straightforward forecasting nor on futurology - is the only viable scientific basis for taking meaningful action and averting what fatalists might consider inescapable. Whatever criticisms may be leveled at the prospective approach, we consider it a necessity.

The Futures Study reflects an innovative approach to the examination of the Sahelian context: to my knowledge, no other region in the developing world has yet undertaken such a study. And yet there seems no doubt than an investigation of this type was a vital step, since it has enabled us to rise above simple intuition and to come face to face with reasoned scenarios of the region's future.

There is little doubt that we needed to go beyond the intuitive approach. Now, for the first time, a document analyzes our past and present influences and encourages us to come to terms with the harsh realities of the Sahel as it is likely to be tomorrow. Written in a lucid and unsensational style, the report argues that it is unacceptable to continue development along current lines, for this "present-trends scenario" will inevitably involve icnreased food dependence, increased financial dependence and increased cultural dependence. Indeed, it could even be referred to as the "dependen scenario".

What is more alarming still is that even the present-trends scenario will only materialize if the rich countries increase the amount of aid they allocate to the region. Increased aid would simply perpetuate the situation and would not bring about any deep-seated change.

The Futures Study has no intention of offering alternative "off-the-peg" solutions for the countries of the CILSS. Member States will judge for themselves how best to make use of the document. Be that as it may, one thing is eminently clear: the "other future" that we are obliged to aim for now will only become a reality if we brace ourselves for a difficult battle ahead, and if we approach the coming years with pragmatism and lucidity. As history has shown us on so many occasions, radical alternatives are unrealistic. Similarly, neither regional introversion nor wholesale surrender to world-market forces can solve the problems we now face. It seems clear that the only judicious solution is to constantly endeavor to achieve harmony and balance in all our undertakings.

The meeting that brought together Sahelian intellectuals on June 7-9, 1988 to discuss the Futures Study reinforced my conviction that the CILSS and the Club du Sahel took a significant step forward when they decided to encourage this prospective reflection on the region. The meeting provided a forum for frank and open discussion, and despite the differences in option on certain analyses made in the report, participants agreed unanimously that the initiative was well founded and necessary.

Today it is for the leaders of our respective countries to make optimum use of the Futures Study, by setting up working parties - as has already been done in Senegal and Cape Verde - to fine-tune the analyses and produce detailed statistics on a country-by-country basis, and to develop scenarios that rely on the clearly defined, courageous policies that we are now obliged to adopt.

Pay attention to this study. Our future depends on it!

Brah Mahamame
Executive Secretary of CILSS

The aim of the "Futures Study" is to aid all those involved in seeking a development strategy for the Sahel. The study is based on a penetrating analysis of Sahelian history and culture that forms the basis for a number of possible scenarios, all of which are disquieting. This exercise -- hitherto unknown in the Sahel -- will contribute to greater clarity and should inspire the search for innovative solutions.

"The Futures Study" is not an end in itself but rather, we hope, the beginning of a new approach towards development. The study has aroused interest among Sahelian Heads of State and Ministers as well as among the heads of cooperation agencies who met in N'Djamena in January 1988 for the 7th Conference of the Club du Sahel, the conclusions of which are included in the Annex. Meeting in June 1988 at Bobo-Dioulasso at the invitation of the CILSS, a number of leading Sahelian government officials and academics requested that the study be widely disseminated and that each CILSS Member State undertake its own futures study in an effort to guide governments in their choice of strategy.

Senegal has already risen to the challenge: a study into the future of that country is currently under way and is due to be completed at the end of next year. The CILSS and the Club du Sahel have agreed to support each country in its efforts to carry out a futures study. The entire region will therefore be better prepared to meet the challenges of the future.

"The Futures Study" is the result of close cooperation between the CILSS (1) and the Club du Sahel (2), and especially the directors of the two organizations -- Mr. Mahamane Brah, currently Executive Secretary of the CILSS, and Mrs. Anne de Lattre, who founded the Club du Sahel and let it until 1988.

---

(1) Made up of nine Sahelian countries: Burkina Faso, Cape Verde, Chad, The Gambia, Guinea Bissau, Mali, Mauritania, Niger and Senegal.

(2) The Club du Sahel brings together CILSS Member States and OECD countries that play an active part in the development of the region: Austria, Canada, Denmark, France, Italy, Japan, the Netherlands, Switzerland, United States and West Germany. The Club is open to donor countries and aid agencies that wish to support its efforts. The Secretariats of the Club du Sahel and the CILSS work in close cooperation.

To ensure the success of the project, the two Secretariats called on a team of experts from the Sahel, the United States and Europe, headed by Mr. Jacques Giri, who drew up the final version of the study. We extend our thanks to all those who participated in preparing, writing, translating and publishing "The Futures Study" for their exemplary work.

Jean-H. Guilmette
Club du Sahel

FOREWORD

This "Futures Study of the Sahel" has a fairly long history.

The initial phase was conducted in 1985 by a team led by Kimon Valaskakis and including Pathé Diagne, Jacques Giri, Michel Godet and Cheikh Bouh Saad Kamara.

Further to comments made on the work accomplished during this initial phase, a second phase was conducted in 1986, still under the leadership of Kimon Valaskakis and with the assistance of Jacques Giri, Cheikh Bouh Saad Kamara and Alioune Sall.

Finally, in early 1987, Jacques Giri took charge of revising, completing and collating the information that had been gathered, and was assisted in this task by Jacques Lesourne, Jean-Paul L'Allier and Alioune Sall.

A draft version of the Futures Study was reviewed in September 1987 by an informal meeting of Sahelian intellectuals (Marcel Inné, Abdoulaye Moumouni, Moulaye Diallo, Boubakar Barry and Chérif Seye), and was subsequently examined by donor representatives at their meeting in Bern in December 1987.

Throughout its history, the Futures Study has benefited from the criticisms that have been made of it, and this criticism has often been flavored by heated discussion. It is through such passionate criticism that progress is made.

The study has also benefited from consultation of a wide corpus of published information (a bibliography can be found at the end of the report, listing the main works to which reference has been made), and from contributions made by persons that have taken the trouble to write memos and papers specifically for the study (a list of these contributions is given on the following page).

The authors would like to take this opportunity to thank all those contributors who have helped, voluntarily or involuntarily, in the production of this report.

The authors would also like to thank the Secretariat of the CILSS, and in particular Mahamane Brah, and the Secretariat of the Club du Sahel, and in particular Anne de Lattre, for having commissioned this study and for having provided invaluable support in the work that has been carried out to produce it.

MEMBERS OF THE TEAM

The following persons have participated in the production of this report (in alphabetical order):

. Pathé Diagne, lecturer, University of Dakar,
. Jacques Giri, SEED, Paris,
. Michel Godet, lecturer, Conservatoire National des Arts et Métiers, Paris,
. Cheikh Bouh Saad Kamara, lecturer, Ecole Nationale d'Administration, Nouakchott,
. Jean-Paul L'Allier, Jean-Paul L'Allier and Associates, Québec,
. Jacque Lesourne, lecturer, Conservatoire National des Arts et Métiers, Paris,
. Alioune Sall, PRODEST, Dakar,
. Kimon Valaskakis, President, Institut GAMMA; lecturer, University of Montreal.

The following persons contributed specific reports: Paris Arnopoulos (Institut GAMMA), Robert Desbiens (CILSS), Iris Fitzpatrick (Institut GAMMA), Jean-Jacques Gabas (Club du Sahel), Scott Gardiner (Institut GAMMA), Patrick Healey (Institut GAMMA), Mamadou Diallo (Paris), Michel Matly (SEED) and Pierre Pradervand (Geneva).

Finally, the authors would like to thank the Canadian International Development Agency, which provided most of the funding for the study, and successive representatives of that organization at the Club du Sahel -- Yves Garneau and Jean Nadeau -- who provided constant support to the teams of "futures studiers" during periods of difficulty.

To our knowledge, no study of the possible futures open to a region of the Third World had been carried out before. The present report, therefore, is in a way the result of a pioneering approach, and those who have been involved in this trail-blazing would use this innovative aspect to explain (not to justify) the gaps and errors that the reader will undoubtedly identify.

The authors hope that other parties will further the consideration that is given to the future of the Sahel, and they of course hope that the present document, however incomplete it might be, will be of use to the Sahelians and to those who wish to help them.

Jacques Giri

CONTENTS

INTRODUCTION 19

    The aims of the futures study 19
    Methodology 20
    The approach adopted 22
    Scope of the study 24

PART I

RETROSPECTIVE VIEW OF THE SAHEL: FROM ANCIENT EMPIRES TO THE PRESENT CRISIS

INTRODUCTION TO THE RETROSPECTIVE VIEW 29

Chapter 1.   THE SAHEL FROM IMPERIAL TIMES TO
                THE EVE OF COLONIZATION 31

    Fragmentation of the power base 31
    Highly structured societies 32
    Rural societies 33
    The role of foreign trade 35
    The slow and difficult advance of Islam 35
    19th century attempts to restore extensive power bases 36

Chapter 2.   THE COLONIAL PERIOD 39

    Development of potential 39
    The slow development of food production 40
    Urban growth and incipient industrialization 41
    The destructuring of traditional societies 42
    The emergence of new values 43
    The birth of a new political class 44

Chapter 3.   POPULATION TRENDS SINCE 1960 47

    Population growth 47
    Geographic distribution 48
    Urbanization 49

Chapter 4.   THE DEVELOPMENT OF AGRICULTURE SINCE 1960   51

    Climate   51
    The rise in food dependence   52
    Export crops: cotton   54
    Export crops: groundnuts   55
    Livestock activities   56
    Fisheries   58

Chapter 5.   THE DISRUPTION OF THE ECOLOGICAL BALANCE   59

    Production systems and the environment   59
    The advance of the desert   60
    Desertification from within   60

Chapter 6.   INDUSTRY, SERVICES AND THE INFORMAL SECTOR   63

    The trends in manufacturing industries   63
    Obstacles to industrialization   64
    Energy   66
    The mining industry   67
    Services and the informal sector   68
    Secondary and tertiary sectors overall   69

Chapter 7.   OVERALL ECONOMIC TRENDS   71

    The public sector   71
    The contradictions of the economy   72
    International aid   73
    External indebtedness   74
    Structural adjustment   76
    An increasingly dependent economy   76
    A disjointed economy   78

Chapter 8.   THE DESTRUCTURING OF RURAL SOCIETY   81

    Permanent features of Sahelian societies   81
    The end of isolation   81
    Rethinking the distribution of roles   82
    Questioning the natural order of things   83
    The feeling of alienation   83
    Introversion or flight   84
    The emergence of new dynamism   85

Chapter 9.   THE INCREASED IMPORTANCE OF URBAN SOCIETY 87

    An increasingly autonomous society 87
    A society of young people 88
    The role of women 89
    The quest for survival 89

Chapter 10.   DEVELOPMENTS IN THE POWER BASE 91

    From colonization to independence 91
    From independence to the present day 92
    The priorities of those in power 93
    Ambitious leaders 95
    Calls for unanimity and power in a vacuum 95
    Recent development 97

Chapter 11.   CONCLUSION: SOCIETIES IN CRISIS 99

PART II

THE TREND SCENARIO:
ECONOMIC STAGNATION AND INCREASING DEPENDENCE

INTRODUCTION TO THE TREND SCENARIO 107

Chapter 12.   THE EVOLUTION OF SOCIETY AS A PRODUCT OF TENSIONS 109

    What is new about the Sahel crisis? 109
    What elements make up the Sahelian crisis? 110
    The interplay of internal tensions 111
    Structural analysis of the Sahelian system 112
    General outline of the approach adopted
        for the Futures Study 115
    The driving variables 117
    Constructing the trend scenario 119

Chapter 13.   THE SAHELIAN ENVIRONMENT: TOMORROW'S CLIMATE 121

    Recent climatic trends in a long-term perspective 121
    Tomorrow's climate 123
    Will climate play a decisive role in the Sahel? 124

Chapter 14.   THE SAHELIAN ENVIRONMENT: TOMORROW'S WORLD   127

　　The Sahel's position in worldwide geopolitical
　　　　and geo-economic interplay   127
　　External financing   130
　　The impact of technologies   131
　　The immediate environment:
　　　　the Arab world and the humid zone   133

Chapter 15.   VALUES AND MENTALITIES:
　　　　　　 SAHELIAN CULTURE IN THE FUTURE   137

　　A set of hypotheses   137
　　What are the consequences for the Sahel?   140
　　Development will be turbulent   141

Chapter 16.   THE FUTURE SHAPE OF POWER   143

　　Variation N°1 on the trend scenario: regimes that are
　　　　neither wholly military nor wholly civilian   143
　　Variation N°2 on the trend scenario:
　　　　"South-Americanization"   145
　　Contrasting scenarios   145
　　The rise of local power: rural power groups   147
　　The rise of local power: urban power groups   148
　　Turbulent development?   149

Chapter 17.   POPULATION   151

　　Fertility   151
　　Mortality   153
　　Emigration to non-Sahelian countries   154
　　The population of 2010   155
　　Urbanization   157

Chapter 18.   THE RURAL WORLD TOMORROW   161

　　World trends in agriculture   161
　　The Sahel in the world context   163
　　Technical progress and Sahelian agriculture   164
　　The future role of biotechnology   166
　　The trend scenario for food crops   168
　　The trend scenario for export agriculture   170
　　The trend scenario for livestock production   171
　　Ecological disaster or the beginnings of recovery?   173
　　The trend scenario in rural areas: change and continuity   174

Chapter 19.   THE INDUSTRIES OF THE FUTURE   175

    Principal worldwide industrial trends   175
    Sahelian industry within that context   177
    The informal sector   180

Chapter 20.   THE TREND SCENARIO: COHERENT,
               PROBABLE AND LEADING TO TENSION   183

    A ccherent scenario   183
    A probable scenario   186
    A scenario of accumulating tensions   187
    Limited adaptation that does not solve fundamental problems ..   188

Chapter 21.   LESS FAVORABLE SCENARIOS   191

    The accentuated-drought scenario   191
    The Aids-explosion scenario   192
    The reduced foreign aid scenario   193
    Scenarios that bring into question
        the current role of the state   193

Chapter 22.   CONCLUSION: IS THE PRESENT
               TRENDS SCENARIO ACCEPTABLE?   195

    Increased restrictions   195
    A difficult future   196
    Which way out?   197

PART III

LOOKING AT POSSIBILITIES FOR THE FUTURE

INTRODUCTION TO POSSIBILITIES FOR THE FUTURE   201

Chapter 23.   POSSIBLE SCENARIOS   203

    Auto-centered development scenarios   203
    Scenarios based on integration in the world market system   206
    Mixed scenarios   208
    Can these scenarios materialize?   209

Chapter 24. THE ROLE OF THE GOVERNMENT AND THE NON-
GOVERNMENTAL SECTOR IN BUILDING A BETTER FUTURE 211

    A new balance between the government
        and the non-governmental sector 211
    Local communities in rural areas 213
    Communities in urban areas 215
    The role of the State 215

Chapter 25. PREREQUISITES FOR ROLE CHANGES 219

    Awareness of the implications 219
    Democratization and national consensus 221

Chapter 26. ROLE CHANGES AND POLICY CHANGES 223

    The rural framework 223
    The urban framework 225
    Food policies 227
    The relationships between Sahelian markets
        and international markets 229

Chapter 27. FOREIGN AID 233

    Official development assistance 233
    Private aid 236

Chapter 28. PREPARING THE FUTURE FOR THE NEXT GENERATION 239

    The formal education system 239
    The informal education system 240
    Population policy 242

FINAL CONCLUSIONS

Chapter 29. CONDITIONS FOR FINDING A WAY OUT OF
THE TREND SCENARIO 245

    Where is the way out? 245
    The actors and the system 246
    Topics for consideration by donors 248
    Topics for consideration by Sahelien elites 249
    Topics for consideration by Western countries
        and by the Sahelian elites 250
    Topics for consideration by NGOs 251
    Conclusion: no magic formula,
        but enough hope to mobilize efforts 252

ANNEXES

1. Summary of Proceedings of the 7th Club du Sahel Meeting, held at N'Djamena, 26-27 January, 1988 257
2. Regional Meeting of Experts from CILSS Member Countries on the Futures Study, Bobo-Dioulasso, 7-9 June, 1988 259
3. Bibliography 263

One day Naré Maghan visited the blacksmith-diviner Noun Fairi, an old blind man. The diviner received the king in the vestibule that served as his workshop. To the king's question, he replied:

"When the seed germinates, growth is not always easy. Great trees grow slowly, but they drive their roots deep into the ground".

Replied the king, "But has the seed germinated?"

And the diviner said, 'I am sure the tree is not growing as fast as you would like. Ah! How impatient man can be!"

> Djibril Tamsir Niane
> (Sounciata)

INTRODUCTION TO THE FUTURES STUDY ON THE SAHEL

The aims of the futures study

The drought that hit the Sahelian countries of West Africa from the beginning of the 1970s and that led to the dramatic situations of which we are all aware, also gave rise to extensive consideration of the region's situation and of its medium- and long-term future.

In 1974 and 1975, several institutions began to examine the Sahel and assess the situation there, and made proposals for actions that could be undertaken for the region to become less vulnerable to climatic fluctuations, less dependent on foreign aid, and more able to emerge from underdevelopment.

After the Sahelians set up the Permanent Interstate Committee for Drought Control in the Sahel (CILSS - Comité Inter-Etats de Lutte contre la Sécheresse dans le Sahel), the international community created the Club du Sahel in 1976 to provide an opportunity for a further and more in-depth look at a number of topics which are crucial for the future of the region, including cereals policies, irrigation development and deforestation. The Club du Sahel also provided an opportunity for adopting a "drought-control and development strategy in the Sahel" that would be approved by Sahelian governments and by the principal donor agencies, and that would be conceived, in principle, to guide their activities.

Despite the consideration and discussion, despite significant increases in international official development assistance, despite an increasing number of positive initiatives taken by NGOs, and despite the efforts of the Sahelians themselves, the situation in the region has scarcely improved. A report submitted in 1983 to the 5th Conference of the Club du Sahel in Brussels concluded that none of the major unfavorable tendencies that had been identified in the development of the countries of the Sahel had yet improved. More recent work pointed to the stagnation -- or even negative growth -- that Sahelian economies were experiencing, and to the continuing deterioration of the environment, which is becoming increasingly worrisome for the future. Problems that were unknown or latent ten years ago have now taken on significant proportions: growing external indebtedness, financial imbalance that calls for "structural adjustments", etc.

Sahelian governments are very well aware of these trends. The CILSS Heads of State, meeting in Dakar in January 1986, reiterated their determination to reverse the unfavorable trends and launched an appeal to the international community to provide increased support for their efforts.

Donors have started to ask themselves questions as to the effectiveness of their actions, and the Secretariats of the Club du Sahel and the CILSS were asked at the Club du Sahel Conferences of 1983 (Brussels) and 1985 (Milan) to continue to consider the problems of the Sahel and to reflect upon which specific strategies to adopt. Recommendations were made for this consideration to form part of a "more global, more forward-looking and more cohesive strategic framework".

The present study is an attempt to answer the questions that governments and donors have been asking themselves in an attempt to act more effectively. In particular, the study attempts to respond to a specific wish that has been expressed: to provide a <u>more global, more forward-looking and more cohesive strategic framework.</u>

The study is an attempt to examine in greater depth and in a more systematic manner than before the mechanisms that have brought about the current situation, to look at the futures that are really feasible for the region over a longer period than is generally considered (the timeframe selected is twenty-five years) and to examine the conditions under which a future that is acceptable to the Sahelians could materialize.

Methodology

What methods are available today in the 1980s to meaningfully explore the futures that are really possible?

Since the beginning of time, men have attempted to probe the future or to sketch out the kind of future they would like to move towards. But since the end of the Second World War, reflection on the future has moved into a different phase and people have felt more and more obliged to come to terms with their destiny. A new type of reflection has been born -- pragmatic reflection -- which is intended to help in making crucial decisions for a largely uncertain future. It is with problems of this type that the Sahelians and those that seek to help them are faced today.

We will not give an exhaustive description here of the methods that have been devised for conducting forward-looking reflection as defined above, and readers wishing further details on methodology should refer to the publications quoted in the bibliography. We will limit ourselves here to giving a few indications of what the future is and of how it can be examined, starting by listing the basic principles that the majority of practitioners of this type of prospective reflection accept today:

-- The future is not a predestined reality that can be examined scientifically. It is the result of human actions;

-- Since the future is shaped by human beings and is not fixed by deterministic factors, it is open to discussion and could take on a variety of forms;

-- If exploration of the future is to be of use in the decision-making process, it must be extensive and farsighted, because the speed of change is increasing in all fields. The Sahel is affected by this accelerating rate of change, even if these changes are not in line with the wishes of those involved;

-- Exploration of the future must rely on scientifically developed analytical methods that take into account the specific features of what is being analyzed: a complex reality that is being conditioned by human choices and that is changing rapidly.

While a consensus on the main principles exists, various schools of thought have developed, and the views they express sometimes differ considerably. Different schools of thought conceive the future of human societies from widely differing standpoints, and it is relevant to our reflection on the Sahel to list these various standpoints:

-- From the economic standpoint, analysis is made first and foremost of macro-economic factors, and of the micro-economic decisions made by actors in the economy, without examining the socio-cultural changes that might or might not be taking place. Almost all studies made since 1974 of the long-term future of the Sahel have been made from the economic standpoint, for example the study of the future of agriculture carried out in 1976 by the FAO, or the study made by the Sahel Institute and the Economic Commission of Africa in 1983;

From a more cultural standpoint, examination is based on a belief that ideas are what makes the world change, and that the changes that are under way or that will come in the future are the result of a profound change in systems of values. To our knowledge, only very partial studies have adopted this approach to examination of the future of the Sahel;

- From a technological standpoint, emphasis is placed on the inevitable consequences of technological change on human societies. This approach could be summarized by the epithet: your society will be as advanced as your technology;

From a more sociological standpoint, the underlying belief is that technology explains nothing about society, but that on the contrary, technology is dependent on social structures. This approach could be summarized by a variant of the epithet given above: your technology will be as advanced as your society.

The distinction could also be drawn between a "school of optimists", which considers that changes that are under way in the world provide an opportunity for mankind to make further progress, and that the sections of human societies that are currently not involved in that progress -- as is the case in the Sahel -- will ultimately join the mainstream and take advantage of these changes; and a "school of pessimists," which tends to think that the future is threatened by serious catastrophes and that decision-makers in the South as well as those in the North have crucial choices to make.

All those who have examined the future of the Sahel have been affected by the different approaches to prospective reflection, and by the different attitudes to the future that underlie those approaches. The persons who were directly or indirectly involved in the present study were understandably no exception.

The approach adopted

In view of these different approaches to prospective reflection and the different attitudes to the future, what stance were we to take in examining the specific case of the Sahel?

-- The point of departure was that <u>the future of the region will basically be what those involved there make of it.</u> Those involved include, first and foremost, the Sahelians, of course, but also the men and women from countries of the North who are in contact with the Sahelians. This does not mean that other factors -- the climate, for example -- will not play a role, but the reactions that we have to the events that occur will be of crucial importance.

-- A second key factor in this reflection was the belief that <u>not all futures are possible.</u> The Sahel in 1987 is what it is, with its land resources, its material resources, and above all its human resources. The adults that will play an active role in the coming quarter-century have already been born, many of them have already received the basic education that makes them what they are, and those who will educate those who are not yet educated are already there.

Before embarking on the prospective reflection as such, it was thus indispensable not only to take stock of the available resources, but also and above all to understand the mechanisms that already exist and that make Sahelian societies what they are today. These mechanisms will not cease to function overnight and must be understood more fully before one can hope to adjust the way they function in an effort to alter the course of the future.

-- Since the study was to cover a whole group of societies, it was essential to <u>take into account the complexity of those societies,</u> and it was thus impossible to limit the study to the economic aspects of the life of these societies. Moreover, too many purely economic and financial remedies have been prescribed in the past by the practitioners that have sought to cure the region's ills, and in view of the poor results achieved, it would not have been credible for the present study to adopt the same approach.

The study thus attempted to go deeper into the matter and to identify the social, political and cultural factors that underlie economic variables, even if by so doing we ventured into areas that are less familiar or even virtually unexplored and highly controversial.

-- Since the futures study involves societies that have not yet taken advantage of the full panoply of techniques that are available, and where the productivity of labor is still very low, it seemed appropriate to adopt a theory whereby social or cultural factors are creating obstacles to the adoption of the most efficient techniques. To summarize this approach, we can say that although the majority of the Sahelians have abandoned the use of the swing plow, which has been known for five thousand years in the Mediterranean basin, it is far from certain that tomorrow's advanced techniques will automatically be adopted with enthusiasm in the Sahel, or that these techniques would provide miracle solutions to the situation in the region.

Although certain members of the team responsible for the study had a different conception, <u>the final report took the stance that the technologies that will effectively be used tomorrow will depend on the state of advancement of the society.</u>

The structure of the report that follows is thus based on these few principles and on the desire to present a complex analysis in the clearest possible way.

<u>Part I is a retrospective view of the Sahel,</u> aiming to highlight not only the major trends that can be identified in the region, but also, as we said above, the mechanisms that have brought on these trends. In doing this, we have attempted to delve deep into the past of the region, beginning our study several centuries ago and giving a brief description of what the Sahel was like before the colonial period. This historical examination is of use in that contemporary Sahelian societies are still rooted in a distant past. We have also attempted to consider economic variables, social structures, values and power bases. This retrospective view highlights a number of trends in the development of the region, many of which are already well known and which everybody agrees are worrisome for the future. Part I also points to the factors that are ultimately likely to change that development.

<u>Part II concentrates on the trend scenario.</u> This scenario is not simply an extrapolation of the trends that have already been identified -- everybody is well aware that the trends that seem the most established always change in the end -- but rather a scenario built on the hypothesis that the mechanisms that currently exist in the Sahel will continue to operate, yet the factors of change that have been identified will not come into play during the period under consideration.

If this hypothesis is correct, the major trends that have been identified will change, but in a direction that is highly unlikely to be judged favorable by the Sahelians or by those that seek to help them. However, that does not mean that the trend scenario is improbable or unlikely to materialize. On the contrary, we will demonstrate that the trend scenario is quite feasible, at least for a certain length of time, which is difficult to estimate, but which will lead more or less inevitably to dramatic crises. We will also demonstrate that the trend scenario is not the worst scenario imaginable.

Having established that the trend scenario is unacceptable in the final analysis, <u>Part III attempts to examine the other scenarios that would be possible,</u> and that would be more acceptable to the Sahelians, in view of the inevitable restrictions for the region and the factors of change that were identified in the retrospective view given in Part I. Part III relies on the principles laid down above in an attempt to make an extensive and farsighted examination, taking into account the fact that the conditions needed for change to take place will not necessarily be present during the next quarter-century, but that this period should be used to create those conditions and to prepare the way for later periods.

No attempt is made to propose a normative scenario that would describe a future that is deemed desirable for the region. The members of the team that have carried out this study did not consider themselves qualified to make such normative proposals. They have limited themselves to trying to shed light on the stumbling blocks that will be encountered by the Sahelians and to attempting to point to ways of avoiding them.

The conclusion to this report thus attempts to identify what have been called the conditions for leaving the trend scenario: what actions can be taken that would lead the Sahel away from this scenario towards another scenario that might be deemed more desirable by those concerned? The study has not come down in favor of any of these more desirable scenarios.

Scope of the study

In view of the objectives that have been set, one initial question must be asked: given the diversity of the Sahel, and in particular the diversity of the communities living in the region, whose political, social and cultural histories have been very different, and who live in different environments, is it reasonable to conduct a futures study of the entire region? Would it not be more meaningful to make a study of the futures open to each of these communities?

For the purposes of this study, we have considered that despite their diversity, seven of the nine CILSS countries (Burkina Faso, Chad, the Gambia, Mali, Mauritania, Niger and Senegal) form a relatively homogeneous unit:

-- Geographically: these countries form the interface between the desert and the tropical rainforest belt of Africa;

-- Historically: the main lines of these countries' pre-colonial, colonial and post-colonial history are relatively similar;

-- Culturally: common cultural traits are found in most of the communities of these countries.

By contrast, the Republic of Cape Verde differs from CILSS members from mainland Sahelian Africa in terms of geography (they are arid, volcanic islands), and in terms of history (the islands were settled by uprooted slaves and Portuguese colonials, and in this respect have more in common with the West Indies than with the Sahel). Finally, decolonization reached Cape Verde rather later (1975) than other Sahelian countries.

In early 1986, when the futures study was already well under way, Guinea-Bissau joined the CILSS. Guinea-Bissau is undoubtedly closer to the other countries of the Sahel -- or at least culturally closer to areas like the Gambia and Casamance -- than the Cape Verde islands. But the country also has very specific characteristics due to its history.

The study thus deals essentially with seven countries of the Sahelian mainland listed above. It gives little coverage to the Cape Verde islands, whose problems are markedly different, and little coverage to Guinea-Bissau, although we have tried to include this country whenever information was available.

Be that as it may, the present study seeks to deal with the Sahel as a region, and it is hoped that the framework it provides can be used for other, more specific futures studies on a given country, or even on a fully homogeneous province. Even if specific studies are not undertaken, the conclusions of this report should be examined in the light of the specific characteristics of each country or province.

PART I

RETROSPECTIVE VIEW OF THE SAHEL:
FROM ANCIENT EMPIRES TO THE PRESENT CRISIS

> Histories run parallel
> but at different speeds.
>
> F. Braudel

INTRODUCTION TO THE RETROSPECTIVE VIEW

The Sahel today is the product of a long and complex historical past, from a complex pastiche of pre-colonial civilizations, through sixty-odd years of colonization (slightly more in Senegal and Gambia) to a quarter-century of independence, when the new States have emerged.

This retrospective view will only refer to those aspects of ancient Sahelian society which have survived to the present day and that are important because they help to explain the present situation and will continue to influence the Sahel's development in the future. The more recent past will also be examined to highlight the mechanisms behind the main trends that have marked this period and that are liable to continue to play a role for some time to come.

Emphasis is also placed on the invaluable contribution of Africans and non-Africans whose work over the last twenty or thirty years has led to a better understanding of pre-colonial Sahelian history and has helped dispel the belief, widespread in colonial times, that Sahelian societies were static. However, it is also stressed that vast areas of the region's past still remain shrouded in mystery and that a great deal still remains to be done to examine comprehensively the history, economic development, social structures, attitudes and means of interaction of different sectors of society.

It should be remembered that most of the basic statistics referring to the last thirty years have particularly large margins of error. Basic population figures, production levels, etc. and even statistics that might be thought accurate, such as the foreign debt figures, should be treated with caution. Nevertheless, cross-checking what available data there is can give a fairly accurate idea of what type of major trends exist, provided estimates of scale are treated with care. Particular caution must be exercised when growth rates (positive or negative) are involved.

Chapter 1

THE SAHEL FROM IMPERIAL TIMES TO THE EVE OF COLONIZATION

Fragmentation of the power base

Without going into too much detail here, it should be remembered that until the late 16th century, the West African Sahel witnessed the rise and fall of powerful empires such as Ghana, Mali and Songhai. These empires united a varying number of kingdoms and at the zenith of their power they stretched from the Atlantic to the Aïr Massif in northern Niger.

In the Central African Sahel, empires were built during the same period: the Kanem empire, and, later, the Bornu empire. These empires were never able to extend their rule over the entire region because some smaller kingdoms managed to resist all attempts at integration made by successive emperors. This is the case of the Mossi kingdoms in what is now Burkina Faso, and of Hausaland, which straddles Niger and Nigeria.

The end of the 16th century marked a turning point in the Sahel's history, with the fall of the Songhai and Bornu empires. No other empire has ever risen again to reunite vast regions of the Sahel under a single authority. The days of the great empires are now no more than a memory.

The former empires disintegrated into large numbers of small kingdoms, or even chieftaincies covering only a handful of villages. Conflict was commonplace between rival powers even under the empires, when the central authority was weak, and war became even more common when the empires finally collapsed, and became almost endemic in certain areas. In these areas, herdsmen and farmers fell prey to a belligerent aristocracy seeking food, cattle and slaves, and insecurity became virtually a way of life.

In a few areas, however, a strong or particularly well structured power base succeeded in maintaining security for varying lengths of time, and in the Mossi kingdoms, for example, lengthy periods of peace were not unknown.

Highly structured societies

Sahelian societies are not static, and since they are scattered over a wide geographic area, differences clearly exist. However, it is possible to identify a few common characteristics that have remained relatively constant throughout the Sahel for several centuries:

- A rigid social structure, comprising nobles, freemen and slaves whose status is fixed from the cradle to the grave. Each family had its place in society and social interaction was strictly codified;
- An equally rigid socio-professional category structure: one was born a farmer, herdsman, blacksmith, fisherman, griot, etc. with no possibility of changing categories;
- Organization based on age groups, within which values such as solidarity and emulation were taught, and which have always played an important role in social and economic life.

In this way, <u>each individual was assigned a well defined place in society</u> by virtue of his lineage and date of birth.

The kinship group united under a single authority all the members of the family as well as the slaves that the family owned and their offspring. The family unit was the basic economic unit of Sahelian society and handled the production of goods, the primary division of labor between men and women, young and old, freemen and slaves. It also undertook the equitable distribution of consumer goods between the working population and the aged who were too old to work, and the children who were not old enough.

Aside from its economic role, the kinship group was the guardian of cultural and spiritual values. Before Islam and Christianity spread into Sahelian societies, the kinship group was sacred, and each family had its family shrine. The hierarchical nature of the kinship group, with its corresponding rights and obligations, reinforced the sacred aspect of the family community. As a general rule, power, responsibility and material privileges decreased the lower one was in the hierarchy, while the obedience and respect demanded grew.

The second level of society was the village community, which comprised several kinship groups that did not necessarily belong to the same ethnic group or culture. However, given that they lived together and exchanged their products, <u>Sahelian societies were pluralistic.</u> The village community played a vital role in economic and social life. Labor underwent further subdivisions within this unit and certain tasks were performed collectively by the entire village or by certain kinship groups.

Village society was <u>both community-oriented and highly restrictive.</u>

- It was community-oriented because decisions were only taken after general consultation (under the palaver tree) during which each member of the community had his say. The elders, however, and especially those from dominant families, usually played a key role in the decision-making process. Village society was a gerontocracy;

-- It was restrictive because the individual could but belong to the group, and had no status outside it. In extreme cases, these societies could even be described as totalitarian. Counterbalancing the restrictions, each member was guaranteed material and moral security, and since each member of the society had integrated the values of his society, the society was not seen as restrictive.

Although they played a key role in production, slaves, who were by definition captured from other ethnic groups, were denied a social identity. Even if they were not mistreated, they were denied a place in the social fabric, and had no chance of ever gaining one. Among the nomadic societies, the clan played roughly the same role as the village in sedentary societies.

Above the village level came various authorities -- chieftaincies, city-states, kingdoms and empires according to time and place. These powers were rarely very strong and traditional rules limited their scope for action in any case.

These authorities brought few advantages to the villages, which were largely self-sufficient. They obtained their revenues not from the villages in their jurisdiction, which usually paid few taxes, but from levies on trade -- especially trans-Saharan trade and trade with the Europeans -- or from plundering neighboring kingdoms. Part of this wealth was redistributed, but aside from this redistribution, the ruling classes were never considered to play a significant role in Sahelian societies, although they were purportedly responsible for maintaining security (but were not always particularly effective).

<u>These societies were open to change,</u> and, while certain social groups had little conception of time other than the cycle of seasons, many did not see history as an immutable cycle, but as the result of constantly changing forces. Each class took its place in the succession of generations and had its specific characteristics. In certain societies, a rite of passage was even celebrated every fifty or sixty years to mark the birth of a new society requiring new values and laws.

Rural societies

The population of the Sahel was relatively small, and was very unevenly distributed geographically. It probably never numbered more than 10 million overall, except perhaps for certain limited periods. The vastly higher figures given by some historians do not tie in with the known facts on population distribution. The middle Niger valley was probably heavily populated, especially at the time of the Songhai empire, but vast uninhabited spaces separated the various kingdoms.

Although a few large towns did exist, Sahelian societies were basically rural.

Agriculture was extensive. Crops were rainfed and production relied solely on human labor. Land lay fallow for long periods to regain fertility. Transhumant livestock activities were practiced over vast areas. This type of production system clearly depended on the availability of virtually unlimited space and was well adapted to the region. Rural Sahelians -- especially the privileged slave-owning minority -- had a great deal of leisure which enabled them to develop a rich social life.

Examples of intensive irrigated agriculture were exceptional. Flood-plain agriculture was practiced in the great river basins and a small amount of irrigated agriculture was introduced. However, compled irrigation schemes were never developed in the Sahel since a strong central authority (as existed very early in Middle Eastern civilizations) would have been required both to set up such schemes and to manage them effectively.

Although productivity was low, the system did generate a surplus that supported a small but not insignificant class of non-food-producers (warriors, oulémas, itinerant traders) and certain categories of craftsmen and griots who worked part time in agriculture.

The production system was very vulnerable to climatic uncertainties, and, although each village could fall back on its own due to strictly regulated food stocks when harvests were poor, prolonged droughts sometimes posed severe problems. Indeed, the devastating famines of the 17th and 18th centuries are still recalled in oral traditions and chronicles.

Agriculture and herding were largely separate activities, and the insecurity that reigned after the collapse of the empires probably consolidated that separation by concentrating herds in the hands of the warriors. Small-scale, non-industrial activities were diversified and highly developed. The bulk of agricultural and small-scale non-industrial production was consumed in the village, but there was room for brisk local and regional trade insofar as the lack of security permitted.

Production methods have remained largely unchanged in rural areas of the Sahel -- to such an extent that the scenes described by 11th century Arab explorers are still common today. However, it should again be stressed that rural Sahelian societies were not impervious to change. As we have seen, society was open to cultural change. And it was also open to technical change, and accepted certain innovations, such as the new varieties of rice that arrived from Asia, and entirely unknown crops such as groundnuts and maize from America.

On the other hand, moves towards intensive agriculture, involving animal-drawn techniques, for example, were rejected because vast open spaces were readily available. In general, innovations requiring a longer production cycle and the accumulation of capital were not accepted. The society did not accumulate capital, except in the form of slaves and livestock.

The role of foreign trade

Trans-Saharan trade probably dates back to before the 10th century, and started with exports of gold and slaves from the Sahel in exchange for salt and crafts from North Africa. The political significance of this trade far outweighed its economic importance since it led to the founding of the powerful trading cities of Koumbi Saleh, Walata, Mali, Gao, Timbuktu, etc. The power of the great empires stemmed from this trade and the sovereigns derived most of their revenues from duties imposed on imports and exports. Trans-Saharan trade also had an important cultural impact on the Sahel, since the caravans spread new ideas, and particularly Islam.

North African merchants had exclusive control over this lucrative trade, thereby preventing the formation of a powerful Sahelian business elite. Local traders only controlled regional trade, which was less profitable.

The Portuguese reached the West African coast in the mid-15th century, but the impact of European trade was insignificant until the beginning of the 17th century, because the Portuguese stayed in the coastal areas. New trading channels for gold and slaves were opened up, but they were probably less important than trans-Saharan channels.

The situation did not change until Portugal lost its monopoly on trade with Africa in the 17th century when other European powers arrived. The situation really only changed in the 18th century, when the Atlantic slave trade reached large proportions.

Slavehunting, which was already practiced by the belligerent aristocracy in the preceding centuries, intensified at this time and increased the insecurity of the region, contributed to the spread of anarchy and to the deterioration of the social fabric. The aristocracy no longer played the role of protector that it was meant to play. Nevertheless, certain areas remained relatively untouched by this slave trade.

There was a backlash to the quest for slaves: the War of Marabouts in Mauritania (17th century) and the Torodo revolution in the Senegal river valley (18th century), which were conducted in the name of Islam but whose underlying motivation was, at least in part, to replace the traditional aristocracy, who had allied itself with the slave-traders with a new authority that would be able to resist the temptation of the slave trade and re-establish security.

The slow and difficult advance of Islam

Islam probably gained a foothold in Ghana and Kanem as early as the 11th century, but for a long period only affected the belligerent aristocracy and itinerant merchants, who were intended to transmit the new religion. Until the 19th century, the bulk of rural Sahelians remained faithful to their own traditional animist beliefs.

The spread of Islam seems to have met with stiff resistance. This is understandable, in that Sahelian cultures had major differences from the Middle Eastern cultures that cradled the Islamic faith:

-- Monotheism was omnipresent in the Sahel, but existed alongside a desire to accommodate the forces of nature and their ancestors, who were thought to watch over the living. Such beliefs are incompatible with orthodox Islam;

-- Sahelian societies have retained a strong matrilineal element, whereas in Mediterranean societies the patrilineal element is dominant. Consequently, Sahelian women often had a higher status than their sisters north of the Sahara.

These differences explain why Islam -- and particularly orthodox Islam -- was slow to penetrate the Sahel. <u>Indeed, the history of Sahelian societies could be described as a struggle between orthodox and an African strain of Islam.</u> (In the early days of the Songhai empire, a striking example of this struggle is provided by the replacement of the Sonni dynasty by the Askya dynasty, which was more faithful to Islam). Arabic never became the <u>lingua franca</u> in the Sahel. For centuries, Islam has even been totally rejected by several ethnic groups such as the Bambara, Mossi and Serer. Some of these tribes even used their traditional religions as the ideological basis for their opposition to the powerful empires.

Conversely, Sahelian societies used Islam as the ideological basis of revolutions aiming to revive a strong centralized power in their disintegrating social fabric. This was the case with the backlash to slave-trading that was mentioned above, and with most of the attempts to revive extensive power bases in the 19th century, which will now be discussed.

19th century attempts to restore extensive power bases

The Atlantic slave trade was abolished in the early 19th century, and foreign trade, which had been largely based on slaves until then, was obliged to adapt. After the abolition of the slave-trade, trade with Europe expanded rapidly, based initially on gum arabic, and from 1850 onwards, on groundnuts, which had begun to be grown as an export crop in Senegal, the Gambia and what is now Guinea-Bissau. Trans-Saharan trade in slaves continued and new goods such as hides and ostrich feathers contributed to the expansion of these trading channels. The 19th century <u>marked the opening up of the Sahel to the outside world and the development of foreign trade.</u> However, vast regions still remained isolated and unaffected by this movement.

This was also a period of political change, and <u>several attempts to re-establish powerful empires</u> were made: the Peul empire of Sokoto, the Macina empire, the El Hadj Omar Tall and the successive Samori empires, and the Rabah empire in Central Africa. These attempts unleashed innumerable wars and insecurity in the region did not diminish. Slave raids were a permanent threat. Certain of these empires were remarkably well organized and were founded by eminent politicians, but they were all short-lived, either because they collapsed spontaneously or because they did not survive colonization.

Until 1885, colonization made little headway except in Senegal and the Gambia.

The situation changed in the last quarter of the 19th century when a crisis, due in part to temporary conditions, slowed trade with Europe. The Europeans feared that the fragmentation of political power and the climate of insecurity would be an obstacle to growth in trade with Africa, and particularly with the Sahel, which they believed to be heavily populated, rich in natural resources and with fantastic potential both as a source of raw materials and as a market for their industrial products. The determination to overcome obstacles to trade, combined with rivalry between the European powers, was one of the main causes of the wave of colonization that swept the region at the end of the century. By 1900, colonization was virtually complete.

What is the legacy of the Sahel's pre-colonial past?

-- The Sahelian States are not part of this legacy, because of the discontinuity between colonization and the emergence of the modern nation States. However, it should be pointed out that <u>the Sahel has never experienced strong States capable of administering land resources or organizing complex water supply systems.</u>

-- On the other hand, <u>the values and the organization of the family and the village,</u> which were highly structured, hierarchical and restrictive, have largely survived to the present day.

-- The extensive production system, <u>which was well suited to unlimited space availability,</u> has remained remarkably intact, and certain aspects have remained as they were at least ten centuries ago.

Chapter 2

THE COLONIAL PERIOD

"Development of potential"

The immediate aim of the colonizers was to "develop the potential" of a region, i.e. to develop exportable production by introducing either industrial crops or by applying the traditional agricultural system to the production of new crops. These aims generally ended in failure. The numerous attempts to grow industrial crops did not succeed: the Compagnie Cotonnière du Niger in Diré and the Compagnie Générale des Oléagineux Tropicaux in Casamance are just two examples.

Local farmers, who were little motivated by the profits they could make from such enterprises, did little or nothing to develop export crops. The colonial administration tried to exert pressure on them, either by imposing taxes in money or by resorting to physical force. The farmers reacted by adopting a passive non-cooperation strategy. Some fled far and wide to set up new villages, while others migrated, particularly to the Gold Coast. Those who stayed behind resorted to passive resistance.

There were two exceptions, however, to this general failure:

-- Groundnuts in Senegal and the Gambia (and later in Mali and Niger, but on a far smaller scale): local farmers helped by a large number of seasonal migrant workers (navétanes) found favorable conditions and developed groundnuts without any administrative pressure. However, groundnut production expanded irregularly. Whenever the prices offered by trading companies were deemed too low, the farmers reduced their deliveries drastically. Farmers withheld their produce and, if prices still did not rise, reduced the areas under cultivation.

Groundnut exports (Senegal, Mali, Niger)
(thousands of tons, unshelled)

1895	1913	1937	1947	1956
52	242	793	380	679

Farmers continued to use the traditional, inefficient methods for the cultivation of groundnuts. However, the comparative advantage Senegal and the Gambia enjoyed was great enough to give their farmers a comfortable income and to generate substantial profits for the trading companies. Elsewhere, farmers were not offered attractive prices because of high transportation costs, and groundnut cultivation developed little or not at all despite the efforts of the colonial administration.

-- **Cotton production in Chad,** which only developed under strong administrative pressure. Elsewhere, most attempts to grow cotton on a large scale as a rainfed crop (or irrigated crop in the Niger river valley) ended in failure. Only low-yield varieties were available, the fiber produced was of mediocre quality, and incomes from cotton production were unattractive.

Cotton Exports
(in thousands of tons of fiber)

	1939	1958
West Africa	4	5
Chad	3	15

Wherever export crops developed, the methods used were extensive and little was done to intensify traditional farming techniques. The development of these crops did not lead to a genuine development of agriculture, and often had a negative impact on the fertility of the soil. In certain provinces of the Sahel, the approach adopted was particularly destructive, and, rather than making an effort to maintain fertility, farmers moved elsewhere as soon as the land became exhausted.

The slow development of food production

The colonial administration wanted to raise productivity in food-crop cultivation in order to further mobilize the labor force to develop the potential of the region. However, traditional agriculture and livestock activities changed very little. Many attempts were made to introduce animal-drawn farming techniques, irrigation and ranching schemes, but met with little success. Moreover, agronomic research into food crops was neglected.

The colonial authorities finally shifted their interest away from food production because it seemed too difficult to introduce changes to the production system. Further, with the exception of a few periods of crisis (the droughts of 1914, 1933, etc), the Sahelians managed to feed themselves without too much trouble.

Overall, <u>the Sahel was self-sufficient.</u> Only Senegal and the Gambia imported rice, but their groundnut exports generated enough foreign exchange to pay for the imports and specialization thus proved worthwhile in the end.

It should be stressed that the <u>Sahelian population was still small and only really started to grow after the Second World War.</u> There were perhaps only 10 million inhabitants at the turn of the century and not until the middle of the century did this figure exceed 15 million.

There was still enough room for the extensive production system, and the cities were still medium-sized. The agricultural system could and did generate a small surplus that satisfied the needs of the urban population groups.

<u>Nevertheless, today's problems were already latent during the colonial period.</u> The production system did not become any more intensive to cope with the growing population and the environment began to suffer from the effects of export crop cultivation and population growth. The groundnut basin of Senegal and the Mossi plateau began to experience soil erosion and depletion.

By the late 1950s, the colonial administration was well aware of the menace hanging over the Sahel, and a 1957 report concluded that it was <u>"imperative to transform rural communities completely."</u> At independence, however, no transformation had yet taken place.

Urban growth and incipient industrialization

In the early days of the colonial period, the Sahel was still a largely rural society and the trading cities of the mid-Niger valley were probably smaller than they were a few centuries earlier.

Urbanization started again during the colonial period, but, with the exception of Dakar, Sahelian cities remained relatively small throughout this period. In 1960, the urban population of the Sahel stood at no more than 1.3 million (7 per cent of the total population). Senegal alone accounted for over half this figure. Mauritania still had no cities with more than 10 000 inhabitants. Again with the exception of Dakar, Sahelian cities had virtually no industries, and served instead as administrative and commercial centers.

Industry was only developed on a significant scale in the Cap-Vert peninsula, where groundnut processing facilities, textile mills, cement works and a few mechanical industries were set up. Senegalese industries supplied the whole of French West Africa with manufactured goods and served as a link between industries in metropolitan France and the colonies.

Systematic exploration of the subsoil was undertaken but for a long time produced disappointing results. Not until independence did large-scale mines open in the Sahel (Miferma in Mauritania and Taiba in Senegal).

The destructuring of traditional societies

Colonization led to the disruption of certain features of Sahelian societies. The traditional hierarchies lost most of their power to the colonials, and at the same time lost some of the prestige they had won through wars and slaves.

A small section of the aristocracy did accept to relay colonial power and Governor General Van Vollenhoven wrote in 1917 that the local chief was merely "an agent of colonial power". Even when the traditional aristocracy was willing to play this subordinate role, however, it had reservations about becoming fully integrated in the system and often refused to send its children to schools run by the colonials. Thus, towards the end of colonial period, the colonial administration increasingly chose local chiefs from other classes that were supposedly more docile.

The abolition of slavery, which effectively took place in certain areas, but was more theoretical in others, profoundly modified the economic balance of Sahelian societies where slaves accounted for a large proportion of the labor force.

Once security was finally re-established, the Sahelians' desire to avoid colonial restrictions -- taxes, obligatory government service (corvée), military service -- led to the creation of smaller, scattered villages and temporary or permanent migration to the coast (Côte d'Ivoire, Gold Coast). The dispersal of villages, together with the beginning of the use of money in the rural economy (cash was needed to pay taxes), resulted in the partial disintegration of the traditional patriarchal kinship group, which tended to split up into smaller units. Money, hitherto unimportant in Sahelian societies, took on a new role and began to have an effect on traditional values.

Although loyalty to kinship groups and villages was never really abandoned, and while a truly individualistic philosophy never developed, the traditional patriarchal family structure was no longer always the most suitable unit of production because of changing socio-economic conditions. Smaller units such as single-family households started to play a more important role and increasingly began to live materially and psychologically for themselves. Some of them even moved out of the family concession, thus effectively escaping ancestral influence.

In most other respects, however, traditional rural societies remained largely untouched by colonization. The colonial school system made no impact on traditional rural societies, since no more than 10 per cent of the population went to school in 1960. This figure was far lower in rural areas and virtually no girls attended school at all. Only in one part of Senegal did schools really have an effect on the population.

In addition, the colonial administration lacked resources and the administrator was a remote figure. For example, there was only one colonial civil servant to every 66 000 inhabitants in Upper Volta during the 1920s. Moreover, there were virtually no means of communication, so villages remained isolated, far from the mainstream of "civilizing influences".

Alongside traditional society, a new urban society was emerging, that was completely divorced from its rural roots.

<u>The schools set up by the colonial administration produced a new social class of ancillary workers</u> such as interpreters, clerks, teachers, nurses, post-office employees etc. This class was relatively privileged, but was often rejected by the population and treated with fear and envy.

A class of technicians -- mechanics and various other technical workers -- was another product of the colonial school system. These technicians did not belong to the traditional castes of craftsmen and there was no continuity between pre-colonial Sahelian techniques and the new techniques introduced by the Europeans.

Small-scale traders played a role in this new society. But large-scale businesses were monopolized by colonial companies and Syrian and Lebanese newcomers. The colonial era was thus no more favorable to the emergence of a local business class than earlier periods had been.

Emphasis should be laid on the extent to which the <u>colonial school system</u> -- however poorly developed it might have been -- <u>was a destructuring influence. Divisions arose between rural population groups and the new class of city-dwellers, rifts appeared between the older generation and the younger generation, to whom knowledge was no longer passed down,</u> and schooling in the colonial system tended to lead to assimilation of European culture.

The emergence of new values

Sahelian societies sought moral and cultural refuge to resist penetration by the colonial powers. <u>Islam</u> was one of these refuges, and the Islamic faith <u>spread at an unprecedented rate</u> despite (or because of) opposition from the colonial administration. There were three aspects to the spread of Islam: <u>geographic expansion,</u> advancing even into regions such as the Mossi kingdoms, which had hitherto rejected the faith; secondly <u>it reached all levels of society,</u> reaching all social classes, rural population groups as well as city-dwellers, and converting men as well as women; and <u>it had a deep-seated effect,</u> as is illustrated by the increase in the number of Koranic schools and Medersas, pilgrimages to Mecca and the creation of Islamic brotherhoods.

Initially, Islam was the ideological force behind armed resistance to colonization, and provided moral guidance to movements of revolt. When resistance was finally crushed, Islam compromised, and acted as a screen to protect the local population groups, and Muslim religious leaders -- particularly the brotherhoods -- acted as intermediaries between the local population and the colonial powers.

It is probably significant that the brotherhoods developed particularly in Senegal, where colonization had started earlier and whose economy was more outward-oriented because of the importance of groundnuts. The Mouride brotherhood, the most important of these brotherhoods, was founded in Senegal in 1890. In exchange for total submission to its "marabout", members of the Mouride brotherhood were guaranteed moral guidance and material support from the social group. The Mourides were instrumental in the development of groundnut cultivation. Other brotherhoods such as the Tidiana played a similarly important role in colonial Senegal.

Christian religions, which were so far practiced by a tiny minority of the population, also started to expand considerably despite the stigma of being linked to the colonizers. Christianity spread mostly into Burkina Faso, southern Chad and a few Senegalese provinces, which had all resisted the advance of Islam and whose past had been punctuated by Muslim raids.

The birth of a new political class

Until the Second World War, there was very little political activity in the Sahel, and the situation only started to change during the post-war period.

Trade unions developed as the new urban classes grew. The first major demonstration of the power of the unions was the five-month strike by Senegalese and Malian railroad workers in 1947. From then on, the colonial administration had to treat unions as a force to be reckoned with.

Moreover, there were increasing demands for self-government and even full independence. The colonizers felt that change was imminent and recognized the need to establish dialogue with the Sahelian educated elite. In the French territories, legislation passed in 1956 (called the Loi-cadre) was a critical milestone in the colonial regime and paved the way for independence.

Throughout the colonial period, a new political class drawn from the civil service and trade unions was taking shape and growing, ready to assume power after the European colonizers had left. This class had been educated in colonial schools and was usually heavily influenced by Western culture.

Colonization caused <u>several major breaks</u> with the past:

-- The aristocracy was stripped of its power by colonial governments who created an entirely new State that was an extension of the State of the colonial rulers.

-- Rapid population growth began after the Second World War.

-- A new urban society emerged, heavily influenced by the colonial school system, and from within that urban society emerged a new political class.

-- Sahelian economies increasingly opened up to international markets.

At the same time, <u>many features of traditional Sahelian societies persisted:</u>

-- While rural societies started to become destructured as a result of the sudden changes, the hierarchical social structures and values were relatively unaffected.

-- The production system did not undergo radical changes. Population growth and the stagnation of the production system disrupted the ecological balance, and, although the signs were not yet fully apparent, the trend had begun and was worrisome for the future.

Chapter 3

POPULATION TRENDS SINCE 1960

Population growth

The population of the Sahel started to grow after the Second World War, and this growth is now exponential. Accurate figures for population size or growth rates do not exist. The statistics that are available do, however, give an approximate picture. Bearing in mind that the figures given for mortality, birth and fertility rates are based on estimates and are not the result of scientific observations, it can be said that the population of the Sahel has doubled in twenty-five years:

    1960   :   18 million
    1985   :   36 million

The population has doubled because:

-- The mortality rate, while remaining high (particularly the infant mortality rate), appears to have declined slowly over the last few decades, although certain observers speak of a counter-offensive over the last few years;

-- The fertility rate has remained high and is perhaps tending to rise. In any case, with the sole exception of certain groups of nomadic pastoralists, it has not declined even in urban areas. Overall fertility rates in the Sahel are among the highest in the world.

One can therefore conclude that population growth is tending to accelerate and had showed no sign of stabilizing by 1985. There are two exceptions to this general rule:

-- Burkina Faso, which has experienced lower growth rates than other Sahelian countries (1.7 per year compared to an average of 2.8 per cent). However, this is entirely due to heavy emigration to coastal countries, particularly to Côte d'Ivoire.

-- The Cape Verde islands, where growth rates seem to have fallen sharply since 1960, owing to high emigration as well as lower fertility. Because of the high population density per unit of cultivable land, the situation in Cape Verde is very different from that in the mainland Sahelian countries.

No governments have yet implemented birth-control policies and the overwhelming majority of Sahelians remain strongly "populationist":

-- The average number of children that each woman wants to have is still very high. According to a 1977 United Nations survey, the figure was 8.9 per woman in Senegal.

-- Most leaders feel that the Sahel is still underpopulated.

Factors that regulate fertility rates and, in ancient times that ensured that generations replaced themselves at the same time as making it possible to "export" people across the Sahara and across the Atlantic while making up for losses due to internal strife, have not yet changed despite the end of exports of people and the reduction in the mortality rate.

Geographic distribution

The population of the Sahel is very unevenly distributed across the region. Population density is a function of average rainfall: from almost zero in the desert, population density increases to the south, and reaches its maximum level in the areas with rainfall of 350-800 mm, decreasing substantially in those parts of the region with the highest rainfall. Southwestern Burkina Faso is less populated than the Mossi plateau, although it has higher rainfall. Similarly, Southeastern Senegal is much less densely populated than the Senegalese groundnut basin.

This uneven distribution is a result of the following factors:

-- Health reasons: onchocerciacis prevented settlement in the Volta valleys;

-- Historical reasons: most of the areas with low population density are the areas where insecurity was rife in pre-colonial times, while areas with the highest population density generally correspond to the centers of well structured ancient empires.

Like earlier periods, the last quarter-century has been marked by internal migration, which is now tending to overcome this uneven distribution. Nevertheless, the distribution is still highly uneven, and a century later, the legacy of the region's pre-colonial past is still far from being effaced. There is a clear tendency in West Africa as a whole for population groups to move towards the high-rainfall coastal areas (Côte d'Ivoire, Ghana, Nigeria), which is an extension in time of a tendency that was already observed during the colonial period. In the areas of the Sahel with the least rainfall, the number of inhabitants is increasing more slowly than elsewhere, and migration is occurring towards the cities, towards the countries with higher rainfall and towards rural areas of the Sahel further south.

Urbanization

<u>Cities have grown 2.5 times faster than the overall population:</u> by close to 7 per cent per year, compared with 2.8 per cent per year for the population as a whole. The urban population has increased from 1.3 million in 1960 to 7 million in 1985.

These figures are estimates, and the margin of uncertainty is high. The countries that were least urbanized in 1960, and particularly Mauritania, have experienced the most pronounced urban growth, and have more or less caught up with the other countries. Senegal is still the most heavily urbanized country in the Sahel, as it was at the end of the colonial era: some 40 per cent of the Senegalese population lives in urban areas.

The causes of this urban growth are natural expansion (the fertility rate is practically as high in the cities as in rural areas) and the rural exodus, which in turn is the result of:

-- <u>Economic factors, which are nevertheless not always decisive:</u> many city-dwellers are in pseudo-employment and have very low incomes, and there is probably a greater proportion of undernourished individuals in the cities than in rural areas.

Nevertheless, drought has destabilized the rural population and has drawn it to the cities for economic reasons. Rural inhabitants, considering that their chances of survival were too low, and realizing that their harvests and stocks were insufficient or even non-existent, or that their livestock had perished, thought they would have a better chance of survival in the cities. After the drought, a proportion of these migrants never moved back to the rural areas. In certain regions, deterioration of land resources also encouraged a proportion of the population to move to the city to assure the incomes that agriculture could no longer provide.

-- <u>Non-economic reasons, which on many occasions have been more decisive factors:</u>

a) a more attractive socio-cultural environment;

b) better health and hygiene conditions;

c) the possibility of providing a better education for children and increasing their chances of moving up in society;

d) <u>fewer social restrictions,</u> which are particularly prevalent in traditional rural society, but which are relaxed in the cities (although solidarity still exists, and is a guarantee of survival).

<u>The urbanization of the Sahel is a largely autonomous phenomenon,</u> and has taken place independently of economic change.

The Sahelian population and the geographic distribution of that population have followed the trends that began during the colonial period. These trends are now accelerating enormously.

<u>The demography of the Sahel changed more between 1960 and 1985 than at any other time in its recent history; the population has doubled, and the urban population has increased by a factor of more than five.</u>

Chapter 4

THE DEVELOPMENT OF AGRICULTURE SINCE 1960

Climate

Since the climate is reputed to play an important role in the development of the region, it would be useful to begin our retrospective examination of Sahelian agriculture by giving an overview of how the climate has changed over recent years. Until at least 1965, and in most areas until 1967, rainfall was good in the Sahel, as it was in the 1950s. Average rainfall was higher in those years than the average since the start of the century.

Since 1968, the region has been experiencing a dry period, which can be summarized as follows:

-- General reduction in rainfall levels since 1968;

-- Two consecutive years that were extremely dry: 1972 and 1973;

-- Irregular rainfall since 1974, certain years with almost normal rainfall (although there have been virtually no years with normal rainfall throughout the region) interspersed with drier years: overall rainfall has been below average;

-- Two consecutive very bad years: 1983, which was worse than 1972 (except in Niger) and which witnessed very poor rainfall in areas further south, where rainfall is generally abundant, and 1984, which was a very bad year throughout the Sahel, although rainfall was somewhat better in the areas further south;

-- Two years in which rainfall has been good overall: 1985 and 1986.

The fact that drought has not only hit the Sahel but has also affected regions with higher average rainfall, and in particular the Fouta Djalon massif in Guinea, has considerably reduced the flow of the major rivers that cross the Sahel: the Senegal and the Niger. Compared with the past dry periods for which figures are available, the recent period can be termed a severe, prolonged drought, but it is not certain whether the recent drought is exceptional, nor whether it indicates that a major climatic change has taken place.

Did 1985 and 1986 mark the end of the drought and the return of a more normal period, even if rainfall has not been abundant? There is no way of knowing. We will return to these two questions in Part II.

The rise in food dependence

It is difficult to evaluate Sahelian food production figures accurately enough to identify reliable trends over the past twenty-five years, given the inadequacies of the statistics services. The only way to assess trends in the food production system is to refer to foreign trade statistics. These figures are a little more precise, although they are not particularly reliable either. For instance, very little is known about trade with coastal countries, although specific studies have shown that it is far from negligible.

The breakdown of annual cereals imports in tons (commercial imports plus food aid) is as follows:

```
. Early 1960s              approx.     200 000
. Average 1970-1971                    540 000
. 1974 (acute drought in 1973)       1 060 000
. Average 1975-1976                    660 000
. Average 1977-78-79                   800 000
. 1982                               1 180 000
. 1983                               1 230 000
. 1984 (acute drought in 1983)       1 730 000
. 1985 (acute drought in 1984)       1 640 000
. 1986                                 925 000
```

Rice and wheat account for the bulk of imports, and urban consumers are increasing their demand for these cereals. Farmers nonetheless continue to grow traditional cereals -- millet and sorghum -- and produce very little rice and practically no wheat.

These figures demonstrate two trends:

-- <u>The region's vulnerability to climatic variations:</u> pronounced drought leads to soaring cereals imports, which nevertheless fail to prevent shortages and even famine;

- <u>Rising food dependence:</u> irrespective of drought-related factors, imports have risen by around 8 per cent per year over the last twenty-five years.

Furthermore, <u>food aid accounts for an increasingly significant proportion of total imports.</u> Unknown before 1970, deliveries stood at:

— 100 000 tons in 1970;

— 750 000 tons after the severe drought of 1973.

Food aid imports declined thereafter but since 1981, they have exceeded 400 000 tons per year and have reached record levels recently:

— More than 870 000 tons in 1984;

— Nearly 1 000 000 tons in 1985;

— Around 340 000 tons in 1986.

It can thus be concluded that:

— <u>Food production</u> is not keeping pace with the expanding population and <u>at best matches rural population growth;</u>

— Production is not meeting the needs of city-dwellers, with their growing demand for rice and wheat;

- Sahelian governments no longer have the foreign exchange to pay for the imports needed to meet these needs.

This trend in food production is largely due to the persistence of the traditional extensive farming system, with its heavy dependence on rainfed agriculture and human labor. Seed selection, the use of fertilizers, etc. are rare and the productivity of farmers is stagnating.

More intensive farming methods remain the exception in rainfed agriculture. Irrigated agriculture continues to play a very minor role in the Sahel, accounting for less than 5 per cent of cereals consumption. These crops have developed little in twenty-five years and their yield is often poor.

City-dwellers (and even certain rural population groups producing export crops) are increasing their consumption of imported wheat and rice, which can be bought more cheaply than locally produced cereals. Although the last two seasons (1985 and 1986) produced millet and sorghum surpluses in several countries, those surpluses could not be moved on the markets in the cities because city-dwellers preferred imported wheat and rice, which was considerably cheaper. It is for this reason that food dependence has only partially declined.

> The overall Sahelian food production system has generally remained very traditional, very vulnerable to drought, and inefficient. It has adapted neither in terms of quantity nor in terms of quality to the needs of a population that has doubled in size, and still less to an urban population whose numbers have more than quintupled.
>
> The region is becoming increasingly dependent on external sources and particularly on food aid. The recent return of favorable climatic conditions has not overcome this dependence.

Export crops: cotton

Cotton production has risen spectacularly since 1960.

(in thousands of tons of fiber)

	61-62	71-72	78-79	79-80	80-81	81-82	82-83	83-84	84-85	85-86
B. Faso	0.8	10.4	22.3	28.7	23.3	21.6	28.8	30.1	34.4	45.8
Chad	17.2	41	50.6	33.1	31.2	26.2	38.1	59.9	35.5	38.5
Mali	2.1	25.3	46.4	52.9	38.1	36.4	47.6	52.2	53.4	67.2
Niger	0.8	3.1	1.5	1.2	1.1	0.7	0.8	1.4	1	1
Senegal	-	7.7	12.7	9.7	7.2	15.3	18.4	11.7	18.9	10.9
TOTAL :	21	87.5	133.5	125.5	101	100	134	155.5	143	163.5

Until 1978-1979, production grew by over 11 per cent per year. This performance was achieved by a spectacular increase in yield achieved through modernization of cropping methods, the use of new varieties, fertilizers, pesticides and the introduction of animal-drawn farming techniques:

61 kg of fiber per hectare in 1961-62
303 kg of fiber per hectare in 1979-80

Meanwhile, the land under cultivation remained constant at approximately 500 000 hectares throughout the 1970s.

Since 1979, growth has been irregular and considerably slower, averaging less than 3 per cent per year. Yield has continued to rise and stood at 380 kg per hectare in 1985-1986, but two factors are holding back production:

-- The war in Chad, where land under cotton production has decreased since the end of the 1970s;

-- The rejection of cotton in certain regions due to competition from cereals, the irksome discipline of pest control, lower revenues, etc.

The collapse of cotton prices, which plummeted from CFA F750 per kilo in 1984 to CFA F275 in 1985, before recovering slightly in 1986, has added a new aspect to the situation. Sahelian countries, with the help of the international community, have endeavored to act as a buffer between lower commodity prices and the farmers. Such policies can only be sustained if the fall in prices is temporary. Moreover, further growth in cotton production poses serious problems, which will be examined in a subsequent chapter.

It should be stressed that cotton production, unlike cereals production, has shown little vulnerability to drought:

-- While 1983-84 and 1984-85 were record years for cotton, food aid sent to several countries also reached unprecedented levels;

-- These simultaneous records clearly indicate that drought does not have the same effects on the two types of crops, probably for technical reasons but also for sociological and socio-economic reasons.

Cotton continues to play a modest role in Sahelian economies, representing only 2 per cent, 4 per cent and 5 per cent of the GNP of Burkina Faso, Mali and Chad respectively.

The exceptional expansion of cotton production demonstrates that Sahelian farmers are not set in their ways but can change with surprising speed: yield has increased fivefold in less than twenty years.

This performance is all the more noteworthy because it was achieved after a long period when, despite the efforts of the colonial administration, production never really took off, and in those areas where it did take off, such as Chad, it did so in response to heavy pressure.

Export crops: groundnuts

Groundnut Exports
(tons of unshelled nuts)

	60-62	70-71	75-76	79-80	80-81	81-82	82-83	83-84	84-85	85-86
Mali	54	74	93	36	91	92	44	20		
Niger	-	186	6	3	2	2	4	2		
Senegal	812	454	1178	393	190	688	913	352		
TOTAL :	865	715	1280	430	280	780	960	370		

Groundnut exports reached a peak in 1975-1976 and have declined rapidly thereafter:

-- In Senegal, the economic importance of groundnuts has declined from 15 per cent of GNP in 1960 to only 3 per cent today;

-- In Niger, the rapid growth in exports during the 1960s was followed by an even swifter slump in the 1970s;

-- In Burkina Faso, groundnuts are now grown almost entirely for local consumption.

The causes of this decline are as follows:

-- Drought, which has resulted in lower yields;

-- Deterioration of the soil, which had already started to occur during the colonial era, particularly in the Senegalese groundnut basin, has now worsened;

-- Competition from food crops;

-- The fall in world prices, which declined by 50 per cent in real terms from 1975 to 1982. Specialization in groundnut production brought economic benefits to Senegal and the Gambia but, as neither yield nor productivity increased much, (while oleaginous crop production was rising in temperate climates), the comparative advantage enjoyed by these countries has been eroded, and other Sahelian countries with less favorable geographic situations, have fared even worse. Today, the cultivation of oleaginous crop production is again relocating to the countries of the North.

Export crops developed rapidly in certain parts of the Sahel. However, low world prices have brought the economic viability of these crops into question.

Livestock activities

Uneven development

Here again, statistics are not particularly reliable, especially since the imposition of livestock taxes for a part of the period under consideration has made estimates of herd sizes questionable. The trends in this sector can be summarized as follows:

> -- <u>Livestock activities grew more rapidly than the human population until the severe drought of 1972</u> owing to a combination of favorable factors:
>
>   a) the reduction of epizootic diseases through systematic vaccination undertaken by governments and donors,
>   b) the introduction of new water points in previously inaccessible grazing lands, again undertaken by governments and donors,
>   c) growing demand.
>
> - <u>A sharp fall in overall herd sizes in 1973</u> (perhaps by as much as one-third) due to reduced grazing land rather than lack of water;
>
> - <u>Herd sizes increased after 1973</u> and, for certain animal species, the pre-drought levels were exceeded;
>
> - <u>A new slump occurred in 1983 and 1984</u> which has not yet been accurately assessed.

The drift towards the South

The drought caused a widespread southward drift of pastoral nomads (the reverse of what happened when both herdsmen and farmers moved north during the previous wet period) which in turn increased conflict between herdsmen and the farming community.

Consumption and exports of livestock products

<u>Meat consumption is falling in the Sahel</u> (from an estimated 18 kg per person per year in the 1960s to around 13 kg today) even though animal-protein intake is already very low.

Live-animal and meat <u>exports</u> to the coastal countries (Côte d'Ivoire, Ghana, Nigeria, Gabon, etc.) <u>have fallen by 50 per cent in real terms in the space of ten years.</u>

The limiting factor: animal feeds

In pastoral areas where herding is virtually the only economic activity, grazing land has attained its maximum stock-carrying capacity (this limit has been surpassed in some instances, leading to the deterioration of grazing land). Biomass is just as efficiently exploited here as in comparable regions of Australia or the United States.

In agricultural areas, there are still very few links between farming and livestock activities. Farmers almost never grow animal feed and animal manure is rarely used as fertilizer for cultivated lands.

<u>Traditional herding methods are still prevalent in the Sahel, and have reached their limits. New techniques to enable herdsmen to meet the needs of the growing population are yet to be introduced.</u>

Fisheries

The table below illustrates the trends in the value of fisheries production in constant CFA francs (source : Study on the Definition of a Common Agricultural Policy for the CEAO).

	(billion CFA F)		
	1960	1970	1980
Burkina Faso	0.6	1	1.4
Mali	13	18	20
Mauritania	17.5	25	28.6
Niger	0.4	1.2	1.8
Senegal	25.6	42.5	75.4
TOTAL	57	88	127

<u>Continental-shelf fisheries</u> account for around 20 per cent of this total. <u>Growth in continental fisheries is sluggish</u> and is far below the rate of population expansion. Indeed, the growth rate is currently falling.

<u>By contrast, deep-sea fishing is growing much faster and the development of this sector has been one of the successes achieved over recent years.</u> However, given the offshore potential of the Sahel (one of the world's richest fishing grounds), only a fraction of its reserves are being exploited for the benefit of the region. The remainder is plundered -- to little advantage for the region -- by the fishing fleets of a few industrialized nations.

Chapter 5

THE DISRUPTION OF THE ECOLOGICAL BALANCE

Production systems and the environment

The tables given in the previous chapter illustrated economic trends without taking account of a phenomenon that was already apparent during the colonial era but that has become progressively more pronounced over the last quarter-century, and that now threatens to compromise the Sahel's future: the disruption of the balance between man and his ecological environment.

Traditional production systems maintained this balance but, conceived when space was virtually limitless, required a certain amount of land availability to function correctly. When population density reaches a certain level -- which varies from one climatic zone to another -- human settlements take more from nature than the ecology can cope with, and this leads to environmental deterioration. Once this deterioration process has started, it continues under its own momentum and natural regulating mechanisms do not come into play.

At the end of the colonial period, population densities in several areas started to exceed tolerable limits, and the environment began to deteriorate. During the course of the last quarter-century, the rural population has continued to grow despite the exodus to the cities, while traditional production systems have changed very little.

Environmental overload has thus worsened in those areas that were already affected and the problem is now spreading to other areas. Whence the spread of phenomena that are indicative of ecological breakdown:

-- Deterioration of grazing land,

-- Reduced fertility of arable land,

-- Disappearance of forests.

Several factors have served either to accentuate or speed the appearance of these phenomena:

-- <u>Drought:</u> the southward shift in the isohyets has meant that certain areas have lost their ability to produce adequate biomass, while the inhabitants of those areas have tended to increase their demand on that biomass. Moreover, the fall in the water table due to several years of poor rainfall has affected vegetation, with catastrophic consequences in certain areas.

-- <u>The destructuring of rural societies:</u> rural inhabitants feel less responsible for preserving their natural resources, feel powerless and lacking in resources in the face of environmental deterioration. This point will be discussed more fully in Chapter 8.

The disruption of the ecological balance is the result of a combination of causes: population growth and the persistence of production systems that are incompatible with the unprecedented levels of population densities that now exist, prolonged drought and the destructuring of rural societies. In addition, even if the current period of good rainfall were to last, the trend would be slow but would not disappear.

The advance of the desert

The disruption of the ecological balance is particularly spectacular in the Sudano-Sahelian zone, i.e. the edge of the desert inhabited by nomadic herders. According to a World Bank study, these grazing grounds can only support a human population density of 0.3 persons/km2 while the average density currently stands at 2.

Herd sizes in this area have grown even more rapidly than the human population. Even before the drought, pockets of overgrazing and soil deterioration were already in evidence. The drought reduced the amount of usable biomass and decimated herds. The remaining animals accelerated the deterioration: the desert is moving south.

It should be pointed out that this region of West Africa, with an estimated population of just one million (3 per cent of Sahelians), is relatively underpopulated.

Desertification from within

Even more alarming is what could be called desertification from within, which is affecting areas that are much more highly populated. The Sudano-Sahelian zone, with its traditional farming and herding systems, can support a population density of only 15 persons/km2 (source: World Bank study). The current level is over 20. Considering that the population is very unevenly distributed, figures are vastly superior in some areas, such as the Senegalese groundnut basin, the Mossi plateau, Zinder-Maradi, etc.

The deterioration of the environment, which was already apparent in this area at the close of the colonial era, has considerably worsened in the last quarter-century. Deterioration of the environment is caused by:

- <u>The felling of trees</u> to obtain more land for an expanding rural population which has failed to intensify its production methods. Indeed, in certain regions, changing family structures (with the multiplication of independent units of production which that involves) has led to methods of cultivation that require even more land. Clearing the land of trees has speeded the disappearance of the remaining natural forests and has led to the total disappearance of trees from cultivated plots (this was never the case before when plots were never fully cleared and the trees left standing helped conserve and regenerate the soil).

- Due to lack of available space, <u>land can no longer lie fallow long enough to recover its fertility.</u> Indeed, in certain areas such as the Mossi plateau, farmers keep poor land under permanent cultivation, moving south when the soil is completely impoverished. Transhumant agriculture has now turned into mere plundering of land.

- <u>Erosion</u> is affecting the land resources that are no longer protected by sufficient vegetation. In the worst affected zones, the topsoil (and in particular humus, which is already scarce) has been completely removed by wind or water: certain soils are now either irreparably damaged or could only be rehabilitated through long-term efforts.

The disruption of the ecological balance is not a marginal problem given that over ten million rural inhabitants -- one-third of the Sahel's rural population -- are affected. Ultimately, neighboring areas will be threatened, and particularly those in the Sudanese zone (average rainfall: over 600 mm). This area is not as heavily populated, but more people are moving there and the plundering of land is on the increase. In several provinces, the destruction of the tree cover is already well under way and in the not-too-distant future, pockets of soil deterioration will appear in the most heavily populated areas, if this has not already happened.

The felling of trees for fuelwood has often been blamed for the deterioration of the environment and sometimes it has even been held up as the main cause. However, it would seem that until recently -- and perhaps in only a few specific areas even now -- the pressure that rural inhabitants have exerted on the environment in seeking to meet their fuelwood requirements has not been a major cause of deforestation. This problem seems to be a result of clearing land for farming, and these activities incidentally provide enough fuelwood for the needs of rural population groups.

On the other hand, there is no doubt that <u>supplying fuelwood to major urban areas</u> has had a direct effect on the environment. A large number of operators are engaged in unbridled forest clearance, sometimes converting the wood into charcoal before transporting it and selling it in the cities. Particularly during droughts, collecting fuelwood to sell to city-dwellers provides certain farmers with financial resources and the wherewithal to survive. Although little is known about it, supplying the cities with fuelwood is an important economic activity in the Sahel, but it is currently encouraging deforestation in an increasingly wide belt around the cities.

Several areas of the Sahel are still underpopulated, or even highly underpopulated (especially certain southern areas which have an annual rainfall of over 800 mm). However, given the current extensive production systems, the rest of the region is either overpopulated or heading rapidly in that direction.

The Sahelian environment is becoming depleted, sometimes to the point of desertification, whereas it should be enriched to cope with population growth.

Drought and the destructuring of rural societies have contributed to the disruption of the balance between Sahelians and their environment.

Chapter 6

INDUSTRY, SERVICES AND THE INFORMAL SECTOR

The trends in manufacturing industries

In 1960, only Senegal had an industrial base of any importance, which had principally been set up to meet the needs of the French West African market. The other countries had only the embryonic industries.

The 1960s were marked by:

-- The adaptation of Senegalese industries to a smaller market;

-- An initial wave of industrialization based on import substitution (textiles, consumer goods) in all other Sahelian countries.

Since 1970, industrial growth has slowed, followed by a recession of varying severity according to the country involved since the early 1980s.

Added Value in the Manufacturing Industries
(constant 1975 $ million)

	1970	1981
Burkina Faso	67	96
Chad	37	21
Mali	44	55
Mauritania	21	36
Niger	54	172
Senegal	276	298
TOTAL	500	678

(Source: World Bank)

Added value in the manufacturing industries grew by 2.8 per cent per year between 1970 and 1981, thereby keeping pace with population growth.

In comparison, Côte d'Ivoire and Tunisia recorded yearly growth of added value of 5.3 per cent and 12.6 per cent respectively during the same period.

	1970	1981
Côte d'Ivoire	398	706
Tunisia	222	820

(Source: World Bank)

Since the beginning of the 1980s, industrial growth has slowed even further, and in all likelihood, the industrial sector has even shrunk in several countries. Senegalese industries, which alone account for 40 per cent of the region's manufacturing industry, have recorded an average yearly growth rate of 1 per cent since 1976:

```
1976  :   100
1983  :   107.6
```

In other words, per capita industrial production has decreased.

Obstacles to industrialization

Several factors account for this trend in the Sahelian industry:

<u>Limited domestic markets</u>

Rural inhabitants have very low purchasing power, which, as we have seen, is stagnating at best. This is a result of:

— The low volume of food sales to the cities, most of whose needs are met by commercial imports and food aid;

— Heavy State taxation on incomes derived from export crops.

Many urban or peri-urban inhabitants are employed in the informal sector and they too have very low purchasing power. City-dwellers with high purchasing power have high demand for goods and services from outside the region.

The weakness of domestic markets is primarily responsible for the slow pace of industrialization, <u>without mass markets, industries cannot develop.</u>

<u>The "Balkanization" of the region</u>

"Balkanization" is often put forward to explain the region's slow industrialization. Clearly, the barriers erected by governments compartmentalize markets and are thus not favorable to the creation of mass markets. However, the "balkanization" of the Sahel is tempered by the permeability (de facto if not official) of frontiers: it would appear that informal trade flows between countries are vastly superior to recorded formal trade flows -- sometimes two or three times higher or in certain instances perhaps even ten times greater.

A secondary factor, especially in the case of heavy goods, is the lack of adaptability of the transportation network. A good trans-Sahelian network is needed to reduce the transportation costs of these products between inland countries.

Nevertheless, bringing together small, stagnant domestic markets would not suffice to create conditions for rapid industrialization.

The high cost of factors of production

In all Sahelian countries the cost of the factors of production -- investment capital, energy, local and expatriate labor etc. -- is high. By way of illustration, the minimum wage in Senegal is 2.5 times higher than in Mauritius, and wages in the textile industry are 1.5 to 2 times higher than those in Pakistan or Bangladesh.

Under these conditions, industrialization with a view to exporting to markets in the developed countries (as has been achieved by several South-East Asian nations) is hardly feasible.

The fragility of new industries

Several Sahelian countries have set up State-financed industries that have proved relatively unprofitable or oversized for the needs of the domestic market which have failed to grow as fast as expected. These industries have become a drain on the State rather than a driving force behind development.

Other factors

Other factors behind the slow pace of industrialization include:

-- A labor force that has not been well prepared by the educational system for working in industry, and that is unfamiliar with this sector (the Dakar urban area is the only exception to this);

-- Inappropriate legislation: investment codes favor capital investments and do not encourage job creation, while a great many new arrivals on the urban job market can only find employment in the informal sector;

-- Western-style regulations which discourage potential local entrepreneurs: laws, accounting procedures, tax legislation, etc, are profoundly alien to Sahelian culture;

-- An ambiguous attitude, ranging from liberal to reactionary, to private investment from abroad, or even from local sources.

Energy

Consumption of "modern" energy sources, basically imported petroleum products and hydroelectricity, is still low.

Consumption of Modern Energy Sources in kilograms of oil equivalent (koe)

	1965	1984
Burkina Faso	8	21
Chad	10	16
Mali	15	26
Niger	8	42
Mauritania	48	127
Senegal	79	118

(Source: World Bank)

The comparable figures for Brazil and the United States are 745 and 7 300 kg respectively.

The higher figures for Senegal, Mauritania and Niger reflect consumption by the mining and industrial sectors of these countries.

Consumption of modern energy in rural areas is still minimal (it is measured in grams and not in kilograms oil equivalent). What increase there has been has occurred mainly in urban areas (industry, transportation, air-conditioning and other applications in the households sector, etc.).

The Sahel is almost totally dependent on imported petroleum products:

-- With the exception of Chad, where oil has been discovered in sufficient quantities to meet domestic needs (although the war has delayed exploitation), no hydrocarbons have yet been found in commercially viable quantities in the region;

-- The only solid-fuel deposits that are currently being exploited are in Niger, but the financial conditions are disastrous;

-- Only Mali has primary energy resources (hydroelectricity) that have really been exploited.

Overall, more than 99 per cent of the region's modern energy sources are imported.

The drain on the economy caused by energy imports has increased with the successive oil shocks. The figures below illustrate the trend in the ratio of energy imports to the value of exports:

	1960	1981
	%	%
Burkina Faso	38	71
Niger	6	23
Senegal	8	77

(Source: World Bank)

However, the importance of energy imports should not be exaggerated: in the least industrialized countries, the cost of food imports now exceeds that of energy imports.

The mining industry

The mining industry (excluding the extraction of fossil fuels) was virtually non-existent in 1960 and has developed considerably since then:

-- Iron ore mining and copper mining (currently being started up again) in Mauritania;

-- Phosphate mining in Senegal;

-- Uranium mining in Niger;

-- Gold mining in Burkina Faso (mines recently reopened).

The mining industry now plays an important role:

-- In the economy of Niger, where it represents 18 per cent of GDP;

-- In Mauritania, where it still contributes 20 per cent to the GDP, compared with more than 40 per cent in the early 1970s.

By contrast, phosphate mining is of only marginal importance in Senegal (3 per cent of GNP).

Relatively few jobs are created in highly capital-intensive mines, and the mining industry's role in the economy of the Sahel is generally overestimated because of the methods used to calculate GNP (which underestimate the economic importance of rural activities). The chief value of the mining sector is that it generates revenues for the State, providing that the deposits are profitable and that the State can appropriate a significant share. This is currently the case only in Niger. Even so, uranium revenues have fallen recently because of falling world-market prices.

Services and the informal sector

The services sector has recorded the fastest growth rates throughout the region (except in Chad, where it seems to have declined). World Bank figures for the annual growth rate in public- and private-sector services from 1970-1982 are as follows:

	Per cent
. Senegal	2.8
. Mauritania	5.2
. Burkina Faso	5.4
. Mali	5.4
. Niger	6.9

The public sector's share in the expansion of services will be discussed in detail in the next chapter.

The informal sector covers all activities that are not officially recorded in the cities. These include:

-- Commercial enterprises, small-scale non-industrial and semi-industrial enterprises, transportation companies and financial companies ("informal banks"). While these companies exist entirely outside the legal framework, they probably play a key role in the urban economy of the Sahel. They operate with very little capital and productivity is usually low. Employees, and especially apprentices, earn very low wages. However, certain entrepreneurs seem to earn substantial incomes, although the exact amount is not known;

-- Companies, usually one-person businesses, which provide more or less real services (small-scale traders, watchmen, etc.) but which enable a sizeable category of city-dwellers to survive.

In fact, economic activities in Sahelian towns range from subsistence-level enterprises to modern businesses and government agencies, and cover an intermediate group that is more often than not in the informal sector.

The informal sector has expanded significantly overall in the last quarter-century to the point where it now accounts for the majority of jobs in urban areas. According to a World Bank study, an estimated 276 000 people were employed in the informal sector in Dakar in 1980, compared with 195 000 in the modern public and non-governmental sector. In Ouagadougou in 1976, it was estimated that 73 per cent of the urban working population was employed in the informal sector. Economic development since the early 1980s, and the droughts of 1983 and 1984 that gave a new momentum to the rural exodus, have probably further increased the size of the informal sector.

Secondary and tertiary sectors overall

The table below illustrates overall trends in the entire secondary and tertiary sectors.

	Overall added value (billion CFAF)		Per capita added value in non-primary sector (thousand CFAF)	
	1970	1980	1970	1980
Burkina Faso	189	261	316	236
Mali	192	315	239	223
Mauritania	118	142	904	333
Niger	126	263	243	305
Senegal	554	766	434	325
TOTAL	1 179	1 747	355	283

(Note: For present purposes, mines are considered part of the secondary sector. The table thus covers manufacturing industries, the mining industry, energy, construction and public works, and services).

Aside from Niger, where the introduction of uranium mining in the 1970s has substantially increased added value in the secondary sector, there has been a marked decline in per capita added value in the cities (-20 per cent in 10 years). The reduction is particularly pronounced in Mauritania, where urbanization had been faster than elsewhere, and where the importance of the mining sector had significantly increased overall levels of added value.

Considering that urbanization has accelerated since 1980 and that industrialization has slowed or begun to shrink, it is quite likely that the per capita added value has fallen even further. Nevertheless, the table above should be revised to take greater account of the production and services of the large informal sector, which is poorly integrated in official statistics. Despite this reservation, it appears that:

-- The growth of productive employment in the modern sector is not keeping pace with the expanding urban population;

-- An increasingly sizeable proportion of this population finds itself either in so-called subsistence employment or in the intermediate informal sector where only low-productivity jobs are available.

It should be stressed that <u>the informal sector,</u> which is expanding without government assistance and sometimes despite administrative harassment, bears witness to the <u>dynamism of the Sahelians in the face of a new situation.</u> Notwithstanding that dynamism, per capita added value in the cities is still very low. The table below provides a comparative view of this:

Per Capita GDP of the Urban Population:
Secondary and Tertiary Sectors
(1982 dollars)

Senegal	960
Côte d'Ivoire	1,500
Tunisia	1,660
Thailand	3,500

(Source: World Bank)

The modern secondary and tertiary sectors are not growing fast enough to keep up with the burgeoning urban population. The per capita added value of the urban population is low and falling.

The phenomenal expansion of the informal sector is enabling city-dwellers to survive. Extremely diverse and hard to classify, the productivity of labor in this sector is generally low, but its development illustrates the dynamism of Sahelian societies.

Chapter 7

OVERALL ECONOMIC TRENDS

The public sector

The Sahelian State took over where colonial rule left off, and the number of civil servants has considerably increased over the last quarter-century.

<u>Growth of the public sector has outstripped growth in the primary and secondary sectors.</u> According to World Bank statistics, the public sector absorbed:

- 14 per cent of GNP in 1965
- 20 per cent of GNP in 1984.

Alongside the public sector, the parastatal sector has also substantially increased in size in order to promote economic development (regional development companies, product-specific marketing boards, services for the creation of industries, etc.) or to take over functions previously performed by the non-governmental sector (marketing of agricultural produce and inputs, etc.).

Until recently, the public and parastatal sectors provided an outlet for high-school and university graduates.

The payroll of this sector has increased particularly rapidly. In Senegal, during the <u>austerity</u> period of 1977-1983, the public-sector payroll increased 2.5 times from CFA F60 billion to 150 billion, while the GDP of the primary sector increased only 1.5 times from 132 billion to 204 billion during the same period. This increased payroll and the fact that at least part of the civil service is relatively highly paid has brought a sharp increase in demand for goods and services from outside the region.

Further, the payroll has increased to the detriment of other operating expenses (purchases of supplies, medicines, etc.), and in particular the upkeep of roads, public buildings and other items under State responsibility.

The public sector has only been able to grow because of:

— **Stiff taxation on the income of productive workers**, especially farm workers with higher-than-average earnings. Taxation is imposed through **stabilization** boards and marketing boards and not through direct taxation;

— **Aid from the international community.**

However, the productive sectors have not generated enough resources and foreign aid has not increased sufficiently for the public sector to grow fast enough to absorb all high-school or university graduates. A degree no longer guarantees a job in the public or parastatal sectors.

The contradictions of the economy

Over the last twenty-five years (and probably even longer) economic development in Sahelian countries has involved a **basic contradiction**:

— **On the one hand, the productive sectors — rural and industrial — have grown very slowly, and more slowly overall than the total population;**

— **On the other hand, growth in the services sector — especially the public and parastatal sectors — has outstripped total population growth;**

— **The resulting redistribution of wealth bears no relation to production.**

The foreign trade deficit increased steadily, at least up to the early 1980s:

— Imports of energy, foodstuffs, consumer goods for middle- and high-income brackets, and of capital goods for the public and parastatal sector, have grown rapidly;

— Exports of agricultural products have not grown as rapidly, exports from the mining sector have remained moderate and exports of manufactured goods are even lower;

— Petroleum price rises and the increased costs of imported industrial goods have only been offset by short-lived price rises for exports such as phosphates, while other major exports such as groundnuts and, more recently, cotton have experienced a persistent slump in prices.

The terms of trade have worsened considerably and this has compounded the downturn in volumes exported, which is itself a consequence of the changes in the Sahelian economy. The trade deficit has been cut and the contradiction referred to above has temporarily been resolved through:

— Increasing levels of aid from the international community;

-- Growing external indebtedness;

-- Since the 1980s, a new form of financing to support the reform program: structural adjustment.

International aid

The trend in official development assistance to Sahelian countries (including Cape Verde and Guinea-Bissau) expressed in current US$ million is as follows:

```
1974 :   756
1975 :   817
1976 : 1,136
1977 : 1,002
1978 : 1,378
1979 : 1,688
1980 : 1,570
1981 : 2,035
1982 : 1,575
1983 : 1,822
1984 : 2,176
1985 : 1,889
```

Expressed in constant prices, aid commitments rose by an average of 3 per cent per year between 1975 and 1980 and by an average of 7 per cent between 1980 and 1985.

Disbursements of official development assistance have more or less followed the same pattern: in the early 1970s this amounted to roughly US $250 million per year, rising to approximately US $700 million from 1974 and US $1 100 from 1978. Disbursements reached a ceiling of about US$ 1,300-1,400 million from 1981 to 1984 and stood at 1,750 million in 1985.

In addition to this official development assistance, private-sector aid, which is difficult to quantify, is accorded by a growing number of non-governmental organizations (NGOs).

The Sahel is now one of the regions of the world that receives the most aid. The following are the figures for aid commitments in 1984 (in dollars per inhabitant):

```
Sahelian countries                  60
Egypt                               38
Sub-Saharan Africa
     (excluding the Sahel)          19
Asia                                 7
```

A growing portion of this aid is used for subsistence purposes (food aid, emergency aid) and to keep the public and parastatal sectors operating: budget assistance, balance-of-payment assistance, food-aid counterpart funds, various contributions to help run Sahelian agencies involved in what are called development projects, etc. From 1975 to 1981, this portion represented 35 per cent of official development assistance, if not more. In 1985, more than 50 per cent of official development assistance was allocated to other items besides projects (mainly budget assistance) and was used to keep the economy of Sahelian countries afloat.

Another portion of aid is used to finance investments, which, however vital, will only become profitable in the long term: transportation and telecommunications infrastructures, education, health, water supply, etc. This portion has accounted for about one-third of overall official development assistance.

The final portion of aid is used for investments that generally become productive relatively quickly. This portion barely exceeds 30 per cent of the total. Of this amount:

-- Roughly 4 per cent has been devoted to the development of rainfed agriculture, which is essential to Sahelians' food requirements;

- Roughly 1.5 per cent has been devoted to reforestation and the restoring of the ecological balance, which are vital to the region's future. After reaching its peak in the early 1980s, this type of aid is now on the decline.

International aid is only very partially adapted to the region's needs.

External indebtedness

The indebtedness of Sahelian countries is illustrated below (in $ million at current prices):

1970 :	450
1875 :	1 070
1980 :	3 680
1982 :	5 830
1984 :	6 880
1985 :	8 120

(Source: OECD-DAC)

As the table below indicates, Sahelian countries owe on average more than one year of their total GDP. The more heavily indebted countries owe two years of their total GDP, which may be a world record.

National Debt ($ million) and Per Capita Debt ($) at December 31, 1985

	National debt	Per capita debt	Debt/GNP ratio
Burkina Faso	580	87	0.51
Cape Verde	92	287	0.92
Chad	167	33	0.41
Gambia	248	335	1.52
Guinea-Bissau	253	287	1.60
Mali	1 503	193	1.38
Mauritania	1 509	893	1.98
Niger	1 138	178	0.89
Senegal	2 653	402	1.06
TOTAL	8 124	225	1.07

Debt servicing depends to a large extent on the debt structure of the individual country: certain countries are chiefly indebted to aid agencies on soft terms, while others have borrowed from the banking sector at market rates. The table below shows that the debt service has considerably increased recently. While the debts have been repaid, a significant portion of aid (about 35 per cent on average but more in certain countries) has had to be used for servicing them.

Servicing of the Foreign Debt

	Debt service effectively paid average 1982-1984 (in million $)	Theoretical debt service due average 1982-1984	
		national (million $)	per capita (dollars)
Burkina Faso	18.6	39.8	6
Cape Verde	3.2	7.1	22
Chad	1.1	5.5	1
Gambia	8.2	16.9	23
Guinea-Bissau	2.7	14.9	17
Mali	12.7	86.2	11
Mauritania	39.6	151.6	90
Niger	83.6	91.4	14
Senegal	65.3	227.9	35
TOTAL	235	641.3	18

Structural adjustment

Structural adjustment emerged at the end of the 1970s in response to the shocks that jolted the world economy at that time (the second oil shock, rise in interest rates, recession in the West). The World Bank's structural adjustment loans were originally a form of aid to those developing countries that agreed to introduce such adjustments.

Structural adjustment programs have now become <u>a way of dealing with the persistent imbalance between domestic demand and total national production plus financeable imports.</u> These programs tackle the problem by providing the financing needed to pay off the deficit that neither conventional aid nor increased foreign indebtedness can now reduce, on the one hand, and by endeavoring, through a series of measures and institutional reforms, to bring an end to the imbalance (conditionality) on the other.

The structural adjustment loans accorded by the World Bank and the Caisse Centrale de Coopération Economique, various forms of IMF assistance, including the recently created structural adjustment facilities, and a certain amount of bilateral aid (particularly from the United States), which are comparable to structural adjustment loans, have played this role since 1980.

Have these loans succeeded in ending the imbalance? To a certain extent, they have. Several countries have reduced their foreign deficits since the beginning of the 1980s. Have they succeeded in creating suitable conditions for sustained growth? There are no clear criteria for answering this question. In Senegal, for example, where large-scale structural adjustment programs have been in existence for some considerable time, it can be said that:

-- The "urban bias" that favors the growth of incomes in the modern urban sector to the detriment of rural population groups has still not diminished after several decades. Certain observers even claim that it has become considerably more pronounced since 1980. In the cities, the bias in favor of the highest income earners has not disappeared either;

-- These programs have had little impact on orientation of investments towards the most productive sectors of the economy.

An increasingly dependent economy

<u>The positive aspects</u> of the Sahel's economic development must be emphasized: the beginnings of industrial development in several countries where no industry existed before 1960, the launching of the mining industry, the exceptional expansion of cotton, the development of deep-sea fisheries, etc.

However, <u>the negative aspects</u> are more numerous, and the overall economic performance of the Sahel has been unimpressive over the past twenty-five years.

After an initial period of development in the 1960s that gave the impression that the Sahel is "on the right tracks", the region has progressively sunk into a crisis situation that has worsened in recent years. This crisis is reflected by the increasingly heavy dependence on the outside world:

-- Food dependence

This is the most visible aspect of dependence. Food self-sufficiency, which Sahelian governments set as a major goal, is highly criticizable from an economist's point of view. In fact, the region is moving further and further away from achieving this objective. These tendencies would not necessarily be unsound if other sectors of activity underpinned food production and provided the foreign exchange needed to buy food and other essential imports. But this is not the case and it is because no other sector has been dynamic enough to take over from the food production sector that rising food imports and food aid is worrisome.

-- Dependence on the outside world to run the public sector

Over the past twenty-five years, Sahelian countries have developed public and parastatal sectors that have grown faster than the productive sectors. The size of the State sector is now out of proportion to the productive base of the economy. Given that the State can no longer appropriate enough funds from the economy to keep the public sector afloat, a growing portion of foreign aid has to be allocated to the State sector, and the foreign debt has made up the shortfall over recent years.

-- Dependence on external sources to finance investments

With the exception of Niger (which for a time generated sizeable income from uranium mining), the economies of Sahelian countries have not generated any savings to finance new investments: those generated by certain economic agents are totally swallowed up in the running of the public and parastatal sectors. The Sahel has come to depend entirely on external sources for investments, which are a prerequisite for future development.

The table below illustrates the trend of rising dependence. In 1965, public- and private-sector consumption and gross investments exceeded the Sahel's GNP by 4 per cent. In 1984, this figure stood at 22 per cent.

Breakdown of GNP
(all Sahelian Countries)

	Public-sector consumption	Private-sector consumption	Gross investments	Total consumption + investment	Consumption + investment − GNP
	%	%	%	%	%
1965	14	72	13	104	4
1984	20	82	20	122	22

(Source: World Bank)

A disjointed economy

Why does such a crisis situation exist?

The international environment of recent years has clearly not been favorable to the Sahel: the oil shocks and the decline in the value of its exports have had an adverse effect on the region. The recent fall in petroleum prices has clearly been good for the Sahel but its positive effects have unfortunately been offset by a slump (unconnected) in cotton prices. In the medium term, therefore, trends in the international environment may be no more favorable to the region than they have been in the recent past.

The international environment has nevertheless allowed aid to increase significantly. In addition, the impact of the international crisis on Sahelian economies, which are not particularly outward-looking (aside from the Gambia and Mauritania, whose exports represent over 40 per cent of GNP), has been less pronounced than on economies that are more geared to the international market.

The drought: The Sahel has undeniably experienced an exceptional dry spell recently and this has sometimes had disastrous consequences on cereals production, livestock activities and the environment. However, the trends in rural production are not the result of the drought. The drought -- like the international environment -- is one factor that has aggravated the crisis. 1983 and 1984 were record years for both food aid and cotton production. Drought -- however acute -- is thus not an inevitable scourge against which all reaction is hopeless.

Further, the years 1985 and 1986 prove that the return of good rainfall is not enough to assure the Sahel's economic recovery. While the good harvests have had a positive effect on the nutrition of rural population groups, they are also behind the price slump affecting traditional cereals, which are not selling well enough, and which are in competition with imported wheat and rice. The financial resources of rural population groups have perhaps never been lower since the early 1960s.

Lack of cohesion between the different sectors of the economy. The development policies pursued by Sahelian governments and supported by donors -- who share the responsibility for the present crisis -- have resulted in disjointed economies. The strong growth of the public sector has only been possible through external aid and through taxation of farmers' revenues, which has led to the impoverishment of a large section of the rural population.

Urban-area population groups, whose numbers are constantly swollen by the rural exodus, have similarly low incomes. Neither group provides a market for manufactured goods, and industrialization cannot thus develop.

The relationships between the different sectors of the economies of Sahelian countries do not constitute a sound framework for sustained economic growth. The Sahel appears to be turning into a mosaic of economic islands: introverted rural communities, an isolated modern urban sector, a growing informal sector and an increasingly alienated public sector. Invisible, little-understood relationships do exist between these islands, but they are not sufficient to create conditions for growth.

Structural adjustment programs have (temporarily) slowed the rise of dependence. They have not put an end to the de-linkaging of the economy. By reducing the demand of the most underprivileged sections of the population, these programs might even have increased dependence in certain instances.

Chapter 8

THE DESTRUCTURING OF RURAL SOCIETY

Permanent features of Sahelian societies

A number of features of contemporary Sahelian societies already existed in pre-colonial times. The pluralist nature of village societies has become even more pronounced: in particular, when population groups migrated to escape the drought, the migrants were received by village communities that were already established.

Membership of a specific line of descendancy and age group, and the solidarity that is linked to that status, have retained the importance they have always had, not only in rural societies but also to a large extent in urban areas.

Belonging to a social class or a caste no longer has the importance that it used to have. In principle, slavery no longer exists, but traditional hierarchies and the complex network of relationships that bound families together is still present in the minds of the Sahelians, and even today plays an important role in daily life.

The structures and mechanisms of traditional societies have remained largely intact. Nevertheless, the destructuring of rural Sahelian society that began in the colonial period has accelerated considerably over the last twenty-five years. The aim of this chapter is to examine the different aspects and consequences of this destructuring process.

The end of isolation

Already in colonial times, rural societies, which had until then been highly isolated, began to open up to the outside world. It was easier to move from one place to another than it had ever been, and this increased potential for mobility brought with it a level of dissemination of information that these societies had never witnessed before. This opening up to the outside world, however, remained limited.

The last quarter-century has been marked by deep-seated changes:

-- Further improvement of the transportation infrastructure, which has further increased people's potential mobility: the cities have become considerably more accessible to rural inhabitants;

-- Most importantly, <u>a technical revolution that has had a direct effect on the villages of the Sahel: the transistor.</u> This breakthrough brought radio to areas where access was formerly unthinkable because the availability of electricity was still exceptional. Nowadays, almost all villages have access to information broadcast not only on national radio stations, but also on international networks. Broadcasts are regularly received in a large number of villages in the Sahel. Even pastoral nomadic groups are linked to the outside world through their transistor radios.

The other mass media are markedly less prevalent in rural Sahelian societies, but the spread of the radio has brought an end to the isolation of these societies. Urban society and its way of life, which until the introduction of the radio were very distant and of marginal interest to rural communities, are now very much closer.

Rethinking the distribution of roles

The use of money, which was imposed during the colonial period, started to disrupt the way in which rural societies functioned, and an importance was attached to money that had never previously existed. The role assigned to each of these societies in turn began to change, and the trend has accelerated considerably over the years.

The difficulties encountered by many rural communities -- due to drought, deterioration of land resources or falling commodity prices -- amplified the rural exodus and the flight to the cities. An increasing number of members of the community started to go to the cities in search of an income that would allow them to live better, or at least to subsist, and that would thereby ensure the survival of the group, which remained behind in the village.

The opening up to the outside world described in the preceding paragraph led to greater awareness of the restrictive nature of traditional society and also encouraged villagers to seek greater liberty elsewhere. Naturally, it was chiefly the younger members of the community that moved away from the villages in this way. Certain of these migrants broke off their relations with the village, but many others migrated only temporarily and continue to participate in community life.

The money or gifts that they send back to the community give them a role in that community that they had never had in ancient times. The independence achieved through distancing and financial resources made it possible for these migrants to escape, at least in part, from the restrictions that the group had formerly imposed on the younger generations. Similarly, incomes generated by cash crops or other activities made it possible for rural inhabitants to escape these restrictions.

In traditional society, the elders kept strict control over the young and over the wealth the young created. The very specific rules, often of great complexity, governing the marriageability of young men and stipulating the size of the dowries to be paid, provided a particularly effective means of control in this respect. Under these conditions it is understandable that the elders feel there is a <u>widening generation gap</u> -- wider than in most contemporary societies. It is not surprising that the elders feel that an entire order has been brought into question, that the end of an era is imminent and that they have little hold over the new era that is being born.

Questioning the natural order of things

Alongside this widespread feeling of radical disruption of rural society, there is a feeling that the new society is breaking with the natural order.

Rural communities are very well aware of the breakdown of the ecological balance, the disappearance of the forests (which is borne out by comparing the present situation with memories of only twenty or thirty years ago), and even more aware of the falling fertility of the land (certain Senegalese farmers speak of "the land ageing"). Rural communities know that the situation is new, or at least that it has considerably worsened in recent years. They know that the situation is dangerous and that the breakdown of the ecological balance inevitably leads to catastrophes. What is more, they feel <u>powerless to change this new situation,</u> since they are too busy ensuring their short-term subsistence to seek longer-term solutions. They are overcome by what they have undergone.

What appears to be a break with the natural order consolidates the feeling that an era is about to give way to a new, worrying, situation. The prolonged, serious drought that has recently hit the Sahel must appear to the rural inhabitants (and no doubt to other Sahelians who no longer live in rural areas) to be the direct consequence of breaking with the world order that governed society itself and its relationships with the environment -- an order that should have been immutable.

The feeling of alienation

Another characteristic feature of many rural communities is the increasing feeling that they are being sacrificed, alienated from a society that is changing, but that is changing in favor of an urban minority.

During the colonial period, the power of the colonizers was often considered a fatality, and the intervention of the colonizers in rural life was unwelcome but inevitable. The new society built by colonial power or that grew up under its influence was a distant phenomenon: it was the white man's world, a universe that was somewhat incomprehensible and inaccessible and that did not particularly appeal to them.

The rise of the urban society, which is much better known because it is brought closer by the means of communication and the media, and which has emerged as the result of the efforts of fellow Sahelians, may also be considered a fatality, but inspires feelings of envy or bitterness.

Rural inhabitants are very conscious of the priority that is attached -- in practice if not in theory -- to the building of a modern society that is essentially urban, to the construction of a State and to industrialization. They feel they are being sacrificed for the purposes of these priorities. Central government has probably never had a particularly favorable image in the rural world. Today, more than ever, the rural world sees central government as distant, rather hostile and in any case indifferent to the destiny of the rural communities, and those communities have become alienated as a result.

Introversion or flight

These breakdowns of relations within rural societies are leading to changes in behavior:

-- Changes in habits that used to seem deeply rooted, such as the propensity to save in preparation for harder times to come: the proximity of city life is encouraging rural inhabitants to attach greater priority to the purchase of the few consumer goods they can afford than to savings;

-- Growing passivity and <u>the introversion of the rural world,</u> which is little motivated to increase production if that additional production is to be sold through official channels; surpluses are often moved through informal channels or through personal, family or ethnic contacts and play an important role, and certain observers have spoken of the development of an economy based on individual affinities;

- <u>The flight of the most dynamic elements of the rural world,</u> whether temporary or permanent, to the cities or abroad; the expansion of schooling into the rural world, and the arrival of a school system that is conceived outside the rural context and that favors the flight to the cities more than the transformation of the village provide further incentives to leave the village and flee to the cities. In certain areas, the flight to the cities is systematic. Villages are deserted by the young people and economic and social life is more apparent than real, and has in fact largely deteriorated.

> The conclusion of the chapter on trends in the economy of the rural world was that the rural world had remained detached from development, and in any case had not reaped the benefits of that development. Trends in the economy and trends in rural society are clearly very closely linked. <u>The demotivation of rural inhabitants passively witnessing the end of an era leads to stagnation in the economy, and a stagnating economy reinforces the feeling of impotence and alienation on the part of these rural communities.</u>

The emergence of new dynamism

Does this imply that the rural world in the Sahel is caught up in a vicious circle from which it cannot escape, and that it is condemned to stagnation while awaiting inevitable ecological catastrophes? The situation is not as cut and dried as it might appear, and we are now going to examine a number of very positive aspects that exist.

Totally independently of government action, initiatives have been taken here and there for a number of years in the rural world. Indeed, in certain cases, this initiative has been taken despite government action. For example, <u>genuine cooperatives or village associations have been set up,</u> particularly for obtaining credit, developing irrigated perimeters, safeguarding land resources and fighting erosion, etc. Since the beginning of the 1980s, the number of organizations of this type -- by whatever name they may be known -- has multiplied.

These new organizations are not set up by traditional village communities, but by individuals that choose to join of their own free will. Many of the organizations have been set up on the initiative of former migrants who have returned to the village, while others have been created by people that have spent some time in the cities and have decided to express their dynamism in their villages rather than trying their luck elsewhere.

In other areas, initiative has been of a more individual nature, and there are signs of the emergence of <u>a class of "rich" farmers</u> each owning several teams of animals and several pieces of equipment for animal-drawn farming, and using techniques that are more productive than traditional farming techniques and employing wage-earners. The social fabric has never been homogeneous in the Sahel, but new differences are now beginning to appear.

This individual or collective initiative is speeding the destructuring of traditional society and is generating new structures. In any case, it demonstrates that <u>passivity is no longer the general rule</u> and that certain rural inhabitants now wish to take their affairs into their own hands. Be that as it may, <u>this initiative is still very insular, and the rural world is still not organized.</u> As we will see, this lack of organization has an effect on the political might of the rural world. Nevertheless, this new initiative may be <u>one of the most promising of the factors</u> that have appeared in the last few years.

Chapter 9

THE INCREASED IMPORTANCE OF URBAN SOCIETY

During the colonial period, a new urban society was born under the influence of the colonizers. The last twenty-five years have been marked by a very sharp acceleration of urbanization, which has not only had an effect on the size of the urban population, but has also had a number of effects on the quality of life: Sahelian urban societies have been deeply changed and the gulf between rural society and urban society has widened.

An increasingly autonomous society

During the colonial period, Sahelian cities played a marginal role in the society, since rural inhabitants outweighed the city-dwellers considerably. The city was a consequence of colonial rule and was subjected to its influences. The city aggravated the discontinuity with traditional social values. However, it could also be claimed that the city was a kind of extension of the rural society, a sort of outgrowth of that society that was caused by contact with the outside world. The only exception to this was Dakar, because of its size, its geographic situation and the role it played as a federal capital.

By 1986, the Sahelian city was no longer marginal. Although it has retained close ties with the rural world, it has taken on a separate identity, and has its own structures, ways of life and values. The media boom shattered the isolation of rural population groups, but the boom was even more pronounced in the cities. Radio developed at least as much in the cities as in the rural areas, and television, cinema and the printed press play a far more important role in the cities than in rural areas. Urban population groups are thus in closer contact than they have ever been with the outside world, with other African countries, with other developing continents, and above all with the West. Western ways of life and values are a daily reality in the cities of the Sahel.

<u>The gulf between rural society and urban society, which began to appear during the colonial period, has now widened.</u>

A society of young people

Exponential population growth and the rural exodus (chiefly involving young people) have led to a situation where more than half of the urban population of the Sahel is under the age of twenty. This society of young people is <u>by and large cut off from traditional values.</u> It does not feel pressured by the family group back in the village, and is little subjected to influence from the adult family group living in the city, which is itself unsure of its values, and whose experience is no longer relied upon and is increasingly challenged.

In contrast to what has happened in other emerging urban societies, traditional Sahelian values were more imposed by the group than interiorized by the individual. There is thus very little "hysteresis", where values that have ceased to be imposed persist for the time being. Even if many young people do not wish to break with tradition, or with what they think is tradition, traditional values play a real role for only a very small minority.

This society of young people is thus <u>in search of new values.</u> A fraction of these people have found -- and are continuing to find -- their new values in different variants of Marxism (Soviet, Chinese or Cuban). Another small section of the population has turned to Islamic fundamentalism. Others have adopted other ideologies. The remainder -- perhaps the majority -- are adopting very hedonistic values and seem more than anything determined to take advantage of the pleasures offered by the Western model.

A large proportion of this society of young people is <u>fascinated by the Western consumer-society model,</u> which is transmitted through the school system and brought closer by the media. This model is not only copied by the minority of Westerners living in or passing through the cities, but also by a privileged minority of Sahelians. Another minority of young people rejects this model on the grounds that it is corrupting African society, and often rejects it in the name of Islam.

In any case, this society of young people <u>cannot afford to follow the Western model.</u> Only a small minority of young people have succeeded in entering the modern economy and can be considered to have access to the Western model. The others are unemployed or are employed in the informal sector, where they often earn subsistence wages (young "apprentices" arriving from the villages are often exploited by the "bosses" in the informal sector, thereby continuing the practices of the traditional society where the young were heavily dependent on the elders).

The fascination with the Western consumer model, the questioning of traditional values and the lack of resources to gain access to the model that is dreamed of has a variety of consequences that are already widely recognized:

-- Confusion in the face of a collapsing system of values: the emotional security afforded by traditional society has disappeared, and young people are seeking integration in a new social group that can provide that security;

-- Worry in the face of an uncertain future: success at school is no longer a guarantee that it will be possible to join the privileged minority, and is no longer a motivating factor; even worse, to fail in school is even more traumatic;

-- Juvenile delinquency in its different forms, and resorting to prostitution to procure the resources that society cannot provide;

-- Escapism through drugs and alcohol, or refuge in sport, music and dance.

These problems are undoubtedly not peculiar to urban societies in the Sahel. Most societies in developing and developed countries are experiencing the same sort of problems to varying degrees. But the speed with which urbanization is taking place, the slow pace of industrialization and the shock of coming into contact with other cultures (which may be more pronounced than elsewhere) undoubtedly make the problems more acute.

The role of women

Within this society that is in the process of changing values, women are taking on a role that they had never had before, or else had lost. Women do not have inferior status in most traditional Sahelian societies, within whose cosmogonies male and female elements had equivalent roles. Aside from women's role in handing down values to the next generation, they played an important part in the fabric of social relationships.

The economic role of women in urban society is tending to increase: women are working in an increasing number of professions outside the home, and earn and spend their own incomes. A significant proportion of informal activities, trade and services -- as well as productive activities -- is now handled by women.

The quest for survival

The urban areas of the Sahel are in a state of flux: values and roles are being brought into question, and new models and new modes of expression are constantly being sought. The urban environment is a complex web of contradictory influences and as such is eminently dynamic. What is dramatic is that this dynamism meets with severe restrictions. The limits to industrialization hamper the creation of new productive jobs in the industrial sector. The development of the public sector is hampered by a lack of resources. Dynamism thus turns to the informal sector and towards the creation of new cultures.

The informal sector provides the means of subsistence. But however important a socio-economic role the informal sector has assumed, it is still marginal and heavily dependent on the modern society, the State and the industrial society. Creativity in the cities finds expression in various different directions: theater, music, occasionally cinema. But it lacks the sound economic basis that it would need to flourish.

Dynamism in the Sahelian urban environment has not yet led to balanced socio-economic development.

<u>Urban society in the Sahel is developing very fast</u> and is moving further and further away from the traditional society. Young people and women are playing an increasingly important role within that society.

<u>Drawn by conflicting influences</u> -- tradition, the West, Islam and many others -- urban society is seeking new values and new ways of life.

<u>The dynamism of this society has not yet led to sustained economic development, because conditions have not been favorable, and the informal sector is the only outlet for that dynamism.</u>

Chapter 10

DEVELOPMENTS IN THE POWER BASE

From colonization to independence

In chapter 2, we saw that the colonial period hampered the emergence of a class of entrepreneurs and merchants. We also examined the demise of the ancient aristocracies, whose power was fragmented by the colonizers. Finally, we examined the birth of a new political class, chiefly fathered by government employees, educated by the colonial school system and heavily influenced by Western culture.

Most of the Sahel moved progressively and relatively smoothly from colonial rule to independence. In French-speaking countries the main stages in this process were as follows: the legislation of 1956 (Loi-cadre), which introduced a certain level of self-government, followed by internal self-goverrment after the referendum of 1958, and finally full independence in 1960.

The new political class naturally found itself in the driving seat of the newly independent States. And the statal structures that were set up by the colonial powers and which were naturally copied from the systems in the colonizers countries, were adopted as the structures of the new States.

Colonization had brought a sudden rupture within the power base: not only had power changed hands, it had also changed its very nature, since the new power was totally alien to Sahelian society. Decolonization did not lead to the same rupture: power changed hands, but the newly independent State governed on the basis of authority they had derived from colonial rulers. We shall refer to this as continuity. At no time was it really possible to choose between this continuity, a return to the earlier forms of rule, and the introduction of new forms of government.

The new Sahelian governments are not the successors to the Mali empire or the Mossi kingdoms, but inherited their power from the colonial administrations. The very conception of the State, its structures, mechanisms and traditions were passed down from the colonial powers, or were at least influenced by Western models. Over the last quarter-century, the State has to a certain extent adapted to the specific conditions of the Sahel, but the initial basis has never been brought into question.

From independence to the present day

1958-1970: Birth of the Republics

The members of the political class that assumed power after independence were from a variety of backgrounds (university graduates, schoolteachers, lawyers or post office employees), but all had something in common: they had all been through the colonial school system, which was non-religious and staunchly republican. That schooling gave the new leaders a sense of mission -- a mission to build modern nations. To accomplish that mission, there was a need to shape the attitudes of their fellow citizens.

This republic of "educators" and "politicians" did not remain in power for long in most countries. By the end of the 1960s in certain countries, and during the 1970s in others, a new social category was to take power: the military.

The 1970s: Republics and military leaders

When they achieved sovereignty, the new States of the Sahel established national armies and signed defense agreements with the former colonial powers under which they received sometimes substantial military assistance. According to the republican tradition, these armies served the executive power base and could under no circumstances replace that power base. In an effort to remove any temptation for the army to intervene in the political life of the country, members of the military establishment were forbidden to hold public office by the constitution. In compensation, they received much higher salaries and greater benefits than their qualification would have allowed them in civilian life.

But this tacit agreement between the civilian political class and the military was not to last. At the end of the 1970s, of all the former French territories in the Sahel, only Senegal was under civilian rule. Everywhere else in the region, the military had taken over the political power base.

The military leaders that took power during this second decade of independence all shared a deep disrespect for "party politics" and scorned the struggles between political factions that in their opinion created disorder in the nation. Even though military intervention was stimulated, not to say encouraged, by appeals from civilians, in all the countries where they took power their first reflex was to abolish the customary forms of political life in the name of "the well-being of the nation, liberation or recovery". But the restrictions they imposed would not last forever. Unable to shake off the economic crisis that was afflicting their countries and face to face with the social contradictions from which the military establishment itself was not exempt, the military was forced to compromise with the elites in one way or another in order to find new directions for their countries. The 1980s dawned in this context.

The 1980s: Decade of reform

Since the beginning of the 1980s, all the power bases in the Sahel -- military or civilian -- have undergone a "face-lift".

-- Senegal in 1981 introduced constitutional reforms (the 16th set of reforms since 1960) and introduced an unlimited multi-party system. This country's image is now that of a liberal democracy, which is exceptional in contemporary Africa.

-- In Mauritania, relatively liberal tendencies have been detected since 1984.

-- In Niger, the creation of a post of Prime Minister, the creation of a "development-oriented society" and the adoption of a National Charter are opening up new possibilities for political expression.

-- In Chad, the creation of the UNIR bears out the determination of the country's rulers to find a political solution to the conflicts of all kinds that have torn the country apart for the last 20 years.

-- In Mali, the creation of the UDPM in 1979 is also a sign of increasing political openness.

-- The military government that took power in Burkina Faso in 1983 clearly wishes to differentiate itself from the successive military oligarchies that held power from 1963 to 1983.

-- In the Gambia, the 1981 treaty instituting the "Confederation of Senegambia" marks a change in direction.

These moves have all brought policy changes, but the extent of real change varies from one country to the next. But despite this checkered history of power in the Sahel, where different governments have come to power or have decided to introduce reforms or face-lifts, a number of factors have remained unaltered, and it would be useful to examine these factors here.

The priorities of those in power

The governments that have been in power since 1960 have all had two major priorities:

<u>The building of the nation</u>

The colonial territories were divided up according to the conquests achieved by the different colonial powers, and certain boundaries were redrawn to make the colonies easier to govern. The siting of these boundaries paid little attention to historical or geographical aspects. During decolonization, administrative frontiers were not changed, and became national borders. Colonial "confederations" such as French West Africa, French Equatorial Africa, which were put together so that the "richest" territories would support the poorest, broke up under the effect of centrifugal forces. And new confederations (e.g. between Senegal and Mali) had but an ephemeral existence.

The primary preoccupations of the national leaders that inherited these heterogeneous territories was to try to stick the parts together to make a nation, and to introduce the structures of a modern nation-state -- structures that had only been established in a cursory fashion during the colonial period.

By acting in this way, the new governments introduced a major disruption in Sahelian history, since these nations had never really existed in the region. The former empires of kingdoms brought together various ethnic groups (and in this respect were as heterogeneous as the colonial territories), but each ethnic group had its own customs within that empire or kingdom. The central authorities did not intervene in the specific laws of the ethnic groups, and respected the legislative autonomy of each one. The "nation", the common State and law common to all the members of the nation are modern concepts in the region, and they were imported from the West.

Modernization of the country

The Sahelian economy was not changed radically by colonization, and the Sahel has remained "underdeveloped". Social infrastructures such as the school and health care systems are still way behind those of the industrialized countries. The new leaders, who are impregnated with Western culture, are very well aware of the backwardness of the economy and of the social services.

Priority is thus attached to modernization of the economy, and modernization is seen as the way of progressively "catching up" with Western countries. Two sectors are receiving particular attention:

- Industry, which is still embryonic, although industrial development is considered a prerequisite for the birth of a modern nation -- , a sort of symbol of modernity;

- Transportation infrastructure, which, according to a doctrine that was generally accepted during the colonial period, is thought to almost automatically generate economic growth.

At the same time, priority is attached to the development of the social services: education, health, mass communications, etc. All these areas have enormous needs. Education, in particular, is often considered to be the top priority of all priorities.

The education system established by the colonial powers along the same lines as education systems in the West, and which trained the new elites that are now in power, is not really being brought into question. It has been re-oriented to a greater or lesser degree, but the basics have remained unaltered: the use of European languages, the low level of adaptation to the economic realities of the local context, etc. The education system is as alien to Sahelian traditions as it is to the needs of development. It is, however, expanding horizontally to reach larger and larger sections of the population, and it is expanding vertically through the development of secondary and higher education.

The obstacles to the development of industry, the development of infrastructures and the development of the social services are above all considered to be problems of investment.

Ambitious leaders

In feeling responsible for building the State and for modernizing the country, the new governments are caught up in the same continuity with the colonial power base that we mentioned earlier. In the eyes of the colonizers, local population groups were incapable of taking their destiny into their own hands and it was the duty of the colonizer to push these local population groups towards "progress", even against their will.

Development was expected to come as a result of government action, and not as a result of initiative taken by the local population. Whatever the ideologies they profess (socialist or not), the new governments adopt highly interventionist policies. Development plans, which more than anything else are investment plans, are devised and implemented. Official organizations are set up to promote development at the rural, national and provincial levels, and to promote industrial development.

These policies were largely inspired and supported by the industrialized countries. These countries were experiencing a period of exceptional prosperity and the ideologies that underpinned government action in the countries of the North were very similar to those found in the Sahelian countries: priority was attached to economic growth, and nobody had yet brought that attitude into question. The government's role in this growth was considered crucial and the influence of Keynesian economics was at its height.

These investment policies required financial resources, which were found:

-- Through foreign aid;

-- Through taxation of the only sector of the economy that generated any substantial level of resources: export crops. Governments started to receive taxes on exports that the trading companies had received during the colonial period, and, in this respect, the producers' situation was not really changed by decolonization.

Calls for unanimity and power in a vacuum

The priority attached to building the nation brought with it a <u>monolithic ideology</u> whereby everybody was to work together in this national construction project. Differences within Sahelian societies, and in particular the division of that society into groups often with conflicting interests, were not recognized.

In certain Sahelian countries, the single-party system is an expression of this ideology. From the end of the 1960s, military governments began to replace civilian governments in the name of the "well-being of the nation" (or some similar concept) in several countries. They suspended the multi-party system and claimed to act in the interests of the entire "people".

Memories of the traditional, community-oriented society strengthen this ideology and compound the belief that it is possible to find a development plan that suits everybody: the single-party system is the modern version of the "palaver tree", beneath which decisions concerning the community were taken. Western-style democracy is considered a risk for nascent national unity and is thought to drain off the energy that should be channeled into the mainstream of development.

Despite the fact that the dominant school of thought is calling for unanimity, the powers -- whether civilian or military -- are going to be largely divorced from the population groups they are intended to govern, and particularly from rural communities, which do not identify with the power base. This divorce is a result of:

-- The origin and nature of the power base, which grew out of Western traditions and is not rooted in Sahelian customs;

-- Moves to build a modern society to the detriment of the rural world: taxation of cash crops, chiefly by food marketing boards, which attempt to exert pressure over prices in order to promote the development of a modern urban society;

-- The adoption of objectives -- however well intentioned -- that have been defined without reference to the population groups. Even when these objectives are compatible with those of the social group concerned, the very fact that they are imposed from outside renders them suspect.

The power base is little closer to an entire category of city-dwellers that has been able to find employment neither in the public sector nor in the modern economy, and which has therefore turned to the informal sector. This section of the population is developing autonomously and clearly wishes as little intervention as possible from the political authorities.

In fact, <u>the Sahelians' attitude to the power base is ambiguous.</u> On the one hand, they continue to feel the need to belong to a group and to identify with a leader that provides security and protection. National leaders -- however often they may change in certain countries -- are thus widely acclaimed by the majority of the population.

On the other hand, <u>the vast majority of Sahelians do not identify with their leaders.</u> They do not feel involved in the objectives sought or in the means of action adopted. In most cases, the changes that have come about, particularly through military coups d'état, do not seem to have had a deep-seated effect on this state of affairs.

Further, <u>the vast majority of the population is still unorganized,</u> incapable of expressing itself politically except through sporadic rioting that is scarcely likely to bring real change. This is true of virtually the entire rural population, and of a large proportion of city-dwellers that do not follow the trade union movement.

In several Sahelian countries, the only press that exists is State-run, and organizations acting as the mouthpiece of an unofficial viewpoint are non-existent. Even in those countries where genuine freedom of expression does exist, <u>there is no powerful opposition</u> because the population is not sufficiently organized.

Recent developments

National leaders confronted with the difficulties of recent years have recognized that a system has become established in the Sahel within which the dynamism of the local population cannot manifest itself, and that the economies are stagnating as a consequence.

The official line has changed, and frequently emphasizes the need for the role of driving force behind development to be handed back to the people themselves, for the aspirations of the population to be taken into account, and for frameworks to be created within which the dynamism of the people can manifest itself. The latest version of the strategy for drought control and development drawn up by the Secretariat of the CILSS and then adopted by the Council of Ministers of that organization provides a good illustration of this recent change.

Several governments have taken moves to encourage dialogue with spokespeople of the people and to involve those spokesmen in the conception of the development plan.

However, it is clear that the habits and restrictions that have been created by the political leanings of the last two decades, combined with the constraints that were inherent in the legacy of the colonial period, cannot be abolished overnight. The priorities adopted immediately after independence have at best begun to be brought into question, and as yet there are no signs of a genuine opposition movement appearing.

Today's <u>Sahelian State</u> has taken over the reins of power from the colonial rulers and is the progeny of an alien tradition. <u>The modern State has set for itself the ambitious objective of building a nation and modernizing the economy.</u>

In view of its origins and of the action it has taken, <u>the State has become detached from the population, and the population does not identify with the State.</u>

Sahelian populations are unorganized, incapable of making themselves heard, and <u>there is no genuine opposition</u> anywhere in the region.

<u>A rift has formed between the power base and the population.</u> Those in power follow their own objectives, while population groups become introverted or else express their dynamism through other channels. Reforms that have been introduced and recent attempts to repair this rift have not yet been particularly successful.

Chapter 11

CONCLUSION: SOCIETIES IN CRISIS

This last chapter of the retrospective view aims to draw together the points that have been brought out so far, and to see how the legacy of the pre-colonial and colonial past of the Sahel fit into the economic, demographic and socio-political picture of the region. An attempt will be made to explain how this has brought about the current situation, and how it can be used as the basis for a study of the region's future.

We will thus examine the history of the last quarter-century, and attempt to see how this picture has been put together.

The legacy of the pre-colonial and colonial past

At independence, <u>Sahelian societies were still largely rural and traditional.</u> Social values and structures were a legacy of the pre-colonial past and were not basically changed by the colonial period. Sahelian economies were not profoundly changed by colonization. The colonial powers introduced export crops, thereby considerably increasing a tendency towards greater outward-orientation that had begun in the century before. But Sahelian economies nonetheless remained largely rural, traditional and <u>underdeveloped.</u>

Colonization <u>sowed the seeds of change</u> within these relatively stable societies: sharp population growth had begun ten or twenty years before, rapid urbanization had started, new values were emerging and the destructuring of traditional society had begun. New social categories were born, including a new political class that was strongly influenced by the colonial school system and Western culture.

Exponential population growth, the development of export crops and the lack of change in rural production systems disrupted the ecological balance, the signs of which were unspectacular but sufficiently evident to be worrisome for the future.

Post-independence Sahel

The move from the colonial era to independence was a gradual process. The power base was formed from the new political class that had emerged during the last years of colonial rule. No attempts were made to return to the pre-colonial status quo; the new leaders perpetuated the colonial regime.

The policies of the new governments were to be largely inspired from a <u>Western-style model of development,</u> which was more or less liberal or more or less socialist in different countries. This was a logical choice for the ruling elites, who had been strongly impregnated with European culture and who did not imagine that any other solution was feasible. The choice corresponded to the deep-seated aspirations of a sector of the population, and the rapidly developing media brought the Western model closer every day. Finally, continuity was encouraged by foreign aid: the European countries were committed to a process of economic development that was considerably more extensive and more lasting than they had ever experienced before. Nobody questioned the wisdom of the moves that were taken.

The priorities at this time were:

-- To find the hard currency needed to import consumer goods from the West, whence the priority attached to export crops, the development of any mineral resources that existed, and to forging links with the former colonial power, which overcame the immediate need for greater integration in the world-market system;

-- To develop industry, which was considered the very symbol of modernity, even if the conditions for this development were not particularly favorable: the ratio of productivity to wages was low, exchange rates were overvalued and did not allow for genuine competitiveness on world markets, whence the introduction of directive, protectionist policies;

-- To construct the infrastructure that was needed for the development of export crops, mining activities and industry;

-- To develop the social services, and in particular health care and education, along Western lines, and to develop the institutions needed to build modern nation-states.

The State acted as the basic driving force behind the conception and implementation of this model of development. International aid backed up aid from the former colonial power and was deeply involved in this process.

The Sahelian community was considered incapable of playing this role of driving force. Lacking necessary training in Western techniques, the community undoubtedly was incapable of playing that role, and contented itself with responding -- with varying degrees of success -- to State initiatives.

These policies led to real development and prosperity for a time, to different extents in different countries. It should be pointed out that these polices were not the result of genuine choices, but were the consequence of the socio-economic conditions of the early post-colonial period.

<u>External shocks and internal contradictions</u>

From the 1970s, external shocks began to disrupt this development and to bare the internal weaknesses or even contradictions of Sahelian economies:

-- <u>Drought</u> demonstrated that food crops had been neglected as much since independence as they had been during the colonial period. Food crop cultivation was still extensive, suffered from low productivity and was vulnerable to climatic fluctuations. But times had changed, and the production system has become incapable of meeting the needs of an expanding population (whence the deterioration of the environment), a growing urban population (whence the increasing structural food deficit) and drought (whence the occurrence of emergency situations).

-- <u>The oil shock and the groundnut shock:</u> Terms of trade deteriorated sharply and demonstrated the dangers of integration into the world market system. Sahelian countries occupied a marginal position on markets and could thus exert virtually no pressure on them, their exports were little diversified and their productivity was growing less fast than the world average. Thus, with the increasing outward-orientation of Sahelian economies, it was those economies that inevitably suffered.

Under the effect of these external shocks, the internal contradictions, which were already latent during the colonial period and which developed considerably after independence, began to become clearer:

-- The need to construct modern economies and the role that the State had assumed in attempting to achieve this objective brought <u>high taxation</u> on the incomes of producers. A few traders and religious leaders amassed substantial fortunes, but no group of rich farmers and no middle class emerged to drive development and consume the output of manufacturing industries.

<u>Overtaxed farmers tended to pull out of the market</u> (at least from the official market), and agricultural production stagnated. <u>Industry also stagnated, or even shrank, because of insufficient markets,</u> and the informal sector developed to allow the growing urban population to subsist.

-- The emphasis laid on the social services and on the building of a modern nation-state swelled the ranks of the public sector, whose size became progressively out of proportion with a productive sector that was growing less fast. The developing school system generated the growth of the public sector, which became the principal outlet for school graduates.

This situation led to:

-- Even stronger pressure on incomes from productive activities, and thus even greater introversion of producers;

-- Increasing calls for foreign aid and thus growing dependence;

-- Rising external indebtedness as a temporary solution.

The situation was developing as if the dynamism that existed in Sahelian society was fragmented, and as if these islands of dynamism were acting independently of one another, and without the coordination needed to build a developing society.

- -- The State and the social groups composing the State were increasing in size in inordinate proportions, absorbing a growing share of the national resources and foreign aid available.

- -- The rural population was migrating or becoming introverted; the more dynamic rural inhabitants were leaving the village individually or in small groups.

- -- City-dwellers other than civil servants were organizing themselves in order to subsist, expressing their dynamism wherever possible, and drawn by contradictory influences.

In the attempts to develop along Western lines, the State and foreign aid ultimately failed to involve the community, and the community did not respond. Social interaction did not bring self-sustained growth but an increasingly dependent economy that began to become disjointed. Indeed, the entire society began to become disjointed, and as time went by the situation in several Sahelian countries was becoming more and more critical.

Even if the policies that have been followed were designed to promote the building of the nation and development of the entire country, these polices have only favored a privileged urban minority. The polices have never really been brought under scrutiny because no organized political opposition has existed.

The situation in 1987

New external shocks -- the rising value of the dollar, rising interest rates, two consecutive years of acute drought -- have further aggravated this critical situation in recent years.

The return of better climatic conditions since 1985 and the current trends in the world economy have had positive effects (the falling value of the dollar and falling petroleum prices) and negative effects (collapse of the cotton price, falling imported cereals prices, which start to compete with local produce on the domestic market).

Irrespective of these outside factors, the internal contradictions within Sahelian societies have not been resolved.

- -- The economies are still disjointed, there is no cross-fertilization between modern cities and rural areas, and the conditions for sharp increases in agricultural and industrial production clearly still do not exist, despite the structural adjustment programs that have been imposed on Sahelian governments.

-- There is a widening gulf between the economic realities and the aspirations of a population that is increasingly attracted by the Western model, and the economic realities are not becoming any more favorable. Indeed, in certain instances, they are worsening.

Sahelian societies are manifestly in crisis.

*
* *

At first sight, the history of the Sahel in the last few decades seems highly erratic. The Sahelians seem to have been buffeted by outside events -- climatic, economic or geopolitical -- over which they have had no hold. However, even though the Sahelians have not succeeded in controlling their future, the analysis made above has attempted to demonstrate the deep-seated logic of their history: the social, economic and political conditions that existed at independence and the interaction of the forces present have not yet made it possible for the foundations of sound growth to be laid.

What is also striking is the fact that trends are going in opposite directions: a population explosion, the destructuring of traditional society and the appearance of certain new values -- all of which are taking place extraordinarily quickly -- while at the same time the economy is stagnating, the environment is deteriorating, and certain aspects of behavior have remained unchanged for centuries. The picture of early European societies painted by Fernand Braudel -- <u>Histories that "run parallel but at different speeds"</u> seems just as applicable to the Sahelian societies today.

It is also striking that the new-found dynamism of the Sahelians, which would have been unimaginable a quarter-century ago, and that is now being expressed in rural areas (through village associations) and in urban areas (through the informal sector), is manifestly incapable of spurring real growth.

<u>The economic development policies that have been adopted since 1960 are consequences of the social, political and economic conditions</u> that existed at independence. Subsequent trends in socio-politico-economic conditions consolidated policy decisions and those policy decisions in turn perpetuated the trends in socio-politico-economic trends.

The policies not only brought <u>disjointed economies but also disjointed societies,</u> marked by a widening gulf between the rural society and the urban society, and a deepening rift between the power base and the population.

Within the existing framework, <u>the dynamism of the rural and urban population groups cannot find expression</u> in terms of economic development. The gap is already opening between a population that is increasingly made up of young people and that is more and more open to the outside world, on the one hand, and the realities of an economy that is not progressing and that is becoming more and more heavily dependent on the outside just to ensure the survival of the members of the community.

PART II

THE TREND SCENARIO

ECONOMIC STAGNATION AND INCREASING DEPENDENCE

"Africa will continue to receive aid, and an "assisted" society is a society that has lost its soul..."

Tidiane Diakité

INTRODUCTION TO THE TREND SCENARIO

In Part I we described the early and more recent history of the Sahel, attempting to identify trends and pinpoint the underlying mechanisms. We shall now tackle the Futures Study proper and try to construct a trend scenario. But to avoid misunderstandings, this term will have to be defined.

We can agree first of all that a scenario is a logical succession of credible but hypothetical events leading from the present to some future date. It might seem tempting to construct a trend scenario for the Sahel simply by extrapolating from the main trends identified in our retrospective study. The trouble with this approach is that extrapolation from trends does not automatically produce a logical sequence of events. With present-day Sahelian societies, as with any society, extending certain trends over a long period, e.g. the quarter-century we have opted for here, leads to some unlikely situations and brings out contradictions that would necessarily have to be resolved; the resulting scenario thus lacks coherence and credibility.

One may say, on the other hand, that one of the few statements we can be sure of in the Sahel today is that present trends cannot continue for very long: the deterioration of the rural environment cannot go on indefinitely, nor can the growing dependence on the outside world.

To construct our trend scenario, we have therefore looked at the Sahel as a social system set in a certain environment, and we have made the following hypotheses about it:

-- There will be no fundamental change in the interaction between forces that has been taking place within Sahelian societies in recent years; adjustments will be made to enable these societies to go on living without major upheavals; in particular, the seeds of change we have found at work in the Sahel will not be able to take on any real significance in the life of the region.

-- The Sahelian environment, both physical (the climate) and socio-economic (including relationships with other countries, in Africa and beyond) will develop along the most likely lines.

By building a trend scenario in this way, we will be able to make a more thorough exploration of some of the mechanisms now operating in the region, thereby completing our retrospective view.

Chapter 12

THE EVOLUTION OF SOCIETY AS A PRODUCT OF TENSIONS

What is new about the Sahel crisis?

To return to our retrospective view, which concluded that these societies are societies in crisis, it might be said that our conclusion lacks originality. All human societies, except perhaps for a few isolated, primitive societies, have always been more or less in crisis, in transition between one state and the next. These crises vary in their degree of severity, and the transitions take place at varying rates. It is basically because there are tensions within them, because they are in crisis, that societies evolve at all.

The Sahel is no exception to this rule; it has applied to all human societies for many centuries, and one can find indications of crisis in the distant past of the region. Re-reading, for example, the author of the Tarikh es Soudan, a man of letters writing in Timbuktu in the 17th century after the fall of the Songhai empire: "Everything changed at that moment, security gave way to danger, opulence to destitution; trouble, calamities and violence took the place of peace and calm. Everywhere people devoured each other; everywhere and in every sense, pillage and depredation reigned, and war spared neither the lives nor the chattels of the inhabitants. Disorder abounded". The sense of living in a crisis situation -- then or now -- could not be better put. The rise of the slave trade in the 18th century, its abolition in the early 19th, colonization and subsequent independence were undoubtedly all moments of crisis for the societies of the Sahel.

What is specific about the present crisis compared to earlier ones? In what respects does it differ from the crises affecting industrialized countries today? What are the tensions that have given rise to it? We need to ask all those questions before tackling the construction of a trend scenario for the region.

The retrospective study provided a few answers to these questions, but it seems important to gain a better grasp of the interplay of tensions within Sahelian societies. The retrospective study brought out one factor in particular, one that necessarily creates tensions: the changes now taking place, at different rates, within these societies. The asynchronous nature of a society's evolution is not a feature of the Sahel alone: the difficulties that Western societies are experiencing in their attempts to adapt to rapid change are often cited as an explanation of crisis situations, and particularly of persistent unemployment. In Western societies as in the Sahel, not everything changes at the same rate.

What, then, are the specific features of the Sahelian crisis?

What elements make up the Sahelian crisis?

Historians and sociologists who have studied the evolution of human societies disagree sharply as to the analytical methods that should be used, and in the analyses they produce. Without entering into scholastic quarrels here, we will simply point out that there does seem to be a certain consensus on the facts we stressed above: that the different elements constituting a society do not evolve at the same rate, that this asynchronism sets up tensions within the society, and that it is partly through these internal tensions, partly through the impact of external jolts, that the society evolves.

There is less consensus when it comes to defining the relevant constituent elements in society. Three such elements often selected, under a variety of names, are culture, social structure and civilization. As these terms are often used differently, and as they do not always mean the same in English and French, we will define their scope as used in the following pages.

— <u>Culture</u> includes values and ways of thinking which determine attitudes and behavior within a society.

— <u>Social structure</u> is a society's division into groups, classes or other aggregates, and the relations between such groups: linked to the social groups are institutions through which the groups attain their aspirations.

— <u>Civilization</u> should be understood as material civilization: whatever is produced by culture through social structures. This includes:

   a) lifestyles,

   b) ways of producing the goods and services required for the lifestyle in question.

In modern Western societies, civilization evolves at a faster pace, driven by technical progress. Overly rigid social structures, and also values and behavior patterns, have evident trouble keeping up with this pace. From this asynchronism spring many tensions.

In Sahelian societies, as in many others which have scarcely begun their agricultural and industrial revolutions, certain aspects of civilization — the lifestyles of certain social groups, for example — change very rapidly, while other aspects — especially modes of production — remain relatively rigid. Culture changes under the impact of outside influences; new values and aspirations emerge, which the slowly developing modes of production cannot satisfy adequately. The rigidity of the social structures hampers the evolution of modes of production.

The experience of societies that have undergone that phase of development shows that the gap between culture and civilization sets up tensions that ultimately become intolerable. A change occurs in the material civilization through the action of agents emerging in the social structure. That change in turn leads to changes in social structure and culture that are often very sudden -- changes that restore the balance so that a new cycle can begin.

The movement of society thus seems to be driven by different elements with different dynamics, producing periods of speeding up and slowing down rather than a continuous process. This pattern may be disrupted by external jolts that can affect any of the three elements we have identified in society.

This is the general scheme we shall adopt in constructing our scenarios for the Sahel. First, however, we shall use it to re-interpret the region's recent history.

The interplay of internal tensions

Over the past two centuries, the rise of Islam has brought significant changes to traditional Sahelian culture, while certain external factors have made a violent impact: the trans-Atlantic and trans-Saharan slave trades and then the end of the trans-Atlantic trade in the early 19th century. The resulting tensions were reflected in attempts to re-establish strong local power bases -- attempts that were to be swept away by the major external jolt of colonization.

This was to have a considerable impact:

- On culture: we have seen the unprecedented expansion of Islam as a reaction to colonization; the rise of Western values due to the presence of Europeans and the colonial school system; the growth of individualism; the replacement of the former notions of prestige by those of wealth and education; the decline of kinship groups and of the ancestor worship that was one of their key manifestations; the weakening of the sense of tribal belonging, etc.

- On the social structure, which underwent major upheavals: the aristocracy lost its power to the colonial rulers; the slaves, who constituted a large section of society, were emancipated; new classes appeared, a political class and a class of auxiliaries to the colonial administration; the social stratification which had previously depended on age, sex and lineage did not change immediately, but the power of the chiefs was already deeply affected.

Despite those more or less violent changes, the Sahel's civilization proved lasting: lifestyles changed to some extent in the cities that were beginning to develop, but they changed little in the rural areas; modes of production remained very stable; conceptions about the land and land tenure, an essential element in rural systems, changed only slowly.

A clear discrepancy appeared between culture, which was beginning to change very rapidly, and civilization, which was lagging behind. The profound upheavals that marked the social structure doubtless contributed to the width of this gap: there were no longer enough people capable of changing lifestyles and modes of production, or else people were traumatized by the upheavals that had just occurred. This is at least a plausible hypothesis. That widening gap clearly sets up tensions, though without those tensions leading to a rupture.

The last quarter-century has brought new changes. First, there have been external jolts, e.g, drought, the oil shocks. Compared to colonization, the impact of those jolts has been minor. The greatest jolt, though slow and insidious, has undoubtedly been the invasion of Western values, and above all the Western models of consumption that are now brought to every village by the media.

As a result, Sahelian culture has probably changed more in the last twenty-five years than it did throughout the colonial period, and those changes have affected the rural areas, which had until then remained in relative isolation, as well as the cities.

The social structure was disrupted again by the abrupt departure of the colonial rulers and the takeover of power by a new ruling class.

The gap between culture and civilization has widened further, and despite the efforts -- or at least the good intentions -- of those concerned, attempts to close it have failed. There has still been no rupture, at least in modes of production.

Where this asynchronous development of culture, civilization and social structure in the Sahel goes next, and how its internal tensions now develop, will be decisive for the region's future. Be that as it may, this scheme of evolution in Sahelian societies is still very general. We need to pinpoint the factors that are likely to play a key role within this overall scheme in the future of Sahelian societies.

Structural analysis of the Sahelian system

Before we develop our scenarios for the future, therefore, it will be useful to complement our retrospective view with a structural analysis, approaching the Sahel's problems from a different angle. We shall see that this analysis does not introduce any really new elements to the retrospective view, but qualifies that view and complements it in several respects.

The retrospective analysis enabled us to identify a number of factors which have shaped, are shaping and will very probably continue to shape the development of Sahelian societies. But Sahelian societies are extremely complex systems set in a complex environment. There are many variables, internal and external to the Sahelian system, interacting with each other and setting up long chains of reaction. Some of these interactions reinforce each other, others cancel each other out. If we select certain of these factors in Sahelian society as playing a driving role in the evolution of the region, as suggested by a first analysis, can we be sure of making the right choice?

Within the complex context we have just described, do certain factors really have the driving role attributed to them? Will their influence not become diluted along the chain of reactions they provoke within the Sahelian systems, while the effects of others are reinforced so that, in the end, those other factors play a decisive role that one would not have expected? What is lacking is a classification of the factors that generate change in the Sahel.

Table A

STRUCTURAL ANALYSIS

The aim of a structural analysis is to highlight the structure of a system (in this case, the Sahel). The approach used includes:

1. Identification of the system

   The system is defined by its internal variables, while its environment is defined by external variables.

2. Defining relationships between variables

   -- This means asking whether variable "i" acts on variable "j" and so on, entering "1" or "0" accordingly in each square of a matrix made up from the selected variables. (Instead of "0" and "1", one might identify strong, medium and weak relationships).

   -- The completed matrix gives a schematic and qualitative picture of the structure of the system under consideration.

3. Determining the driving force of the variables

   From the structural matrix one can:

   -- Classify the variables as driving or dependent according to the number of relationships in which they are directly involved;

   -- Classify the variables according to their total number of relations, direct and indirect (i.e. through one or more intermediary variables);

   -- Classify the variables according to the number of relationships in which they may be involved in the future (variables with potential driving force);

   -- These classifications are worked out mathematically from the matrix, thereby revealing the consequences implicitly contained in its structure.

Structural analysis, without claiming to be strictly accurate -- the social sciences are of course not capable of strict accuracy -- aims to explore the role (more or less a driving role, more or less a dependent role) of each variable in a human society. Basically it is an exercise in systematic reflection on the role of those variables.

Our analysis primarily consisted in asking a panel of experts to identify the variables in the Sahelian system and its environment, and then asking them which variables act on which others and drawing conclusions from their answers.

Clearly, this introduces no element other than those already to be found in the experts' opinions. But it does make it possible to identify the variables that the experts consider to be involved in the greatest number of direct and indirect relationships that affect the system in question -- and this appraisal does not always coincide with one's initial, intuitive conclusions.

Table A above gives a brief description of the method of structural analysis employed.

General outline of the approach adopted for the Futures Study

The introduction of a structural analysis enables us to give a more precise overview of the approach adopted by the Sahel Futures Study, an approach that is illustrated in the diagram below and that could be summed up as follows:

-- The retrospective analysis brings out, on the one hand, the main trends in the region's development and the forces at work within the Sahel and, on the other hand, the seeds of possible change.

-- The structural analysis pinpoints the variables which seem to act most strongly as driving forces and which will probably play a decisive part in the region's future, whatever that may prove to be.

-- A trend scenario is constructed from the factors that emerge from these two analyses, and by applying our general scheme for the evolution of Sahelian society under the influence of its internal tensions. The trend scenario takes account of the forces at work in the Sahel and the seeds of change which, even if they do not play a crucial role, cannot be ignored.

-- Also on the basis of the factors brought out by these two analyses, we then identify the factors for change that might lead the region towards other futures than the one described in our trend scenario, and we explore these possible futures.

-- Some of those futures seem undesirable, others desirable. We try to identify the conditions that will have to to be met if the region is to develop in a desirable way.

METHOD OF APPROACH TO FUTURES STUDY

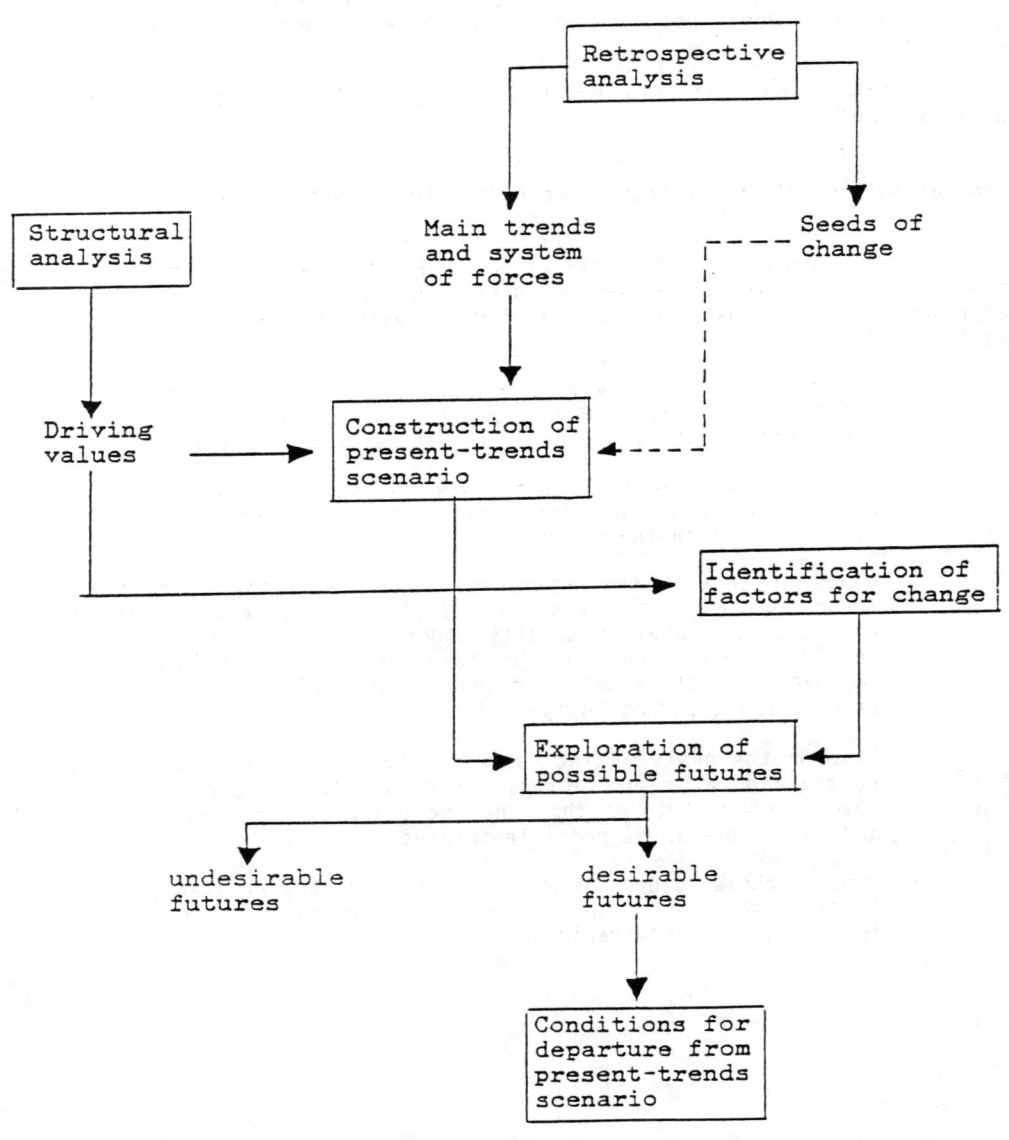

The driving variables

Table B gives the most interesting results of our structural analysis. We would once again stress in passing that these results must be treated with caution, as they reflect no more than the opinions of a panel of experts. The table shows:

-- The ten variables that seem to have the strongest driving role in the "direct" classification, i.e. looking only at variables acting directly on other variables without intermediaries;

-- The ten variables that seem to have the strongest driving role in the "indirect" classification, i.e. taking account of chains of reaction and loops of variables acting on each other;

-- The ten variables that seem to have the strongest driving role in a classification of potential, i.e. taking into consideration not only the direct and indirect relations which (in the experts' opinions) actually exist, but also those that are embryonic or non-existent today but could be significant in the near or distant future.

These lists of variables may seem a motley combination of sociological, political, economic, technological and other factors. This is because, to set out all the characteristics of the Sahelian system and its environment without omitting variables that might play an essential part, we have made a wide sweep, bringing in variables of all kinds.

Table B

Variables with the Strongest Driving Role for the Sahel, as Identified by Structural Analysis

Direct classification	Indirect classification	Potential classification
Values & mentalities	Values & mentalities	Information technologies
Role of State	Role of State	Type of regime
Aid to Sahel	Type of regime	Biotechnologies
Type of regime	Aid to Sahel	Values & mentalities
Family structures	Family structures	North/South relations
Energy technologies	North/South relations	Role of State
Rainfall	Rainfall	Aid to Sahel
North/South relations	Information technologies	Northern values & lifestyles
Agriculture	Influence of France	Family structures
Role of local powers	International trade	International trade

This table merits a few comments:

-- **Values and mentalities** emerge as a strong driving force whatever type of classification is taken. That variable includes more or less what we were referring to above as "culture," and it is no surprise to find it among the driving variables. Another result, which is not illustrated by Table B, is that this variable also emerges as a highly dependent one, i.e, many other variables, internal and external to the Sahelian system, act on values and mentalities through direct or indirect relationships. We have seen, for example, the influence of Islam and the West on Sahelian values and mentalities. Values and mentalities seem to emerge as an unstable variable, whose effect on the Sahelian system is probably of prime importance, but which can also be subject to strong outside influences and unexpected feedback effects. This needs to be borne in mind in building our scenarios.

-- **Role of the State, type of regime.** It is not surprising, given the many analyses that have been carried out on this topic, that the structural analysis points to the driving role that these variables play in the evolution of Sahelian societies. On the other hand, they do not emerge as very dependent variables.

-- **Family structures.** The driving role of this variable is not clearly distinguishable. The results of the structural analysis can be compared to the thesis recently put forward by Emmanuel Todd in "L'Enfance du Monde", on the role of family systems in the creation of the world's centers of development over the past two centuries and the spread of development from those centers.

-- **The role of local power groups** comes 10th in the direct classification and 11th in the indirect classification, drawing attention to a variable one might not have thought of spontaneously.

These four variables -- the role of the State, type of regime, family structures, the role of local power groups -- are part of what we have been calling "social structures". The structural analysis draws attention to the role of these particular factors within the structures.

-- **Aid to the Sahel, North-South relations and international trade.** Here we enter the field of the Sahel's environment and the impact of the environment on the region. In the same field we find that the variable **influence of France** plays a significant role, while other similar variables one might have thought would play a driving role do not emerge so clearly among the driving variables (e.g. the role of neighboring African countries, especially Nigeria, which carries great economic and demographic weight -- 50 per cent of West Africa's population -- or the role of the Arab states).

-- Another variable external to the Sahel and part of its environment is **rainfall**; it would have been surprising not to find that factor among those listed.

-- A group of variables one might call <u>technological variables</u> emerge as driving forces -- energy technology, information technology, biotechnology -- carrying what would seem to be disproportionate weight compared to the part they play at present in the Sahel. The structural analysis in fact has the merit of drawing attention to <u>the potential role</u> these variables could play in the region; the circumstances under which this potential might become reality need to be identified.

-- Lastly, it is rather surprising to find that certain variables the experts had selected as characteristic of the Sahel system, with the more or less explicit idea that they might play a driving role, do not show up among the strongest driving forces. One such variable is the role of women, who, aside from their important productive role, play a specific part in the transmission of values and mentalities from one generation to the next, and in the evolution of those values and mentalities; i.e. the role of education.

It will be helpful to look at these variables to see why they do not emerge as driving forces from the structural analysis.

Constructing the trend scenario

According to the general outline set out above, and taking into account what the structural analysis has to add, we shall set about constructing the trend scenario in the following way:

-- We shall first examine the environment of the Sahel, including in this concept both climatic conditions and the political and economic context, immediate and more distant; and we shall examine its influence on the region and the new jolts it may yet inflict on the Sahel. Taking the results of the structural analysis into account, we shall pay particular attention to the external environment and the role the new technologies might play in the Sahel of tomorrow.

-- Then we shall study how the culture -- the values and mentalities that govern human behavior in the Sahel -- is liable to develop.

-- The next chapter will cover the evolution of social structures and power structures.

-- We shall then examine demographic problems: fertility, birthrate, migration from the rural areas to the cities.

-- Then we shall look at civilization: rural production systems (of crops and livestock), urban production systems (industry, services and the informal sector).

-- Lastly, we shall examine the conditions under which the different elements in our trend scenario could combine to form a cohesive and plausible whole, and then, having explored in passing the possible materialization of scenarios that are less favorable than the trend scenario, we shall conclude with an attempt to answer the question of whether such a future is acceptable.

Chapter 13

THE SAHELIAN ENVIRONMENT: TOMORROW'S CLIMATE

Recent climatic trends in a long-term perspective

Recent climatic trends in the Sahel, which are outlined in chapter 4, can be interpreted in two ways:

-- Either the twenty-year dry period the region has just experienced is part of long-term climatic trend which can be reconstituted from the historical data available;

-- Or the dry period marks a break in the known trend.

It is clear that the interpretation we choose will make a significant difference to our view of tomorrow's climate.

The continuity hypothesis

It row seems to be clearly established that, ever since the Quaternary era began, the Sahel has experienced fluctuations in climate. This is probably due to two periodic astronomic phenomena: precession of the equinoxes and variation in the eccentricity of the earth's orbit, both of which influence the amount of energy received by each of the earth's hemispheres.

It seems to be established that during the last ice age twenty thousand years ago, what is now the Sahel had a Saharan climate, and that this period of extreme drought was followed by one of high humidity which reached its optimum about 8,000 BC. During this period most of the Sahara was covered by vast stretches of savanna and huge lakes, Lake Chad being all that remains of one of these. The Sahel received significantly more rain than it does now, and its great rivers flowed more abundantly than today.

The climate began to become drier around 4000 BC and this process accelerated over subsequent centuries. The most spectacular consequence was the creation of the desert, basically completed around 2000 BC. Since then, the available data is fairly consistent, allowing us to confirm that the climate is gradually becoming drier through an irregular process typified by two kinds cf fluctuation:

-- Fairly slight, long-term fluctuations lasting a century or a few centuries: at the time of the Ghanaian and Malian empires, the climate was probably wetter, on average, than today, and the observations of 17th century travelers lead us to believe that the same was true at that time;

-- The short-term, more marked fluctuations referred to as droughts. We know from oral traditions that there have always been droughts, perhaps going back more than two thousand years. There are many eyewitness accounts of terrible droughts, for example between 1639 and 1643 and between 1738 and 1756. More recently, there were several droughts during the colonial period, particularly the 1913 drought which proved disastrous across much of the Sahel.

One may consider that the recent drought is a further such short-term fluctuation in the Sahel's climatic history. It seems to have been more severe than earlier droughts -- at least, there are a number of indications to this effect, the most spectacular of which is that the river Niger practically ran dry in Niamey in 1985, a striking event of which we have no earlier record from written accounts or folk tales, and which therefore cannot have happened before in human memory. But one may regard the greater severity of the last drought as unexceptional, being part of the general trend towards a drier climate in the region: it was merely a little more severe than those that went before, as might be expected in a trend that unfolds over a thousand years.

The change-in-trend hypothesis

Another hypothesis can be, and has been, put forward: that this last drought is the sign of a recent change in the trend, a sharp acceleration of the drying process which all partisans of this hypothesis attribute not to natural causes but to human activity.

This change can be attributed to two causes:

-- Deforestation and, more generally, alterations made to the vegetation cover in the Sahelian regions themselves, modifying the reflective power (or albedo) of the land and changing the energy balance in the atmosphere above these regions, which could have an effect on the amount of rainfall they receive. However, while we understand that variation in the albedo can have an effect on the distribution of monsoon rains, it is not so easy to see how it could influence the monsoon itself, the northward movement of the inter-tropical front which, if insufficient or ill-timed, leads to drought in the Sahel. Albedo measurements for the Sahelian regions, taken from satellites since 1973, have shown no correlation with rainfall. The drop in albedo recorded between 1973 and 1979 did not lead to higher rainfall as might have been expected. Also, the negative feedback hypothesis -- i.e. drought leading to a reduction in vegetation cover and hence to a rise in albedo, which in turn leads to a fresh reduction in rainfall -- is yet to be verified.

-- The massive deforestation of the humid tropical regions south of the Sahel. The galloping disappearance of the tropical rain forest in the coastal regions, replaced with plantations or with more or less sterile savanna, is a recognized fact. It is estimated that in Côte d'Ivoire the forest covered more than 15 million hectares at the beginning of this century, no more than 12 million by 1956, and 9 million by 1966. In 1985, it apparently covered not much more than 3 million hectares. That forest, it is argued, constitutes a reservoir of moisture: its disappearance has an effect on the amount of water present in the atmosphere of the coastal regions during the monsoon season, and consequently on the amount of water that the south wind carries northward into the Sahel. This view also is hypothetical -- a plausible hypothesis, but unverified.

The return of two years of good rains in 1985 and 1986 makes the change-in-trend thesis less attractive, but it certainly does not allow one to exclude the possibility of a shift in the general climatic trend, an acceleration of the centuries-long drying process caused by human activity. Massive deforestation in the humid coastal regions is at present the most plausible cause of such an acceleration.

Tomorrow's climate

Whichever hypothesis is adopted, one fact seems virtually certain: there is no reason to question the basic fact that the Sahelian climate is irregular. There are thus grounds to believe that the futures will be identical to the past in this respect, where more or less dry periods are followed by periods with more or less good rainfall, and where this succession of periods is relatively irregular and non-cyclical. This means that the recurrence of drought over the next quarter-century must be seen as a virtually normal part of the pattern.

A logical consequence is that the Sahel must be prepared for recurrent drought. Is this a trite conclusion? Perhaps not, if one agrees that human beings tend to attribute all their ills to a natural scourge while it is present, including those for which it is not responsible -- and then forget it as soon as it has temporarily receded.

The question is whether the next twenty-five years will be, on average, wetter or drier than the last twenty-five years. There are three possible hypotheses:

1. <u>The continuity hypothesis</u> developed above. If one agrees with this, then twenty-five years is too short a period to show a significant reduction in average rainfall. But, given the high degree of irregularity observed in the past, one cannot exclude the possibility of a long dry period equivalent to that of the 1970s and 1980s, or perhaps even a little drier.

2. <u>The hypothesis of a rupture in the climatic trend</u> would be reflected in an accelerated drop in rainfall. If this rupture is due to the disappearance of forests in the coastal region, it is unlikely that the new trend will correct itself over the period under

consideration. According to this hypothesis it is possible, and indeed very likely, that the next quarter-century will be markedly drier on average than the last quarter-century, with even more marked dry periods -- perhaps so marked as to constitute major catastrophes.

3. There is a third hypothesis that cannot be excluded: that of a break in planet-wide climatic trends due to human activities. Most experts are in agreement that an altered planet-wide trend would be towards a warmer planet. The trend would be the result of two phenomena: an increase in the carbon dioxide content of the atmosphere due to massive use of fossil fuels; and the presence of freons -- gases used in many applications and which accumulate in the upper atmosphere -- amplifying the greenhouse effect around the planet. While there is no doubt that these phenomena are real, opinions are divided on the questions of when and how much we can expect the planet to warm up. If such a process were to be significant over the period under consideration, its effects should tend towards an increase of rainfall in the Sahel. But at the present time nobody seems to be in a position to say on what scale this increase will occur.

Of course, this third hypothesis is independent of the first two. It could run concurrently with the first, modifying or reversing the region's centuries-long drying trend. Or it could combine with the second and considerably reduce the effects of the break-in-trend hypothesis.

For our trend scenario, since we cannot give a reasoned argument in favor of one or another hypothesis, it would seem best to opt for the continuity hypothesis, i.e. a slow drying process, not significant at the level of one human generation but involving more or less pronounced dry periods, unpredictable in our present state of knowledge but very likely to occur within the next twenty-five years.

Will climate play a decisive role in the Sahel?

It is clear that climatic developments since the end of the 1960s have played an important part in the Sahel. It is also clear that these developments have accelerated and highlighted certain developments which would have happened in any case, drought or no drought: deterioration of the environment, rise in dependence on food aid, etc. Will the climate play an equally important part in the future?

There is no single answer to this question. Locally, climatic developments may be decisive for the future of human communities. In marginal zones, a drop in average rainfall or a prolonged drought may have major effects: lack of sufficient biomass would make it impossible to continue the type of herding practiced for centuries, and the traditional rainfed crops would become impracticable. The migration of a whole section of the population to areas with more abundant rainfall might be unavoidable.

But at a Sahel-wide level, the decisive nature of the climate is less certain. Lower average rainfall will create a certain southward shift of activities and population groups, and no doubt lead to a less favorable scenario than the trend scenario (see chapter 28). But with more abundant rains, would the Sahel do more than join the ranks of African countries that do not suffer from drought but are nonetheless going through a severe crisis? Would it not find itself back in the position it was in during those years of relatively good rains, the 1950s and 1960s, i.e. a situation of obvious underdevelopment?

One important measure of underdevelopment is a lack of control over the natural environment. Natural disasters strike Third-World countries as much as the rest, but no more; what is different about the Third World is its vulnerability when such disasters strike. As L. Timberlake shows, natural disasters these days have little effect in the industrialized world, while in the Third World they are almost always catastrophic. In 1972 an earthquake hit Managua and killed 5 000 people; in 1971, an earthquake of comparable intensity on the Richter scale in the San Francisco valley, California, killed 65. In the "average" natural disaster in Japan the death-toll is 63; in Peru it is 2 900. Drought occurs periodically in the southwestern United States: it makes life a little less comfortable for the people who live there. In the Sahel, drought leads to acute famine and makes massive food aid indispensable if a massive death-toll is to be avoided.

The role of the climate as a driving force, though undeniable in the most fragile areas, especially those along the desert fringe, must not be overestimated. A "miracle-rain" scenario, involving a long period of good rainfall, would not solve all the Sahel's problems. Certainly it would turn the region green again, but it would not even solve the problems of deterioration of the natural environment. Population pressure would persist, and the Sahel would merely enjoy a few years' respite to solve its problems. One may even ask whether, by reducing the urgency of finding a new ecological balance and giving the illusion that problems were going to solve themselves, the "miracle rain" scenario might in the long run do more harm than good for the region's development.

The importance of climate for the region's future must not be ignored, but neither must it be overestimated.

We shall adopt the hypothesis that there will be no rupture in climatic trends, i.e, there will be no significant drop in average rainfall over the next twenty-five years, but that the irregularity of the climate will persist and that new droughts, more or less prolonged, are highly probable.

Chapter 14

THE SAHELIAN ENVIRONMENT: TOMORROW'S WORLD

In a world where interdependence is constantly increasing, no region will be free from the influence of the international environment, but that influence will take very specific forms in the Sahel:

- Because of the way in which that region fits into the worldwide geopolitical and geo-economic interplay.

- Because of the nature of the Sahel's relations with the industrial world; the present chapter will deal with financial relations and with the impact of the technology proposed by Northern countries; commercial relations will be examined in chapters 18 and 19;

- Because of the nature of the region's relations with its immediate environment: the Arab world to the North and the West and Central African countries to the South.

The Sahel's position in worldwide geopolitical and geo-economic interplay

For future generations of historians, 1970 will doubtless stand out, at the global level, as the year when sustained and relatively regular economic growth made way for a series of major fluctuations. The time taken by markets and governments to bring those movements under control was sufficiently long to allow other profound imbalances to appear. In this way, the Latin American debt crisis was, to a great extent, the legacy of the two oil shocks; and the current decline of the U.S. dollar is due to that currency's rise during the 1980s, itself caused by the fight against inflation that followed as a consequence of the second oil shock.

These movements of the world economy are most probably due to the confluence of two phenomena:

- <u>Rising interdependence,</u> which involves movements of persons and information, transfers of financial resources, and interchange of natural resources or manufactured goods;

-- The emergence within the world of market economies of a USA/EEC/Japan triad; a corollary to that development has been <u>the weakening of the regulatory role</u> played by the United States in the post-war economy.

Under these conditions, interdependence makes it increasingly necessary to seek cooperation between governments in an effort to regulate international markets, and especially exchange markets, at a time when the progress of that cooperation is hindered by the growing number of governments involved on the international scene.

If this analysis is accurate, the development of the world economy over the coming twenty-five years will most probably continue to be marked by profound imbalances. The forces that underpin this rising interdependence seem so powerful that the movement will continue to develop even if protectionist measures were to temporarily slow down or halt the process.

Two other trends, independent of the above phenomena, should progressively alter the face of the world economy:

-- <u>Growing differentiation</u> among different countries and regions;

-- The current <u>development of technical advances.</u>

During the 1950s and 1960s, numerous economists accepted the idea of a gradual convergence of national per capita incomes; the growth within less developed countries would be more rapid, in line with the model provided by Western Europe and Japan, which eventually caught up with United States incomes. However, the most striking lesson to be learned from the experience of the past twenty years is that each region or country has its own dynamics, which depend on the behavior of its social groups and the policies of its various governments. The differentiation within the Third World has emerged as a firmly established trend, and the most probable hypothesis is that the movement will continue over the coming twenty to thirty years. Future developments will be very different in the industrial countries of South East Asia, in continent-nations such as India or China, in the countries of Latin America, in the Arab world, and in sub-Saharan Africa.

At the same time, if technological innovations are subdivided -- as C. Freeman suggests -- into marginal innovations, radical innovations, technological revolutions, and socio-technical paradigm shifts, it becomes necessary to recognize that the rapid expansion of information technologies, which was already under way in the early 1960s, unquestionably belongs to the fourth category. Those technologies have brought about profound modifications in technical processes, in conditions of competition, in geographic distribution of productive activities, in the relative rarity of different categories of labor, and in job structures. Although biotechnologies are still in the very early stages of development, it is reasonable to think that this initial phase will lead to technical revolutions in the sectors of agriculture, livestock activities, human and animal hygiene, food processing, and chemistry.

Finally, the coming twenty-five years will most probably continue to be marked by permanent East-West rivalry, irrespective of the development of relations between the Soviet Union and the United States. One consequence of this is the risk of open or covert internationalization of the civil wars or conflicts that may appear in sub-Saharan Africa.

What is the significance for the Sahel of these principal trends in the world outlook?

-- The European Community, with which the Sahel (and more especially West Africa), maintains close relations, will find itself increasingly torn between two sets of interests. On the one hand, the Community's own economic interests, underscored by growing competition within the developed world, will incite its business sector to set up interests in South East Asia, in North America, and even in South America. On the other hand, the cultural and strategic interests of the Community will force European governments to attach importance to their relations with the Mediterranean world and with sub-Saharan Africa. That dichotomy will inevitably lead to a dispersal of European priorities.

-- At another level, the outlook for European countries until the end of the century points to relatively low rates of growth and high unemployment. The major reasons for the high number of jobless are slow growth rates and the structural inflexibility of European economies. The above conditions, and the size of the public-sector debt, mean that budget constraints will remain severe in Europe, that immigration policies will probably become more restrictive, and that free-trade policies will be unadventurous.

-- The most dynamic countries, especially those in the Third World, will especially benefit from the intense competition prevalent on world markets for manufactured goods and tropical agricultural products, while prices on international cereals markets will depend on the degree of protection imposed by the governments of developed countries on their agriculture sectors.

-- <u>The problem of the Sahel, and more especially of the poorest sub-Saharan countries, will become increasingly specific compared to those of the Third World as a whole.</u> This evolution of specific problems is <u>risky and fortunate</u> at the same time: it is risky because the actors in the international environment may be forced to neglect, even more than at present, the consequences of their decisions for the Sahel; it is fortunate since the international community may be led to adopt for the Sahel, and for sparsely populated countries in general, solutions that would otherwise be rejected if they were to be applied to a larger and richer segment of the world population.

External financing

The three sources that will converge to contribute to the external financing of Sahelian countries are direct investments, bank loans, and official and private development aid.

Direct investments will depend to a large extent on an evaluation of the risks posed by each country and on the intrinsic profitability of the economic activities that are chosen for financing. The guarantees of monetary stability and convertibility that are inherent in the fact that five Sahelian countries belong to the franc area represent a definite advantage when risks are being evaluated. However, that advantage is virtually eliminated by a number of dissuasive factors, including the exiguity of domestic markets, high production costs, poor development prospects and clumsy interventionism by national governments. It is accepted that, under the trend scenario, direct investments will not be a driving force in the economy, nor will they play a significant role in external financing. Further, it will be seen that funding for new large-scale extractive or industrial projects is unlikely to materialize.

Bank loans will be allocated with caution. Banking policies will long be influenced by the memory of the general debt crisis in the Third World during the present decade. We have already remarked on the high level of indebtedness of Sahelian States in relation to the capacity of their economies and their capacity to export. Those States are not alone in bearing the responsibility for the debt situation, and banking institutions have been at best incautious in granting major loans to certain of those countries. However, even if satisfactory solutions are found to today's foreign debt problems, the banking system will have gained experience from both the general crisis and from the specific crisis of the Sahelian countries; and it is unlikely that those countries will be able any longer to take out such massive loans.

Official development assistance is the third source of financing; however, in the light of the budgetary constraints affecting OECD countries, it seems unlikely that the members of that Organization will greatly increase the portion of their economies that is earmarked for official development assistance. In view of the probable evolution of oil prices, the same observation holds true for OPEC countries.

However, within the overall context of official development assistance, the amount that is received by the Sahel is naturally likely to vary, and the observation made at the end of the last paragraph concerning the specific character of the region and of the positive aspect of that specificity can equally be applied to this sector. Public aid (supplemented to a significant extent by private aid) plays a vital role in development, and we shall therefore examine the factors that can affect the level of that aid.

The impact of technologies

Major worldwide trends

Technical progress in Northern countries is advancing at great speed, fueled by major innovations that have occurred in so-called "generic" or basic technologies, principally in the fields of energy, new materials, data processing and biotechnology. Those technologies are capable of penetrating and transforming numerous fields of activity. The introduction of these advances into sectors that hitherto appeared fully developed and disinclined to change has created competitive advantages that may be decisive. Information technology in particular has proved to be particularly suitable to such sectors because of the great flexibility of the microprocessor on which that technology is based.

The scope of the changes brought about by these new technologies has inspired certain observers to talk of a third industrial revolution, following those engendered by the steam engine in the 18th century and by the widespread use of electricity at the end of the 19th century. The Third World in general, and the Sahel in particular, will inevitably feel the consequences of the third revolution in two different ways:

-- The changes will have a strong impact on world markets, on the structure of comparative advantage throughout the world and thus on the division of labor at the international level. We will examine that impact in a later section (chapter 18 on agriculture and 19 on industry).

-- The Third World will have access to a broader range of technologies (although that access will generally not be free of cost). Will the Third World be really capable of applying those technologies, and what will be the impact on its development of this broader panoply?

The impact on the Sahel

Certain experts claim that recent technical progress, especially in information technology, will allow for wider dissemination of new technologies, making them accessible to everyone; and that future problems of technology transfer will be very different from those of today.

This is undoubtedly true to a certain extent; it is now possible to learn to operate a microcomputer in a very short space of time and with no specific knowledge of electronics or data processing. However, it is dangerous to confuse the use of a new technology by consumers, which can be non-specific (it is simple to board a Boeing 747), with the use of that technology by the system of production (it is more difficult to fly or to service the same Boeing 747). Indeed, the problem of technology transfer between the North and the South may continue to be presented in terms of acceptability (which includes profitability) and of ability to use the technology (which includes the ability to maintain).

There is an essential distinction, initially proposed by Schumpeter, to be drawn between:

-- <u>Invention,</u> i.e. the discovery of a new principle or process that is more effective and that can be applied to the system of production; and

-- <u>Innovation,</u> i.e. the dissemination of invention throughout the system of production.

This distinction applies as much to Sahelian societies as to human societies in general; they possess "inventions", certain of which have existed for a very long time (e.g. mechanized or animal-drawn agriculture, the use of pesticides and of natural or artificial fertilizers), that will make it possible to intensify the production system and to alleviate pressure on the environment. It is clear that "innovation" has not occurred or is insufficiently developed to respond to the problems posed by climatic uncertainties, population pressure and improved quality of life.

Certain innovations were widespread in ancient times: this was the case with the cultivation of maize, cassava or groundnuts, which are all of American origin; or more recently the development of cotton production. Other innovations were much less widely disseminated, such as the use of farm animals or of fertilizers. It can be said that, at the global level, dissemination of innovation has been unsuccessful in the Sahel over the last few decades.

In the future, the parameters of the problem of technology transfer will not be fundamentally different from those of today, and future inventions will not necessarily become innovations in Sahelian societies. The specific question of technology transfer in the agricultural sector (and in particular the future role of biotechnologies) and in the industrial sector will be dealt with in greater depth in chapters 18 and 19. A number of general remarks will suffice for the present time:

-- When new technologies can be used profitably inside the Sahelian socio-economic context, and without the need for a material or intellectual support infrastructure, the Sahel will easily be able to adapt and to benefit from those technologies.

-- On the contrary, new technologies that necessitate research or maintenance facilities and highly skilled labor will become increasingly difficult, if not impossible, to use.

-- At the worldwide level, the basic thrust of technical research will be oriented to match the size of potential markets. The Sahel will therefore experience difficulty in attaining access to satisfactory technical solutions when the problems to be solved are specific to that region; a research effort into specific regional problems will be necessary.

-- On the other hand, new technologies will often make it possible to overcome the problems of economies of scale, which in the past have formed virtually impenetrable barriers to the development of certain industrial activities in the Third World.

The immediate environment: the Arab world and the humid zone

The Arab World

The first problem affecting relations between the Sahel and the Arab world is that of neighborly relations. In the northern extremity of the desert, decolonization has revived the old dream of extending hegemony to the southern fringes: the land of gold and slaves. That dream was instrumental in the demise of the Songhai empire, while Chad and, to a lesser extent, Mauritania have recently learned from experience that their neighbors are not without ambition. Despite the fact that such ambitions are anachronistic in the latter part of the 20th century, periods of troubled relations on both sides of the Sahara are a possibility in the future.

Whatever the state of relations, the Sahelian States will not be able to ignore the weight of North Africa -- the Maghreb will have 85 million inhabitants by 2010, with a per capita income far higher than that in the Sahel; added to that figure are some one hundred million Egyptians and Libyans.

Cultural influences constitute the second problem. In the past, Islam reached the Sahel through the desert. Religious ties between the northern and southern fringes have never been broken and are doubtless far stronger today than ever before. Thus the currents that are stirring throughout the Arab world, and in particular Islamic fundamentalism, are having ineluctable repercussions on the Sahel.

The question of aid is more or less linked to the two above problems. The oil-producing Arab states considerably increased their levels of aid to the Sahel during the 1970s. Mauritania is a member of the Arab League and is considered part of the Arab world; the country thus enjoys a privileged position when aid is allocated. Arab financial aid and technical assistance have played a vital role in the country's development and have enabled it to emerge from a period of some difficulty. In other countries, that aid and assistance have played a less important role, and have further diminished due to falling oil revenues. It is unlikely that levels of aid will once again become significant in the medium term. However, it is difficult to predict the attitude of oil-rich countries if there is an upswing in oil revenues. The environment of those countries is so complex and changeable that any prediction as to what interest they may hold for the Sahel in the future is fraught with uncertainty.

Trans-Saharan trade, which made the Arab world the Sahel's major trading partner for centuries, has virtually disappeared. Despite the improvement in roads through the Sahara, commercial exchanges between the two worlds remain insignificant and, because of the high cost of transportation, will probably remain so in the future. More generally, the level of complementarity of the two economic areas is currently low: neither produces sufficient cereals, and neither ranks among the major industrial exporters. Ultimately, the economic potential of the Sahel in general, and of Mali in particular, is greater than that of the Maghreb, and it is feasible to imagine the Niger valley becoming the storehouse for a Maghreb suffering from major shortfalls in cereals production. However, in view of the current state of world markets, which will be described further on, it seems doubtful that this complementarity will be able to find an adequate framework which can be translated into actions.

Côte d'Ivoire, Ghana, Nigeria

The sustained growth experienced by Côte d'Ivoire up until the beginning of the the 1980s attracted a wave of migration from the Sahel. Following a marked recession, the country appears to have returned to a healthier situation, even though the size of its foreign debt currently acts as a handicap to further growth. Prospects for development in Côte d'Ivoire are great, due to the presence of diverse resources and a dynamic farming community. However, the example of neighboring Ghana, which is equally well endowed, has highlighted the fragility of development.

The Ghanaian economy has not fulfilled the promise it showed at the beginning of the 1980s, and has not been able to play out its potential role in West Africa. However, the country has begun the process of recovery and could possibly become a focus for development in the region in the near future.

Nigeria, which contains half the population (approximately 100 million inhabitants in 1985, and a probable total of 200 million in 2010) and half of the oil resources of West Africa, is the giant of the region. Politically, it is a feeble giant: the country is a federation that has subdivided into increasingly numerous and culturally disparate States. However, Nigeria appears to have returned to a certain balance, and it is safe to predict that the country will not disintegrate in the foreseeable future.

The giant is economically fragile: Nigeria's agriculture has literally collapsed, and the country that was the world's largest producer of oleaginous crops at the beginning of the 1960s has now become a net importer. Oil revenues had a profound effect on an economy that was unprepared to benefit from them, and led to a massive surge in imports. The fall in revenues submitted the economy to a further -- and severe -- shock, from which the country now appears to be recovering. Like its Ghanaian counterpart, the Nigerian economy is currently undergoing a period of recovery and is fully capable of playing a leading role in the region in the near future.

Because of their monetary policies, Ghana and Nigeria have played a special role in Sahelian economies. For two decades, the currencies of both countries were non-convertible, poorly managed and, in general, highly overvalued. The countries of the franc area that had convertible and less overvalued currencies took maximum advantage of the situation. A large volume of trade flows developed between Ghana and Nigeria and the countries of the franc area, largely for monetary reasons. However, since trade was largely informal, the flows were not recorded and were therefore not widely known. The franc-area countries, including the Sahelian countries, were the major beneficiaries of those flows.

Under pressure from international institutions, and doubtless chastened by past experience, Ghana and Nigeria appear to have altered their monetary policies. Since the populous and dynamic merchant classes in those countries have taken maximum advantage of a currency with favorable parity (and which was even undervalued), and are henceforth in a position to win acceptance for their point of view, it is far from unfeasible that the future monetary situation of West Africa will be very different from that of the last two decades. If this should be the case, the pattern of trade flows would alter enormously and the countries of the franc area would lose the commercial advantages they enjoyed in the past.

The CFA franc is currently the basis of an underground economy, the ramifications of which extend throughout French- and English-speaking West Africa. However, it should be remembered that the role currently played by the CFA franc was foreshadowed by the West African Currency Board pound. The currencies that have followed on from the pound can also one day adopt that role.

It is thus plausible to imagine a scenario where <u>a Nigeria and/or a Ghana,</u> having made a strong economic recovery, <u>constitute(s) an area of prosperity and intense commercial activity, thereby forcing the Sahelian countries into a secondary position in an economy that dominates the region.</u>

This scenario, though plausible, is far from certain. The experience of recent years has been one of uneven development and has demonstrated how rapidly situations can be reversed in those countries, and especially in Nigeria. Moreover, total collapse of whole sections of their economies can in no way be excluded.

One final hypothesis that cannot be excluded, although it appears improbable at the present time, consists in the Sahel being trapped between a Maghreb and a Nigeria that are in a state of, if not open conflict, at least fierce rivalry (although the hypothesis of an armed conflict cannot be totally dismissed). Under this hypothesis, the Sahel becomes the stake in a conflict between two powers with vastly superior economic and political weight.

Chapter 15

VALUES AND MENTALITIES: SAHELIAN CULTURE IN THE FUTURE

Having examined the probable development of the environment of the Sahel, we shall now look at the future of Sahelian societies by studying what we have called their culture, i.e. their values and modes of thought, which forms the very basis of those societies.

We will not attempt to draw subtle distinctions between values, mentalities, aspirations, etc, and we will consider culture to be what H. de Jouvenel calls "the underlying preferences of individuals, the profound motives on which they base their judgments, their hopes and their fears". Although it is obvious that these mental sets vary greatly from one individual to another, we have long since realized that the distribution of attitudes within a society is not a haphazard process, but that those attitudes represent the characteristic configurations of the society at a given point in time.

A set of hypotheses

The retrospective study illustrated the ongoing changes in Sahelian culture, the gradual disappearance of the values on which the traditional society was constructed, the rise of new values, and the permanent values that resist change. That analysis suggests a number of hypotheses concerning future development. We have chosen four of those hypotheses:

<u>Islamic fundamentalism will not become the dominant force</u>

The rise of Islam has taken place over a very long period. It began in ancient times and accelerated rapidly during the colonial period and following independence. We have also observed that the conflict between "Africanized" Islam and the more traditional form of Islam is rooted in the distant past. In recent years, numerous observers have stressed the breakthrough of Islamic fundamentalism, which has gained impetus from the difficulties experienced by Sahelian societies. Those difficulties have been put down to behavior patterns that are considered to be over-influenced by Western culture. Total devotion to Islam is presented as the remedy to all the ills that currently beset Sahelian societies. However, the breakthrough of fundamentalism involves a limited number of persons.

We shall put forward the hypothesis that Islamic fundamentalism will not become the dominant force; there are four reasons for that postulate:

-- Specifically African values remain indestructible;

-- Islamic brotherhoods are only truly organized in a limited area of the Sahel (principally in Senegal, and, to a lesser extent, in Mali, Mauritania and Niger);

-- The authorities in those countries have adopted a strategy of reintegration and/or containment of religious leaders;

-- The political aggressiveness of oil-producing Islamic countries is destined for relative decline.

Those four reasons will remain valid except in two cases:

-- If the situation of the Sahel is significantly modified and the crisis becomes acute, Islamic fundamentalism could become a refuge, as has happened several times in the past;

-- If fundamentalism comes to power in the Maghreb and engages in more or less open conflict with the West, the Sahel could in all probability come under strong pressure to follow the same path and to abandon its links with Western countries.

Cultural nationalism will not develop significantly

The colonial and immediately post-colonial periods were favorable to the rise of cultural nationalism, which sought to establish an authentic African identity as a reaction to the European presence, considered as oppressive if not intolerable. Times have changed. After twenty-five years of independence, the presence of Europeans in Africa has become less of an obsession.

It will be demonstrated that a trend scenario is only viable if links with the West are maintained and developed. It is more than likely that Sahelian elites, increasingly influenced by Western culture, will not take the risk of severing ties with the West.

Finally, an aggravated form of cultural nationalism could open the way for displays of micro-nationalism and basic ethnicity that are unacceptable to governments anxious to consolidate national unity and to construct modern nations. Governments will not therefore take the risk of encouraging cultural nationalism.

The destructuring of traditional society will continue

We have examined the role of the radio, which put an end to the isolation of the rural world and which made a significant contribution to the process of destructuring traditional society that began in the colonial era. That role will not decline; on the contrary, it may be greatly enhanced by the role of television, which is a far more powerful tool of cultural penetration than the radio.

Up until the present time, the spread of television throughout the rural world remained very limited. Television broadcasting networks cover only limited parts of different countries, but the principal restraining factor has been the lack of power supply to villages. The technical revolution brought about by the transistor has enabled radio to overcome this handicap. Battery power has become sufficiently inexpensive to be compatible with the monetary resources of rural populations. But the energy consumption of television receivers is such that batteries cannot be used to power them. The greater availability of photovoltaic solar panels, at a cost which today hardly exceeds the purchase price of a television set, will bring about a urther revolution by bringing television to villages and to peri-urban areas that have not so far been connected to national grids. The extension of television broadcasting networks will in all probability mean that donor agencies in Western countries will compete for the privilege of aiding Sahelian countries to develop such networks.

In addition, the rural exodus will continue. To date, most of the people who migrated to cities have maintained links with rural society, for which they acted as representatives. They never cease to belong to the rural society, returning to marry in the traditional manner in their villages, for example. In a number of cases, membership of that society has remained real and firmly rooted in personal attitudes, but in others it has become more of a formality. For the latter group, it is an imaginary world where the young pretend to submit to their elders and where the elders behave as if times had not changed. It is probable that this allegiance to traditional society will become increasingly formalistic and will eventually disappear. A further reason that will compound the disappearance of this allegiance is the fact that a large number of rural dwellers, including some of those who play or who should play a dominant role in traditional organization, no longer have sufficient strength or conviction to retain their power, and even less to win it back.

Western influence will increase

The media that transmit Western culture play a significant role in the Sahel, and that role is certain to grow. We have highlighted the probable increased development of television, which is certain to transmit more Western culture than African authenticity or Islamic fundamentalism. The probable expansion of satellite broadcasting will further reinforce the presence of Western culture in Sahelian cities and villages. The role of other media such as cinema and radio will also grow.

Lower air fares should also facilitate the penetration of Western culture by encouraging the development of a European tourist industry in search of exotic places, and by increasing the size of the minority that are currently able to afford to travel to Europe.

This penetration is easy to criticize in ideological terms as the source of all the problems that beset individuals. But such criticism is not sufficient to stifle the rise of Western values. This situation will change only if living conditions were to decline significantly; in that case, recourse to other values and a return to authentically African values could provide an alternative solution to Islamic fundamentalism.

The situation could also change if strong currents of xenophobia were to surface in Western countries, leading to a sudden and massive expulsion of Sahelians, who in turn could awaken feelings of cultural nationalism in that region. Such a hypothesis appears improbable today, but cannot be ruled out.

What will be the content of the Western culture transmitted by the media and by direct contact with Westerners? It is probable that Western values will be a mixture of materialistic values and of post-materialistic values, which have developed around those whom the consumer society has left with an after-taste of dissatisfaction. These new values have not swept away the values of the consumer society, which appeared to be the case at the end of the 1960s, and there is little likelihood that young people in the West will give up their attachment to material possessions. Indeed, the consumer society has adopted the values of conviviality, self-fulfillment, the importance of relationships, the quality of the environment, etc, that emerged as a result of the turbulence of the late 1960s, and has applied those values to the purchase of commercial goods and services.

What are the consequences for the Sahel?

If the preceding hypotheses are accepted, how are Sahelian values and attitudes likely to develop? First, it is probable that the concept of the relationship among people and between them and their environment will gradually be modified. Characteristic features of Sahelian societies, such as the metaphysical dimension of the family or the vital importance of mythical or symbolic kinship, will gradually become blurred. The rise of individualism, which began in the colonial era and which carried on after independence, will continue: the Sahelians will feel less and less a part of a social entity, and more and more responsible for their own individual destinies.

This should find its expression in a reduction in the prejudices linked to birth (caste, slave ancestry), and in the increasing importance attached to individual success. At the same time, the world will become more secular -- less a place where obscure forces, especially those of the ancestors, fight for control, and more a reality that is responsive to human actions.

The Sahelian will thus be freed from the constraints that once assigned him a fixed place in a social group, and from the restrictions that doomed to failure any intervention in the physical reality of the world. These future generations of Sahelians -- whether of rural or urban origin -- will possess a more "entrepreneurial" mentality, in the broadest sense of the term.

Similarly, certain traditional links will gradually disappear. Those links ensured that every civil servant or salaried worker was also (or primarily) a member of a network, and membership in the network had a multitude of impacts on his professional tasks. It is possible to imagine the consequences of these impacts on the quest for additional income and the distribution of that income, on work schedules, on the employment of other members of the network, etc. Mythical or symbolic kinship will also become less restrictive and will possibly make way for blood relationships.

The negative aspect of this process may be a loss of conviviality in Sahelian societies and a weakening of the solidarity that survived the vicissitudes of colonization and independence.

A further consequence will be <u>a widening of the generation gap</u> and a lessening of the educative role of the family. Unexpected modifications may appear, e.g. a "transformation" of values among youth groups, under the influence of the media or local leaders.

Finally, all these developments will have hardly any effect on the rural exodus. The Sahelian (or non-Sahelian) city will probably retain all its fascination, in spite of the drawbacks of life in urban areas. On the contrary, <u>the rural exodus will probably be vindicated</u> in the eyes of society.

Thankfully, however, <u>it would be a grave mistake to believe that Sahelian culture will be replaced by imported culture</u> over the coming quarter-century.

Traditional Sahelian cultures were composed of extremely coherent entities that resisted outside pressure and that were effectively passed down from generation to generation. Despite the severe trials through which these cultures have been put for over a century, their profound vitality is startling. On a minor but nonetheless significant point, it is startling to note the lack of influence that Western art has had on Sahelian culture. While it is possible to find Chinese orchestras that play Western classical music, no such Sahelian orchestra exists, and, indeed, the influence of African music has spread to other continents.

Although Sahelian cultures will doubtless continue to be submitted to severe trials over the coming twenty-five years, and despite the fact that the mechanisms for transmitting lore and values down through the generations are gradually weakening, the vitality of Sahelian cultures is unlikely to disappear. It is highly improbable that, in twenty-five years' time, Sahelian values and attitudes will be a mere reflection of their Western counterparts.

Inter-cultural conflicts will not disappear either. Is it possible, in particular, that the different concepts of time and history in which certain researchers find major sources of conflict between African cultures and Western cultures will disappear? We consider this to be unlikely, especially since those concepts are acquired at a very early age. The generation of Sahelians that will play a leading role over the coming quarter-century has already received its initial education. It is fair to hypothesize that the generation in question will be even more strongly marked by traditional concepts in this domain, and this is not without consequence for the development of societies and their economies.

Development will be turbulent

The experience of the past twenty-five years has shown that values now change rapidly in the West, and that the values of the 1960s, which replaced the middle-class values of the past and which were naïvely supposed to survive for decades, were partially rejected by subsequent generations. In the coming twenty-five years, many changes may affect the values transmitted by the West, and many of those changes may be unexpected.

There is even more reason to believe, therefore, that values in societies with an exceptionally high proportion of young people will not develop smoothly!

The preceding hypotheses simply outline probable general orientations. But within that general movement, numerous specific movements, which either follow or go against the current, are inevitable.

Discussions among young Sahelians of today are full of nascent contradictions. A great degree of tolerance towards issues of drugs and sexuality, and aspirations of freedom, are mixed with a nostalgia for order and discipline that could be exploited to political ends. A desire for emancipation, which centers around the free choice of a spouse, is mitigated by a lack of receptiveness to the liberation of the woman. There is involvement, sometimes direct involvement, with delinquency but at the same time a firm condemnation of corruption; universalist aspirations are tempered by ethnic reflexes and a sometimes aggravated national rivalry.

The set of hypotheses that we have put forward and the conclusions that we have drawn should be considered with some circumspection. The evolution of Sahelian values and attitudes could well develop in unexpected ways. It is possible to conclude that there is only one certainty: adult value systems have lost their credibility and the values of the future will be different from those of the past.

Chapter 16

THE FUTURE SHAPE OF POWER

Chapter 10 outlined the development of political power bases since independence, and demonstrated that the last twenty years have been marked by the arrival of the Army in the forefront of the political scene and by the removal of the politicians who emerged from the colonial period. The regimes that have come to power since the beginning of the 1980s are neither wholly military nor wholly civilian. A first possibility for the future is the development and the consolidation of such regimes: this will be variation number 1 on the trend scenario.

The permanence of those regimes most probably indicates that the internal situation of Sahelian countries is not in serious decline. If growing difficulties appear a second variation, which does not actually abandon the hypotheses that constitute the trend scenario, would better describe the political situation of certain Sahelian countries. We shall refer to this variation as "South-Americanization". We will demonstrate that these two possible variations on the trend scenario share a number of common characteristics.

It is possible to envisage other scenarios, e.g. secessionist regimes, fundamentalist regimes and multi-party democratic regimes that contrast with the trend scenario. We have already briefly reviewed those scenarios.

One final Sahelian phenomenon has also been highlighted: the rise of local power bases.

Variation N°1 on the trend scenario: regimes that are neither wholly military nor wholly civilian

Four of the eight countries covered by this study are currently headed by a military leader. In a fifth country, the presence of the military at the head of the government was forestalled only by the armed intervention of a neighboring country. In two other countries, the civilians who are currently in power were all, at one time or another, military leaders involved in guerrilla activity. There is only one country in which the civilian authorities have not yet been replaced by the military, and which projects a liberal image.

This massive military or quasi-military presence at the head of the majority of the Sahelian countries is partly balanced out by the recent inclusion of civilians in the exercise of political power. A number of recent developments seem to point towards a search for a new balance between military and civilian power. Those developments include the abolition of the Comité Militaire de Libération Nationale and the creation of a political party (the UDPM) in Mali, the creation of the Conseil National de Développement in Niger, the opening of the Conseil National de la Révolution in Burkina Faso to civilians from recognized political formations (even though those formations no longer exist legally), and the organization of municipal elections in Mauritania.

By contrast, the Army is playing an increasing role in civilian regimes, where it is presented as an institution within the participatory structures set up by those regimes. The Army is not, or is no longer, solely an instrument in the hands of the executive, as would be the case in the republican tradition of Western countries. The current trend is thus towards a certain "civilization" of military regimes, and the militarization of civilian regimes; we are witnessing a consolidation of political regimes whose dominant characteristic in the future may be their hybrid nature: they are neither wholly military nor wholly civilian.

This "hybrid" characteristic is unlikely to disappear in the future, as long as the basic hypotheses of the trend scenario apply. The political class has developed and diversified considerably since the early 1960s, and today is far from being homogeneous. That class embraces the politico-administrative middle classes, officers, businessmen, and religious oligarchs; and each of those categories has its own specific interests. The crisis, or at least the stagnation of the economy, has heightened competition among the different groups, despite the existence of a certain consensus on general political orientations.

In that context, the Army will probably act as the arbiter in conflicts of interest (as much or even more so than in the past), and will come to play an increasingly important role -- even in countries where civilians are, and will remain, the dominant force. However, it is in the interest of the Army, which is only one of the elements of the political class, to share power with civilians (if only because of the negative image that purely military regimes project) except in cases where conflicts deteriorate considerably.

For those reasons, it is plausible to imagine that regimes which are neither wholly military nor wholly civilian will continue to hold sway, and indeed will be reinforced. It is evident that the respective positions and levels of influence of military and civilian members of the political regimes that emerge from the above dynamic will depend on a number of variables (social, cultural, economic, political, etc.), and that those variables will differ from country to country.

If that prospect becomes reality, periods of politico-military upheaval will alternate with periods of relative calm, in cycles that are clearly impossible to predict. However, if this scenario is acted out, two developments can be predicted with near certainty. First, there will be a broadening of the elites already in power, with a more active co-opting of technocrats who have no firm political affiliation. (The corollary to this development is that the countries' youth loses interest in political activity). Second, military spending will rise sharply, and the military as an institution will regain the attraction it once held for the educated minorities, which will look on the Army as a provider of employment at a period when the civil service has reached saturation.

Variation N°2 on the trend scenario: "South-Americanization"

The variation we call "South-Americanization" involves a reinforced role for military and paramilitary institutions, and regimes that are more dictatorial than the mixed civil-military regimes discussed in the first variation. The second variation on the trend scenario could come about in the event of internal troubles provoked by a serious decline in the economic situation, or by a rise in secessionist feelings; or in the event of external threats from any of the countries in the region. South-Americanization would be characterized by the disappearance of political parties that are not affiliated to the single party in power, or to its equivalent.

The civilian/military regime and the South-Americanization variations share a number of common features:

— Both variations suppose that <u>there is no basic modification in existing political forces</u> (which is the basic hypothesis of the trend scenario); this means that rural elites (whether traditional or emerging) do not acquire sufficient weight to represent a significant political force, or that those elites are absorbed by the existing powers.

— Both variations are characterized by <u>the maintained hegemony of the existing political class</u> and by the persistence of what is called the <u>urban bias</u> in economic policies (which does not exclude the possibility that the rhetoric of the political class can be slightly different from its policies).

— Both variations are characterized by <u>increased competition within the political class,</u> which can lead to palace coups that shift the responsibility for power from one group to another within a same class, without provoking major modifications in policy.

Contrasting scenarios

The conditions that underpin the continuation of a trend scenario, and in particular the maintained hegemony of the ruling political class, will not necessarily be met. Other dominant forces may emerge to create other scenarios that contrast with the trend scenario. We shall examine three of those scenarios.

Secessionist Regimes

In the early days of independence, all Sahelian leaders made construction of national unity one of their major priorities. Twenty-five years later, national integration has not been achieved everywhere. Numerous groups retain a keen awareness of the disparities that characterize the different countries. It is both simple and tempting to attribute the responsibility for those disparities to colonial policies, which concentrated investments in "useful" areas of countries while leaving other areas to fend for themselves. But the regions that are backward compared to the rest of a nation do not easily accept that argument: they are tempted to make up for lost time and to demand a more equitable share of the fruits of growth (when growth exists).

By contrast, the better endowed regions may feel that they are not obtaining their full share of rightful benefits from the nation. Both types of region may be tempted by what African politicians call, characteristically, "the specter of secession". If that temptation were yielded to, the map of the Sahel would be altered so radically that it is impossible today to imagine the new perimeters.

It is clear that the emergence of secessionist regimes would be favored by increasing economic difficulties due, for example, to the stringent application of structural adjustment programs that discourage investment in social infrastructures in deprived areas; or by the discovery of a new "miraculous resource" in a province.

Fundamentalist regimes

The helplessness of Sahelian societies in the face of an increasingly acute crisis -- a situation in which Islam could once again appear as a refuge -- combined with the political aggressiveness of Islamic countries (whether or not they benefit from oil revenues) could lead certain religious leaders, dissatisfied with their place in societies that advocate secularism, to attempt to institute "mullah republics" in the Sahel.

Numerous events and tendencies suggest that the possible emergence of fundamentalist regimes is more than just a theory. Among those phenomena let us mention the attempts to establish a major Islamic party in Senegal, the pressures within Mauritania to introduce strict observance of the sharia, the acceptance of enclaves where law and order is enforced by Islamic militias, and the basic tendency of the Islamic faith to act as a temporal power that organizes the lives of the faithful.

Democratic regimes

One constant feature of Sahelian politics since independence has been the search for unanimity. Western-style democracy, involving a number of political parties competing for power, reputedly bears the risk of dispersing energies and of provoking national disintegration. Only two countries, Senegal and the Gambia, currently have legally recognized opposition parties, although it should be stressed that the majority parties in both countries are overwhelmingly dominant. Democratic transition of power has not yet come about in any Sahelian country.

However, the medium- and long-term possibilities of seeing Sahelian politics evolve towards a form of democracy that is closer to Western concepts, including real democratic transition of power, are not nonexistent.

A number of changes have been made along these lines. The theoreticians of Sahelian unanimity have always considered that the single-party regime was not a panacea but a stop-gap measure that had to be accepted in the early stages of development. Those single parties are in no way free from internal contradictions, and the conflicting tendencies that arise within those parties are often expressed in violent form. One obvious way of defusing such conflicts would be to move towards a state of genuine political plurality. The increased sensitivity in the West to human rights issues and the pressures that will be applied to countries receiving aid will also further the movement towards democratization.

Among the factors that will contribute to the institution of multi-party democratic regimes in the Sahel we should cite the demands of the Sahelians themselves. The majority of Sahelians have not lived through the colonial period and are therefore unable to appreciate that the current situation of limited democracy is a marked improvement over the situation during colonial times. These new generations will be increasingly disinclined to appreciate that progress since they will have increased access to information concerning events on other continents where free and democratic expression is considered as a vital condition for existence. Any kind of restriction on democracy will probably appear unacceptable to the majority of tomorrow's young people, all the more so because those restrictions emanate from a State that is more or less incapable of assuming the role of provider.

The rise of local power: rural power groups

The retrospective study discussed the decline of local power since the colonial era, and showed that the decline has continued since independence. Rural elites today comprise the descendants of the families that traditionally held power and the descendants of the chieftaincies established by the colonial authorities. Those elites no longer have the means to constitute a genuine power base, and those who still enjoy a small degree of power would find it suicidal to give up the additional resources that can be obtained through integration into, or allegiance with, the modern State. Those elites must either function as relays for central government power or disappear; they do not constitute a real local power base, independent of the central authorities.

The key event of recent years has been <u>the emergence of genuine local power bases.</u> Chapter 8 highlighted the growing importance of the self-organization movement in the rural world. As the ENDA mentioned in a recent publication on that theme, those initiatives "contradict the image of resignation, of submission, of fatalism, of routine, or of imperviousness to change. Farmers have decided to speak out, which means that they are no longer prepared to remain silent, and that they expect to be listened to with genuine attention rather than with feigned interest. The farmers are speaking as people who are responsible for their own destinies".

Between the beginning of 1985, when the Futures Study began, and mid-1987, when the actual report was written, the rural self-organization movement seemed to have rapidly gained impetus and to have swelled to considerable proportions. Several thousands of village associations most probably exist in the Sahel. (Figures include between 800 and 1 000 associations in Senegal, 9 000 in Burkina Faso, including 4 500 that are officially recognized, and 2 500 associations in the Yatenga alone).

That movement is due to the actions of new elites, former migrants to other countries, and former migrants to the cities who have returned to their places of origin and have played an instrumental role in the development of village associations. Those ex-migrants are often descendants of families that had a subservient place in traditional village organization, or they are youngest sons who are not destined to become the heads of their families. However, they are in no way members of the elites described earlier in this study. Women, who are traditionally excluded from holding local power, are beginning to play a new and sometimes important role in these associations. A whole new elite is beginning to emerge within rural society.

Those village associations are naturally very heterogeneous. Some were created with a view to improving living conditions within the village community, and to initiating economic and social action or to reversing the deterioration of land resources. Other associations have more limited objectives and more restricted fields of action. Although these associations are heterogeneous, they all share one common feature. Whereas the aim of traditional power was to ensure the survival of the group and to preserve its structures, village associations are more <u>open to the outside world and more receptive to change.</u>

To date, these new initiatives remain local in scope, and associations have not grouped together in such a way as to provide each other with mutual assistance and thereby constitute a genuine power base at the national level. (One exception is Senegal, where a federation of non-governmental organizations has been created). The State thus has great latitude to neutralize any initiatives that are too opposed to its policies, to absorb those initiatives, or to revive traditional elites that feel threatened by the emergence of new centers of power. <u>Rural power groups have not yet played a political role at the national level.</u> But even if those groups have not yet played a political or dissident role, it is important to note that <u>they are playing a constructive role,</u> a limited but growing part in the construction of a new rural society.

The rise of local power: urban power groups

New dynamics are not confined to the rural environment. We have stressed the growing importance of the informal sector, and the scope and the variety of the initiatives taken within that sector. However, those initiatives have not yet led to a self-organization movement or to the beginnings of a new power base. But other indicators point to the fact that these urban areas are not passive, and are capable of organizing themselves through a number of types of action, e.g. rent strikes in certain unsanitary areas, illegal connections to electricity grids, protests by women against the rising costs of staples, etc.

These urban "power groups" are often short-lived and have <u>a dissident character</u> that is not shared by their rural counterparts. They are feared by the ruling political forces, which protect themselves by attempting to defuse protests and by adopting a panoply of measures that effectively distance the population from the nerve center of power. Sudden "relocation" is a particularly significant measure within this context.

Turbulent development?

Under the trend scenario, we will put forward the hypothesis that these new, emerging power groups -- whether urban or rural -- will not drastically alter the political scene. <u>But even according to that hypothesis, recent developments make it impossible to gainsay the importance of the emergence of these new groups.</u>

In the rural environment, the most likely scenario is that those new power groups will play a role that may become important on the local level, but that they will not be able to unite to form a political force at the national level. The most probable hypothesis is that, instead of a peasants' revolt, there will be peaceful co-existence between the central government and the rural masses, which feel unconcerned by political activity since they consider it to be an issue for urban dwellers.

In the urban context, new power groups will continue to be feared by the established authorities, but will not manage to play a political role other than that of pressure groups mobilized temporarily by one rival group or another during the palace coups discussed at the end of chapter 16.

Even if those new power groups do not ultimately have a significant impact on national policies, their action at the local level, which is carried on with State support or which benefits from State neutrality or indifference, must be increasingly taken into account. A quarter-century is a significant length of time, a period during which a whole generation of young people -- more numerous than any preceding generation -- will reach maturity. The values of that new generation will represent more than ever before a significant break with the past. During those twenty-five years, it is unlikely that the emergence and rise of local power will cease of its own accord, or that it will be halted by earlier generations now in power. The movement may take forms that are unthought of at the present time, and this possibility must be borne in mind within the context of the trend scenario.

The fact that the emergence and development of local power groups may divert us altogether from the trend scenario must also be considered. That hypothesis will be discussed in Part Three of the study.

This chapter on power groups and power bases leads almost naturally to a conclusion relatively similar to that of the chapter concerning values and mentalities. Moreover, the two themes are closely connected.

The interplay of a complex set of factors would seem to ensure that a number of surprises are in store for the Sahel and that <u>a degree of turbulence is almost certain.</u> Among those factors, we have seen the desire of the political class to conserve its power and the resources it possesses to ensure that end; the demands of the young for more democracy; the desire of other groups (including the young) for more affirmative government; the temptations of secessionism; and the emergence of local power bases both in the cities and in rural areas.

Even if the most likely hypothesis is adopted -- that there will be <u>no basic modification in the political power base -- there is likely to be considerable competition between respective groups, and the balances that are achieved will be delicate.</u>

Chapter 17

POPULATION

Although population variations are influenced by economic events, they are principally determined by cultural factors. For that reason, we shall examine the cultural aspect of population variation before studying the development of Sahelian economies.

Population development is the direct consequence of the evolution of two factors, both of which are largely unknown in the Sahel: fertility and mortality. Migration from the region may qualify the impact of those two indicators.

Fertility

Calculations based on available census data give birthrates of between forty-four and fifty-one per thousand in the Sahel(1). Over the past two decades, it would appear that those rates have tended to increase, but it is impossible to say whether the figures reflect the true situation or whether they are based on inaccurate statistics.

Fertility is thus extremely high, i.e. between six and seven children for each woman, and the small amount of data available (concerning Dakar) appears to indicate an upward trend in major cities, while fertility seems to have declined among nomadic population groups. On the whole, it appears that the tendency is towards increased fertility, which would confirm the upward trend in birthrates.

It is important to note that high fertility is actively desired in Sahelian societies. A woman's fertility is considered a blessing, while sterility is looked on as a curse; there appears to be no significant change in the value attached to fertility in those societies.

Although fertility is high, it is far from the maximum natural fertility rate; it is regulated by a set of customs, including post partum abstinence, and especially a prolonged period of breast-feeding, which leads to a relatively long period of amenorrhea. The interval between two births is thus approximately three years. In larger Sahelian cities, that interval is declining. It is possible to conclude that a high fertility rate is not accidental: it is the result of a deliberate choice that is made by the society and that is strongly interiorized. Women want a large number of children, with periods of three years between births, and they generally manage to achieve that aim.

That social choice and the high level of fertility both have their roots in the distant past, at a time when mortality -- and especially infant mortality -- was high, and when other societies would take slaves, either for their own use or for the external slave trade. For those reasons, a high fertility rate was necessary to the survival of each society. Conditions have changed, but societies only gradually become aware of major changes, especially since those societies have, up until now, solved the problems posed by high fertility, both at the global and the individual levels.

At the global level, the problems posed by population growth have been solved by peopling the land available in most Sahelian provinces, and especially by migration to the cities.

At the individual level, adults rely on their children to take care of them in old age; and, considering the very high rate of infant mortality (and the fact that the drop in that rate is only gradually being integrated into Sahelian mentalities), a large number of children is a guarantee of dignified old age. Migration to the cities reinforces that behavior pattern. The migrant is considered as a "delegate", who has left in search of a more promising future that he will share with his community of origin. But not all migrants "succeed" -- in fact, very few of them succeed. Children doubtless hold the key to the future of the family unit, but the future is like a lottery: it is safer to have a large number of tickets, and thus a large number of children. The probabilistic logic behind this equation is incontestable.

What are the prospects for this individual and collective logic, which leads to the deliberate choice of a high fertility rate?

Can the level of fertility increase?

The lessening likelihood of success among migrants to cities could lead to an increase in the number of children desired. This would be a logical extension of the individual, probabilistic way of thinking mentioned above. But at the collective level, such behavior would hardly be rational; it is probable that other factors would come into play and that adults would eventually be obliged to depend less on their children to support them in old age and to find solutions other than migration, which has proved to be less effective.

Increased fertility is more likely to be the consequence of a modification in the behavior regulating the interval between births. For example, the custom of post partum abstinence may be abandoned and, more especially, the duration and the technique of breast feeding -- the principal factor in determining the interval between births -- could be altered. In the short and medium terms, any such modification would inevitably lead to increased fertility. However, there are currently no indications that changes will occur in the near future, and, if such changes are indeed to come about, it is likely that other forms of regulatory behavior would eventually become predominant.

Let us suppose that a significant and lasting increase in fertility is improbable.

Can the level of fertility decrease?

The arguments in favor of high fertility outlined above remain strong, and the link between the deterioration of the natural environment and population growth does not appear obvious. Given those conditions, will a low level of fertility be achieved spontaneously or will there be a favorable response to actions to encourage a longer interval between births?

The speed of population growth and its associated disadvantages are gradually being perceived. Those disadvantages would be more clearly perceived if the outlets provided by occupation of new lands and rural exodus were to be closed, and especially if a sharp decline in urban living conditions were to put a halt to the flow of migrants towards the cities.

The desire to send children to school, which has always been considered a factor in social achievement, could also help parents to realize the interest of limiting the number of children per family in order to ensure a suitable standard of education for all.

If that interest is perceived, for one reason or another, it is therefore probable that Sahelian societies will make use of a whole range of recognized methods for limiting the size of the family, e.g. avoiding early marriage, increasing the length of post partum abstinence. It is only in cases where those methods appear inadequate or too difficult to use that "imported" family planning methods have any chance of being accepted to any significant extent.

Let us suppose, under the trend scenario, that factors of change will not have any significant impact on the level of fertility for most of the coming quarter-century.

Mortality

Mortality rates are approximately 20 per thousand, and statistics published by the United Nations reflect a slow but steady decline in that rate, and thus a regular rise in life expectancy. As we have already pointed out, however, certain observers have cast doubt on the declining mortality rate, which is more likely a result of approximate calculations than of analysis of comprehensive data (Cape Verde is alone in recording deaths in a thorough manner); those observers speak of a 'mortality rate counter-offensive".

Specific studies (e.g. study on Senegal, Garenne, 1985) do not provide clear evidence of declining mortality: "Since the data is inaccurate, there is no definite proof of a decline in mortality at the national level. In particular, the infant mortality rate appears to have remained stable between 1960 and 1978 in both urban and rural environments, even in Dakar". In Dakar, where civil registers were kept with remarkable assiduity until recently, observers even noticed a renewed rise in infant mortality at the end of the period under consideration. Since that time, little or no use has been made of data from the civil registers.

A mortality rate counter-offensive appears plausible. The diseases that afflict the Sahel have not been brought under control, despite numerous efforts. Illnesses that had not affected the region over the last decades have recently begun to appear (e.g. cholera). Malnutrition and its consequences have probably not receded, because limited resources prevent governments from satisfactorily operating existing medical equipment and from purchasing vital medicines.

Future implications make it impossible to ignore the presence of AIDS in the world. The spread of the disease in West Africa currently seems more limited than in other regions of the world, but we remain unaware of the true extent of the disease(2). We are also unaware of the speed with which the virus is spread, not only through sexual relations but also through medical procedures (blood transfusions and even vaccinations) that are carried out with insufficient precautions. It is possible, though far from certain given the current state of knowledge, that the future spread of the AIDS virus will be naturally limited to certain high-risk social groups -- especially urban groups -- and that the illness will not affect rural areas. It is also possible that an effective vaccine will be found rapidly. But we must also reckon with the possibility of a full-scale demographic catastrophe in the future, which was unthinkable two or three years ago. We shall examine that hypothesis further on.

It is also probable that the "extended vaccination program", draw up by the United Nations and aimed at vaccinating the entire infant population of the Third World by 1990, will not be implemented.

Let us suppose, under the trend scenario, that the decline in mortality will not continue, but that mortality rates will stabilize at approximately the level reached in the 1980s; however, that hypothesis may be somewhat optimistic.

Emigration to non-Sahelian countries

The two Sahelian countries that have high rates of emigration to non-Sahelian countries are Burkina Faso and, to a lesser extent, Mali(3). In 1975, there were a reported 1 700 000 Burkinabe living outside their country, especially in Côte d'Ivoire. There is an almost total absence of data that would make it possible to follow the development of migration over the last ten years.

Several factors must be taken into consideration before constructing hypotheses concerning migratory flows:

-- Western European countries are highly unlikely to open their borders to immigrants from the Sahel (see chapter 14); it is therefore probable that this type of migration, which to date has not taken on any significant proportions in the Sahel, will not fundamentally alter the demographic situation in the future.

However, even if migration to Western Europe does not represent a problem of quantity, it does represent a problem of quality. <u>The brain drain</u> -- the exodus of graduates who are unable to find in the Sahel the living conditions that conform to their ambitions -- will most probably accelerate.

-- The situation is radically different with migration to the coastal countries of the humid zone of West Africa, and in particular to Côte d'Ivoire. Will that country begin to reject migrants, who are considered too numerous, as Nigeria did in 1983 and again in 1985? Or will the coastal countries continue to find an economic advantage in this addition to the labor force? Africa has always experienced major currents of migration, and it would be surprising if the situation were to change overnight. But the frontiers that were drawn up by the colonists and that were declared inviolable are in fact a novelty. Nationalism is a growing reality. Strong demographic growth and the problems posed by shrinking living space are also realities for the coastal countries. It would therefore be surprising if the migration of Sahelians to the countries of the humid zone were to continue unchecked.

-- Will emigration to Côte d'Ivoire, Nigeria and Ghana be replaced by emigration to more distant countries? In the long term, it is difficult to imagine that the highly populous regions of West Africa (Nigeria, with over 200 million inhabitants by 2010, will have a population density of more than 220 per km^2, and the density of several Sahelian provinces will exceed 120 per km^2) will be able to coexist alongside almost-deserted regions of Central Africa (with a handful of inhabitants per km^2), where the annual population growth rate is lower than countries in West Africa. However, migration to those distant countries, which are culturally quite different to the Sahel, will not be as simple.

Let us suppose, under the trend scenario, that there will be no sudden halt to emigration, and even less a massive repatriation of emigrants; however, <u>migration will not accelerate, and the long-term outlook is a for a gradual slowing of the movement.</u>

The population in 2010

Let us first mention a number of forecasts of the Sahelian population in 2000, based on 1980 data:

-- The SEQI [Service d'Etudes et de Questions Internationales (Studies and International Questions Service)] at the French Cooperation

Ministry] forecast projected a figure for the mainland Sahel (excluding Cape Verde and Guinea Bissau) of 46.75 million Sahelians (i.e. an average annual growth rate of 2.1 per cent).

-- The SCET-SEDES group (A Long-Term Image of Sub-Saharan Africa) projected figures for the same region of 49.6 million for 2000 (annual growth rate: 2.3 per cent) and 62 million for 2010 (annual growth rate: 2.25 per cent).

-- The United Nations figures for the same region are 54.17 million (annual growth rate: 2.8 per cent).

The first two estimates are not consistent with the hypotheses of the trend scenario. Stable fertility and mortality, and slower migration suggest an average annual growth rate of around 2.8 per cent.

By taking that rate and adopting United Nations population estimates for mid-1985, i.e.:

<u>35.7 million Sahelians</u>

figures for 2010 will be:

<u>70 million Sahelians</u>

which could be <u>the estimate of the trend scenario.</u>

Based on that figure, what are the upper and lower limits of possible estimates, remaining within the bounds of reasonable hypotheses?

-- If we accept that fertility will remain high (or will even increase slightly), that mortality rates are falling, and that foreign migration has practically come to a halt, we arrive at a possible average population growth rate of 3 per cent, which means that there will be <u>75 million Sahelians in 2010.</u> We will accept that these figures form the highest feasible scenario.

-- If we accept a significant decline in fertility, a slight increase in mortality (a sharp increase would not be consistent with a marked fall in fertility), and constant levels of migration, it seems difficult to envisage an average annual growth rate lower than 2.1 per cent, which would give a figure of <u>60 million</u> inhabitants in 2010. This is doubtless the <u>lowest conceivable possible scenario</u> at the present time.

Given the number of imponderables that affect the actual volume of the population, its birth and mortality rates, we accept that the trend scenario leads to a population of between 66 and 77 million inhabitants in 2010; and that, beyond those limits, we would find ourselves in the lower or upper scenarios.

Urbanization

With 7 million city dwellers in 1985 (although that figure may well be largely underestimated), the Sahel has an urbanization rate of approximately 20 per cent, lower than that of the African continent as a whole, which is doubtless some 30 per cent.

The number of city dwellers was multiplied by a factor of more than 5 between 1960 and 1985. If that trend were to continue, the number of Sahelians living in cities would reach almost 38 million in 2010, i.e. an urbanization rate of 54 per cent. Is such an extrapolation plausible?

First, an urbanization rate of 54 per cent in 2010 would still be lower than the rate in developed countries (67 per cent) and in Latin America (65 per cent) in 1985. But it would still be higher than United Nations estimates, which put the urbanization rate for the African continent as a whole at around 46 per cent in 2010.

We saw in chapter 3 the non-economic factors that lead to a major rural exodus, which is unlikely to be braked by the hypotheses concerning the development of Sahelian values. On the contrary, we saw in chapter 15 that the migrants who abandon traditional village society may feel vindicated in their action.

In the future, slowing urban growth can only be caused by economic factors: a relative deterioration in urban living conditions compared to those in rural areas. We will see that, under the trend scenario, rural incomes have little chance of improving substantially, whereas urban incomes, including those in peri-urban areas, should not deteriorate excessively, at least for some time. (This is contingent on the hypothesis that foreign aid will remain at a high level).

Certain observers claim to detect signs that the rural exodus is slowing down in several Sahelian provinces under the influence of NGOs, which are giving new life back to the villages. Certain observers even claim that, in certain cases, migratory flows have been reversed. By contrast, new forms of migration to the cities are now being observed: young Dogon girls have begun to migrate over the last few years for example -- a hitherto unknown phenomenon.

Today, we are obliged to accept that there is a lack of reliable data on a possible shift in the rural exodus.

The hypotheses that form the basis of the trend scenario lead to the following urbanization scenario:

-- In the medium term, let us say up until the end of the 1990s, no crucial factors will emerge to slow the rural exodus, and urbanization will continue at more or less the same annual rate observed in the early 1970s.

-- Beyond that date, the exodus may slow down due to the deterioration of living conditions in peri-urban areas.

Taking the estimate of 7 million city dwellers in 1985 as a base, and an annual growth rate for urban populations of 7 per cent up until 2000 and of 5 per cent after that date, urban population will be:

31.5 million inhabitants in 2010(4)

i.e. an urbanization rate of 45 per cent. The Sahel will therefore fall into line with the average urbanization rate for the African continent at around that date. But it is important to stress the fragility of that estimate.

It is likely that the growth of very large urban areas will be slowed by the difficulties of life in the cities, and that, on the contrary, the growth of medium-sized urban areas will accelerate. Despite that differentiation (the extent of which is difficult to calculate) it seems inevitable that <u>certain urban areas will suffer from overexpansion.</u> The estimates of the SCET-SEDES, reproduced below, are plausible, but we must stress their hypothetical nature.

(in thousands of inhabitants)

	1980	2010
Dakar	1 300	6 200
Bamako	536	3 200
Niamey	300	2 100
N'Djamena	330	1 500
Ouagadougou	251	1 550
Nouakchott	210	750
Banjul	60	350
Bissau	116	400

NOTES AND REFERENCES

1. Source: 1985 UN estimates.
   The situation of the Cape Verde islands is different; certain sources estimate that the birthrate has dropped from forty to less than thirty per thousand. However, United Nations figures show that Cape Verde had a birthrate of thirty-six per thousand in 1985.

2. Only the Gambia has officially declared the presence of AIDS in the country to the WHO, but it is probable that the virus is present in all Sahelian countries.

3. Cape Verde is a special case: there are reportedly at least 420 000 Cape Verdians in America, Europe and Africa; compared with 350 000 in Cape Verde itself.

4. The SCET-SEDES group study (op cit) also gave the figure of 31.5 million, but with an overall population estimate of 62 million, the urbanization rate would reach 51 per cent in 2010.

Chapter 18

THE RURAL WORLD TOMORROW

We shall first describe the world context for Sahelian agriculture in the coming period, paying particular attention to food production (especially cereals, which are, as we know, crucial for the region) and to the technological changes that will affect agricultural activities around the world.

What impact will these developments have on the Sahel? What might be the trends in the different component parts (food crops, export crops, livestock) of the Sahelian agricultural system? What consequences will this evolution have on the rural environment? We shall try to find answers to all these questions.

World trends in agriculture

The technological revolution which began in 18th-century England has accelerated and spread to many parts of the world in the last few decades. It has transformed agriculture in such a way that the problem is not, as had been feared, one of deficit but rather one of surplus. The technical advances of the near future will probably have even more spectacular effects.

Since 1950, world agriculture has followed two main trends:

-- Increase in the surface area of grain crops from 590 million hectares in 1950 to 720 million in 1976, a figure which has remained stable since that time. This 22 per cent growth rate may seem modest, but it is probably far greater than any recorded in the past.

-- Considerable increase in yield and productivity due to the introduction of new crop varieties and improvements in cropping methods. World consumption has risen from 14 million metric tons in 1950 to 131 million in 1986. Output per person working in agriculture has grown at an average rate of 4 per cent per annum.

Progress in production has been very unevenly spread around the globe. It has been especially strong in North America and Western Europe. That part of the world has progressed from a deficit situation in 1950 to one of considerable surplus today.

The Eastern European countries, by contrast, have not managed to increase their output sufficiently and still have a considerable deficit. Many Asian countries have benefited from the "green revolution", a number having become self-sufficient or even becoming exporters. Progress has been less marked in Latin America and even less in Africa, which has developed a structural deficit because, since the beginning of the 1960s, growth in production has failed to keep pace with population growth.

At the world level, progress in food production has been such that the main problem in world agriculture is one of surplus rather than the deficit that was still feared in the early 1970s, when some experts predicted famine on a world scale.

The agricultural revolution is certainly far from complete. Some experts even think that the better part of this revolution is still to come. In any case, the introduction of new technologies will probably continue to lead to considerable increases in the productivity of crops and livestock (appropriate biotechnology applications, and also information technology both within the chain of production and in the marketing channels).

Technological progress has not been coupled with comparable progress in control over world markets, which are in a state of growing disorder. It is unlikely that conflict situations will become fewer in the future, and the disorder is liable to continue.

World agriculture has to face up to a major structural problem: solvent demand is growing only gradually, while advances in productivity entail, and in the coming years will doubtless continue to entail, a much faster increase in supply. In theory, only the rural exodus will bring levels of supply down, closer to the level of demand, and so avoid overproduction, falling prices and falling incomes in the agricultural sector. But there are powerful sociological factors that may prevent the rural exodus proceeding fast enough. Hence a downward trend in farm incomes, which those concerned consider unacceptable. Hence today's income redistribution policies channeling more towards the agriculture sector, with farm subsidies paid out by all the main industrial countries (the United States, the European Community and Japan). (Farm subsidies in the OECD countries amount to 70 billion dollars, twice the amount supplied as development aid to the Third World). Hence also the tenacious and growing protectionism in the field of farm produce, running counter to the tendency towards free trade, and the policy of massive farm produce export subsidies adopted by the United States and the EEC.

This has profoundly upset world markets in agricultural produce in several ways:

-- First, the distribution of agricultural produce is undoubtedly irrational in economic terms; to a large extent international trade is determined by the resources different States can allocate to subsidizing their exports, rather than by comparative advantage.

-- Fragmentation of the market: for most products, there is no longer a world market in the true sense. What is called the world market is in fact a residual market involving only those surpluses for which there is no place either in national markets or in preferential agreements between countries.

-- Unstable prices, showing a downward trend and now only remotely related to real production costs.

The United States and the European Community have begun to recognize the absurdity of farm policies which create ever-growing surpluses that must be more and more heavily subsidized if they are to be sold on the export markets. Up to now, this recognition has not led to any substantial change in policy.

United States agriculture plays a dominant role on international markets. In recent years its expansion has led to massive surpluses, has put U.S. farmers in debt to an extent that makes the Sahel's foreign debt look insignificant, and has led to equally massive government subsidies. Congress has rejected the agricultural policy reform Bill proposed by the U.S. Administration. The EEC's Common Agricultural Policy is in comparable difficulties: the Community has become the world's second largest exporter, but there are surpluses and financing problems. The intention is to reform this policy, but this will certainly prove difficult.

In fact, as long as agriculture is regarded as a very special activity not comparable to the activities of industry or the services (the farmer being seen as rooted in the land rather than as manager of a production unit), no solution will be found to the problems outlined above.

This means that the disorder in the world markets is not on the verge of resolution. As regards cereals in particular, forecasts point to a fresh drop in prices. For 1980-2000 the IIASA forecasts an annual price change of:

- 0.4 per cent for wheat,
+ 0.1 per cent for rice,
- 0.5 per cent for secondary cereals.

N.B. These are naturally meant as trends, and do not exclude some degree of year-to-year fluctuation.

Only for animal products does the Institute forecast price rises: + 2.2 per cent for meat and + 1.6 per cent for dairy products over the same period.

The Sahel in the world context

<u>The Sahel's grain deficit is relatively small, and does not upset the overall world balance between supply and demand.</u>

Since the beginning of the 1980s, the Soviet Union has had grain deficits in the order of 30 to 40 million metric tons per annum. North Africa and the Middle East have deficits of around 25 million metric tons. The Sahel's deficits, however important they may be from a local point of view, are marginal from the global viewpoint. Even if the upward trend that began in the early 1960s continues, food aid and the world market will have no major difficulty in making up the Sahel's grain deficit, either in years of normal rainfall or in drought years, for a good many years to come.

Except in the case of cotton, the gap between the Sahel's agricultural output and world agricultural productivity is widening.

The contrast between stagnating production in the Sahel and the rapid increase in the productivity of labor in world agriculture is startling. Productivity in world agriculture has every chance of continuing to increase if, as we have suggested, the technological revolution is far from being complete in this sector.

This means that, independently of the dislocation in prices due to disorganized world markets, the terms of international trade can only deteriorate for Sahelian produce. Imported grain appears, and will continue to appear, on the Sahel's domestic markets at ever more competitive prices. At the beginning of this century, groundnuts grown in Senegal earned substantial incomes for the growers and attracted many foreign seasonal workers, while also earning handsome profits for the European trading firms and providing a large part of the budget not just for the Colony of Senegal but also for French West Africa. Today, while the productivity of oleaginous crops in the Northern countries has risen considerably, the productivity of Senegalese groundnuts has remained static, or even regressed because of land degradation; the crop still enables some religious leaders to make handsome profits, but it brings growers only a bare living and provides only a meager income for the Senegalese government. No miracle is to be expected, and even if the world markets were better organized this would do nothing to halt the deterioration in the terms of trade, which is due to structural causes.

Cotton, the only crop for which productivity has increased considerably in the Sahel since the beginning of the 1960s, is also the product for which the terms of trade have deteriorated least, on average (leaving aside the recent drop in world prices, which is no doubt accidental).

Technical progress and Sahelian agriculture

If the main part of the technological revolution in agriculture is still ahead of us, there is no doubt that the advances yet to come will concern Sahelian agriculture. Moreover, some experts think the rise of biotechnology could play a decisive part in the future of Sahelian societies, enabling their production systems to make a huge leap forward and bypass much of the long route taken by Northern farmers.

But, before we examine the part future technical advances may play in the Sahel, perhaps we should ask why past technical progress has had so little impact on the region's agriculture. As has already been stressed, techniques have been available for years, or even for centuries (animal-drawn agriculture), without having the same impact in the Sahel as they have had elsewhere. The Sahel's farming system has not stood still, but it has not developed fast enough to cope with new needs. Generally speaking, one may say technology has failed.

What are the reasons for this failure?

<u>Because rural dwellers do not want it?</u> There are conservative forces at work in the rural environment of the Sahel, as in rural areas all over the world. But there is nothing to suggest they are stronger here than elsewhere, to the extent of blocking innovation. And examples of successful innovation show that the Sahel's rural dwellers are open to change. Today, a new awareness of the dead end towards which Sahelian societies are moving, the destructuring of these societies and the fast-growing numbers of initiatives taken, undoubtedly make rural society more open to change than ever before.

<u>Because rural dwellers do not know that more effective technologies exist?</u> It is obvious that an effort needs, or will need, to be made to disseminate information on available or forthcoming techniques. But the failure of a certain number of projects that included extension work shows that knowledge of the existence of a technique is a necessary condition, but not the only condition, for that technique to be adopted.

<u>Because rural dwellers do not know how to use more efficient techniques?</u> This is certainly true of complex technologies whose use requires basic knowledge that Sahelian rural dwellers do not at present possess (e.g. the literacy needed to read users' instructions). But the fact that simple technologies such as the use of animal-drawn tillage and compost have only very reluctantly been adopted and in fact often rejected, shows that this factor alone cannot explain why Sahelian agriculture lags so far behind in technology.

<u>Because the "inventions" concerned are inappropriate?</u> Certainly, a great deal of effort has gone into disseminating inappropriate inventions: plows unsuitable for fragile soils, plant varieties that present too high a risk in case of drought, etc. But this cannot be true in all cases.

<u>Because it is not in the interests of rural dwellers?</u> This is probably one of the commonest reasons why innovations are not made. Most innovations require either investment or additional work (or both), and farmers consider that adopting the innovation would not compensate their efforts. They prefer the status quo, i.e. the extension of current cropping systems to new land, or other alternatives such as migration to cities or to the coastal countries if the former option is impracticable.

The failure of the transfer of technology to Sahelian agriculture is no doubt due to a complex set of reasons, in which a major part is played by the <u>economic environment</u> within which the agricultural systems (and government policies) operate, and in which <u>the lack of research appropriate</u> to Sahelian conditions and <u>insufficient basic education and training for rural dwellers</u> also play a part.

What is to be expected of the coming technological revolution in this very specific domain of agricultural techniques, in which the Sahel lags such a colossal distance behind the more advanced countries?

The future role of biotechnology

In this section we shall focus on the role of biotechnology, because it is usually regarded -- and quite rightly so -- as the field of technological progress that will have most impact, though it is of course not the only such field that concerns the Sahel. Information technology, for example, is certainly capable of improving the productivity of Sahelian agriculture. In particular, it is possible to imagine how, used in combination with remote sensing and weather forecasting, information technology could play an important part in maximizing production in accordance with the particular climatic conditions of the year at hand (giving the optimum dates for sowing and other operations in the fields), thereby reducing the vulnerability of Sahelian agriculture.

Biotechnology covers all techniques that exploit the capabilities of micro-organisms for economic ends. Emphasis will be laid on the fact that these new techniques are liable to play a "structuring" role, i.e. it is thought that their development will not only affect the processes of production but will have an effect on the very society that uses them.

What can the Sahel expect of biotechnology?

First, more rapid development of new plant varieties and animal breeds, better suited to the particular conditions of the region or even species unknown in the Sahel at present but which could play a part in tomorrow's diet (algae and fungi in particular).

Next -- and this is perhaps the most important contribution one can imagine for the region -- direct fixation of airborne nitrogen by micro-organisms. In a region where problems of soil fertility and environmental deterioration are becoming very worrisome, and where increased productivity in food crops is a vital necessity, the only options for progress open at the present time are:

-- Chemical fertilizers, clearly too expensive to be used on a large scale;

-- Natural fertilizers (compost, animal manure, rock phosphates etc), which demand a considerable human investment which rural dwellers will not make as long as they have an alternative escape route;

-- Acacia albida, a tree which enriches the soil naturally.

If biotechnology were to open up a fourth option, involving neither prohibitive cost nor prohibitive effort and equivalent to making the Acacia albida formula universal, this would be a major revolution for the Sahel.

Lastly, biotechnology can change the ways in which plant and animal products are used, especially through the new products they herald for the food industries. <u>Processing of local products to adapt them to the new tastes of urban consumers</u> could undergo a revolution by these means, so reducing the Sahel's dependence. But the possibilities of biotechnology will no doubt go further still. It is estimated that, at the present time, human beings can use only 50 per cent of the molecules manufactured by plants, the other 50 per cent being "packaging", mainly of lignin and cellulose, which the fermentation industries of tomorrow will be able to use.

Biotechnology could also revolutionize the relation between agriculture and energy. New fermentation processes could transform vegetable matter into fuels, making it possible to conceive of true "energy crops".

However, the negative aspects also needs to be shown, stressing the fact that today and very probably for most of the next twenty-five years, biotechnology will essentially be developed by the industrialized countries for their own requirements, which do not necessarily coincide with the needs of developing countries in general or the Sahel in particular. Recent developments in the production of new sugars from starch have struck a significant blow against Third World sugar production. An example that concerns the Sahel directly: an American firm has recently developed a new product with the same properties as gum arabic, produced by biological methods and costing far less to produce than natural gum. In the past, gum arabic made the fortunes of traders in the Senegal River valley; today it plays only a very modest role in the Sahelian economy, but this discovery makes any revival of gum growing impossible. However, not all the effects of biotechnology on the region's economy will be positive.

We would also emphasize that the work being carried out in biotechnology around the world primarily concerns products sold through the international markets, a field in which the commercial stakes are enormously high; far less work is being done on food crops.

Up to now, private enterprise has shown little interest in research into direct nitrogen fixation because of the difficulty of patenting the results. Governments in the Sahel, and donors especially, could of course decide to put a major effort into biotechnology applications that would be of immediate value to the Sahel's production systems. It is doubtful whether this effort would be comparable to the efforts of the private corporations in the fields that interest them (the American corporation Du Pont has an annual biotechnology research and development budget of US$ 120 million).

Some experts see the emergence of biotechnology mainly as a threat to the Third World which, they argue, will become even more dependent on the industrialized world. While not excluding that viewpoint, it is also possible to consider biotechnology as an opportunity to be seized. But one can reasonably assume that such an opportunity will not come automatically or succeed miraculously: the countries of the Sahel will have to take action if they are not to be left behind in the race to develop biotechnology.

As regards direct nitrogen fixation in particular, it is difficult to say when a technique might become operational in the Sahel. Given the current state of research, plus the fact that progress in biotechnology seems to be slower than in other sectors such as information technology, a concrete application would seem to be ruled out until well into the 1990s. Biotechnology will probably not play a significant role in the Sahel, if it ever does, before the 21st century.

The trend scenario for food crops

Our basic assumption that existing mechanisms in the Sahel will continue to operate has straightforward implications for food crop production, and gives the following scenario: the policies that have led governments to try and supply the towns cheaply with imported foodstuffs will not change significantly over the period under consideration, especially since a world context of oversupply, with the big industrialized countries making great efforts to dispose of their surpluses on export markets and with prices remaining depressed, would make policies of this kind as attractive as ever, or more so. Under these conditions, there would be nothing to halt the shift in urban dwellers' food habits or lessen their taste for imported products. This shift will accelerate all the more with the growing cultural influence of the West, with the increasingly powerful "modern" image imported products convey, and the fact that compared to imported foodstuffs, the prices of most products offered by local farmers are unattractive.

Governments will not react to this competition from imported products, since they will be increasingly aware of the threat the emerging urban social forces represent and will be successful in countering the rural social forces, which will not have managed to unite as one force.

The rural areas will supply the Sahel's cities with grain only in a marginal fashion. <u>Farmers will become inward-looking and will grow for their own requirements.</u> The urban market will offer them no incentive to adopt more intensive cropping methods, and the tendency will be for extensive farming to continue. In particular, <u>irrigated grain crops</u> are uncompetitive and can survive only with the help of massive subsidies provided, under a variety of labels, from external aid. Production will therefore increase only slowly in the large irrigated areas devoted to cereals.

Years of good or even normal rainfall would be catastrophic for the farmers as they can only sell their surplus at absurdly low prices. This will confirm their belief that the urban markets have nothing to offer them and that they must turn to other strategies if they want a money income.

Few farmers have the necessary stocks or range of crops to profit from the high market prices in drought years. In any case these prices would quickly be undermined by grain imports and food aid. This will confirm yet again the farmers' belief that urban markets are totally unreliable.

Is this scenario, with its continuation of current trends, viable over a twenty-five year period? We will here investigate how urban dwellers are to pay for the imported food products; this is a problem we shall be returning to.

Meanwhile, the rural population is still growing; in some regions of the Sahel where there is still unoccupied or sparsely populated land available (in Mali and Chad especially and, to a lesser extent, in Burkina Faso and Senegal), the problem of feeding this rural population is resolved by extending the area of farmland.

In the other regions (Mauritania, Niger and parts of Burkina Faso), overexploitation of the land is worsening, while farmers have increasingly pressing reasons to look to other sources of revenue, migration to major cities especially.

In some provinces, deterioration of natural resources reaches such a stage that the farmers organize themselves to tackle the problem, at the instigation of their local leaders and with the help of a few foreign NGOs. Experiments of this kind that already exist are being expanded. Forms of agriculture that treat the natural environment with greater respect and are doubtless a little more productive, diversified and intensive, are developing and spreading. But this is subsistence agriculture, requiring considerable human effort to halt and reverse the deterioration of the soils. Its produce is generally not competitive with imported produce. It is not a form of agriculture suited to urban markets.

In other provinces where the population is more individualistic, farmers go on working the land until it is completely exhausted, paving the way for an ecological disaster, though perhaps the disaster will not actually strike within the twenty-five years of our scenario. Some farmers extend their cropland more and more, making no changes to their cropping methods and using extremely low-paid labor. As has happened before in other continents, there are ever-increasing numbers of landless laborers and farmers with very little land. Social differentiation is accelerating. The landless can find no salaried work at home and the rural exodus is also accelerating: a prelude to an even more massive exodus once the land is completely exhausted and unredeemable. It is possible that before this extreme is reached, the bigger farmers will realize that disaster is imminent and individually opt for farming methods that treat the environment with greater respect; but this too will be subsistence agriculture.

In both these cases, biotechnology, and especially direct nitrogen fixation, may perhaps help to establish a more ecologically sound form of farming that is less exploitative of the land.

Alongside this subsistence farming, <u>a type of agriculture geared to meeting urban needs in certain fields (fruit, vegetables, poultry etc), is expanding considerably,</u> as these markets have better natural protection against foreign competition than the grain market. The people who earn profits from this, sometimes considerable profits, are the "rich" farmers, the most dynamic cooperatives, and also urban dwellers working partly in farm enterprises. This new type of agriculture is undergoing modernization, making increasing use of fertilizers, mechanization, irrigation techniques, etc. While major irrigation schemes do not develop, small-scale schemes on the contrary are flourishing spontaneously, though they usually do not involve cereals.

Food habits continue to diversify in both urban and rural areas, but this is a slow process. Cereals -- local cereals in rural areas, largely imported grain in the cities -- remain the staple food. Further, <u>food imports, and grain imports especially, have to increase to feed the population of the towns.</u> They probably do not grow as fast as the urban population itself, since some urban dwellers continue to be supplied at least partly from rural areas through relatively informal networks.

This is particularly true of people who have recently arrived and who maintain their traditional dietary habits and strong ties to the village. Diversification of food habits is also slowing the growth of cereals imports. Under this scenario, let us suggest the following estimate for the amount of cereals that will have to be imported in years of good or average rainfall, based on the figures for average imports in recent years and an annual rate of growth a little lower than the growth rate of the urban population:

Scenario for growth of cereals imports
in an average year
(in thousands of tons)

1985	2000	2010
900	2 100	3 400

Assuming the year 2000 to be one of average rainfall, the Sahel will have to import more grain than in 1984 and 1985, which were years marked by the effects of a severe drought.

For a dry year, and especially in the event of a series of dry years, those estimates must be considerably increased. The flow of food from rural to urban areas does not merely dry up in this case: it is reversed, as food aid is sent out from the cities to the villages through official or informal channels.

The trend scenario for export agriculture

As far as export agriculture is concerned, the basic assumptions of the trend scenario point to the governments continuing to tax export produce -- more or less heavily and more or less covertly -- to finance their growing needs.

For some products like oleaginous crops, the structural deterioration in the terms of trade will continue for a while. Productivity will continue to rise in the North, while research to increase the productivity of groundnuts or new crops like soybeans will lag a long way behind. The income to be divided between the State, the intermediaries (who provide extension workers, inputs, marketing and processing) and the producers will shrink steadily. Currencies will have to be considerably devalued to allow for the differing trends in productivity of the various crops. But within the Sahel countries there are powerful forces opposed to such a solution, which would run counter to their immediate interests. As the State and the intermediaries would put up strong resistance to any reduction in their revenue, it is the growers' incomes that would decline, and this would hardly encourage them to make investments to increase output. The decline in the role played by groundnuts in the Sahelian economies -- a process which has already run its course in the countries of the interior and has begun in the coastal countries since the early 1970s -- will continue over the period in question. It is only towards the end of this period that oil crop production will be revived, perhaps with soybeans rather than groundnuts, as newly available research results enable productivity to increase significantly and the Sahelian governments become resigned to taking a much reduced share of the income from the trade. But Northern oleaginous crops have made such a vast leap forward, and land in the Sahel has become so exhausted by decades of over-exploitation, that the reconquest of foreign markets will prove a difficult task.

The situation may be different for cotton. The Sahel's cotton crop will manage, at least for a time, to maintain its competitiveness. But the governments tend to rely too heavily on cotton, one of the few crops that "do well" and one of their few sources of foreign currency. They will therefore increase their share of income from the trade to cover their financial needs. This means that farmers are less motivated. The Sahelian countries will also have difficulty sustaining a comparable rate of growth in productivity to that of the major cotton producers, the USA, USSR and China. The Sahelian economies' income from cotton will tend to fall. Cotton will expand far less rapidly than in the preceding twenty-five year period. This expansion will slow even further, flatten out, and possibly begin to reverse. One cannot exclude the possibility of a technological revolution that will cause a collapse in world cotton prices, leaving the Sahel helpless and incapable of reacting to this new situation.

In global terms, it is likely that <u>agricultural exports,</u> in terms of both quantity and value, <u>will fall far behind population growth.</u>

The trend scenario for livestock production

A distinction needs to be made between nomadic herding on the fringes of the Sahara and sedentary livestock farming further South.

Nomadic herding, in our trend scenario, does not die out. It is the very raison d'être of some population groups, and they will not give it up easily. It is also an excellent way of exploiting the limited resources of the desert fringes, although it provides only a very modest income for the pastoralists. As it is not possible to increase the yield per hectare of this type of livestock production to any significant extent, its role within the Sahel's economies must necessarily decline. On the other hand, productivity per producer could be increased, though there are a number of obstacles to this:

-- The nomads too are affected by the spread of Western culture and the attraction of the cities. But migration is not fast enough for the population along the fringe of the Sahara to shrink rapidly, and that population may even grow. Under these conditions, there can be no increase in average productivity.

-- The recent drought and those to come will combine with overpopulation to speed up the deterioration of the rangelands and reduce yield per hectare. This will help bring down the incomes of pastoralists, since they will not be able to take advantage of the prices obtained for animal products, which are somewhat more favorable than those for crops.

Under our scenario, therefore, <u>nomadic herding looks increasingly like a relic of the past.</u> Trapped between a desertification process partly caused by herding itself and crop farming, which tends to move north as far as it can, and which is practiced by too many people for the available natural resources, pastoralism is <u>an area of growing poverty,</u> not to say total destitution, or in any case an area in which NGOs find a number of opportunities for their charitable activities.

There is a further possibility that we cannot exclude. Towards the end of the period the nomadic pastoralists' living conditions may grow much worse, with a massive flight to the cities. The new population groups settling in urban areas bring with them the extreme poverty of the rangelands. Since they have made a direct leap from their former nomadic life to urban life, they may experience great difficulty, perhaps for the space of a generation, in adapting to their new living conditions.

In the agricultural areas further south, the picture is quite different. In these provinces, the extension of cropland will inexorably eat into the area available for traditional grazing as practiced by the Peul pastoralists. Only truly sterile areas, unusable by cropfarmers, are left exclusively for the herds. Even then, the herds are severely restricted in their movements since the land is used for cropfarming, and clashes between farmers and pastoralists, perhaps violent clashes, will occur.

The future of livestock activities in these areas is likely to lie in mixed farming of crops and livestock. Conditions should be relatively favorable for this. The growth of the cities in the non-Sahelian coastal countries should open up markets for meat, and rising prices on the world meat markets should make imports from the Sahel countries a more attractive proposition. But stagnating cropping systems are likely to considerably slow down a joint development of cropfarming and livestock activities with each activity fertilizing the other. Even so, we shall postulate that <u>integrated mixed farming will develop to some extent</u> and that in the long run Sahelian livestock activities <u>will to some extent recapture coastal markets.</u> But this will be only a partial reconquest; the coastal countries will continue to import meat from Latin America and Europe, and exports of cattle and meat will not be restored to the place they used to hold in the Sahelian economies in the early 1960s. Nor can we exclude the possibility that in some of the major urban areas of the Sahel, imported meat will take a share of the market.

Ecological disaster or the beginnings of recovery?

Most experts who have studied the future of the Sahel's natural environment in recent years have been very pessimistic. All those experts have described the continued deterioration of the environment, a process accelerated by obvious feedback effects. As the quality of the environment deteriorates, the population is obliged to try to obtain more from it in order to subsist: they have to exploit it more, which worsens the degradation. But this is not the process we have described above. What are the reasons for this?

In fact, rather than postulate widespread deterioration in the Sahelian environment, one can ask whether a <u>somewhat more moderate hypothesis</u> does not fit better into the trend scenario. The following scenario could be put forward:

-- In some parts of the Sahel, the possibility of redressing the ecological imbalance seems too slim to consider. This may be the case in many pastoral areas and in some crop-growing areas where farmers are too individualistic to undertake collective action for ecological improvement. The societies concerned will turn increasingly to "flight" strategies: by exploiting the land even more, by migrating to the cities, or by turning to non-agricultural activities.

One can be equally pessimistic about the possibility of halting deforestation. The experiences of many societies on a number of continents show that as long as there is land left to clear and wood to cut for domestic purposes, it is difficult to turn to other solutions.

-- On the other hand, one has to take account of the movement now flourishing in several provinces of the Sahel, aimed at halting the deterioration of the environment and enhancing the fertility of the land by simple methods such as composting and bunds or levees in the fields -- methods that are sometimes ancient practices rediscovered. <u>The most pessimistic forecasts are not necessarily the most likely.</u>

It is probable that the drought of 1972 and 1973, by considerably accelerating environmental deterioration, aroused awareness of the dead end towards which the Sahel's farming system was headed, and that Sahelian societies reacted with the usual time-lag of a few years, while the drought of 1983 and 1984 has strengthened the reaction. Be that as it may, this new attitude now seems to have taken root quite firmly.

It is the rural dwellers themselves, with help from foreign NGOs, who are taking action to defend or restore the environment. The governments and the donors, who have many other preoccupations and who have experienced many failures in this type of operation, are only marginally interested.

The trend scenario in rural areas: change and continuity

The hypotheses we have made in constructing our trend scenario do not lead to the ecological disasters some experts predict, nor to the dramatic and widespread pauperization of rural population groups predicted by some others (though their incomes do, in our scenario, remain very low).

The trend scenario shows <u>continuity</u>, in that a large part of the rural population becomes <u>inward-looking</u>, disconnected from the life and activities of the cities and indifferent to any action taken by the government; in the <u>low crop productivity levels</u> that entail very low average money incomes and in a turning towards a <u>strategy of diversification</u> into non-agricultural activities; and in <u>the persistent deterioration of the natural environment</u>.

But there are also changes: <u>in those products for which natural protection from foreign competition is better than for cereals, local agriculture and livestock expand and modernize; rural dwellers react to environmental deterioration and their declining living conditions.</u>

The new initiatives in the rural world, which began in the preceding period, <u>are accelerating.</u>

Chapter 19

THE INDUSTRIES OF THE FUTURE

This chapter will follow the same lines as the section on the rural world, and will present the future context of the Sahel. We shall then examine the perspectives for the development of Sahelian industry and of the informal sector.

Principal worldwide industrial trends

Extractive industries

Following the period of price rises between 1973 and 1977, the early 1980s heralded a decline in the international prices of raw minerals; the studies of prospects that have been conducted to date have demonstrated that the situation of world markets is unlikely to improve by the end of the century.

Three factors will influence demand for metals: a slower rate of growth in metal-consuming industries, lower specific consumption of metals due to improved labor techniques, and the development of new materials (e.g. engineering plastics, composites, ceramics). The influence of those factors will be reflected in a moderate increase in world demand, which can be met -- at least up until the end of the 1990s -- by a simple increase in the production of existing mines, without undertaking any major new mining projects.

World demand for uranium (of particular concern to Niger) will grow only slowly until 2010 because installed nuclear capacity throughout the world peaked in 1986 and has dropped off sharply since then.

Energy

The world economy took more than ten years to adapt to the consequences of the 1973 rise in oil prices. In the space of six years, factors such as slowed growth, energy savings, the replacement of oil by other primary sources of energy, and the changing patterns of production in industrial countries have turned around the oil market and forced a sharp decrease in prices.

However, knowledgeable operators in the petroleum world do not rule out further price increases in the second half of the 1990s, due to the confluence of three factors:

— The current low prices, which have discouraged efforts by developed countries to save energy and to replace oil by other primary sources;

— The inevitable rise in consumption in Third-World countries;

— The increase in the percentage of world reserves held by Middle Eastern countries.

Manufacturing industries

Manufacturing industries will be affected by the structural changes that began towards the end of the 1970s. We shall restrict ourselves to a presentation of the broad outlines of the general picture, highlighting anything that may be of concern to the Sahel:

— The decline of a number of traditional industries in Northern countries, especially the production of steel and building materials. By contrast, those industries will continue to develop in the South under the effects of population growth and of unsatisfied demand. There will be a gradual shift of such industries from North to South.

— The growth of new industries, the so-called hi-tech industries, which include information technology, the production of complex molecules using chemical or biotechnological techniques, the manufacture of new materials, etc. The majority of those industries, and in particular those industries that are at the forefront of technical development, will be located in Northern countries, since it is in the North that the research and development efforts that lead to the creation of such industries will be concentrated. Newly industrialized countries, and doubtless those Third-World countries that manage to achieve comparative advantage and to make their mark on a highly competitive market, will also participate in the development of these new industries.

— The ascension of the service industries, including services to individuals but more especially those to industry. The world is heading for a major industrial transformation, where solutions (i.e. techniques of organization and communication) will play an increasingly important role. We have called this upcoming transformation the "tertiarization" of industry.

— At the global level, the effects of development should be reflected in lower manpower levels in Northern countries, while the number of industrial-sector jobs in the South will increase.

— Because of technological development, there should be <u>no massive relocation of labor-intensive industries from the North to the South,</u> as was predicted in the 1970s. The robotization and computerization of production are transforming labor-intensive industries into capital-intensive industries, and are eliminating the comparative advantage that Southern countries believed they enjoyed. The governments of Northern countries, which are faced with sometimes acute problems of structural unemployment, cannot be relied on to oppose these industrial changes.

-- By contrast, technological development will reduce the scope of the scale effect. The era of gigantic industrial groups is over. <u>New technologies will make smaller-scale, decentralized production units more feasible and more profitable.</u> For example, the construction of conventional steel plants, equipped with blast furnaces and coking plants and producing millions of tons of steel every year, is unlikely to continue; their place will be taken in the future by smaller facilities that rely on direct reduction processes and that are equipped with electric furnaces.

Developing countries should benefit from the movement towards small-scale production facilities and flexible workshops, which are capable of producing limited runs of manufactured goods under highly competitive conditions. The countries that should benefit the most will be those with moderate-sized domestic markets.

Sahelian industry within that context

In chapter 6 we analyzed the disincentives to industrialization in the Sahel and saw that, in spite of the progress made to overcome those disincentives, the region remains under-industrialized, and in fact has been experiencing de-industrialization for several years. What may the Sahel reasonably expect within the context we described earlier?

Extractive industries

In view of the current world situation of the extractive industries, which we described earlier, it would be unwise to expect any major developments in that sector. Exploitation of the iron ore deposits in Western Senegal seems impossible before the year 2000, and unlikely beyond that date. New developments in the uranium-bearing province of Niger also seem unlikely. However, circumstantial developments do seem possible but the effects on Sahelian economies will be negligible. For centuries, the Sahel has been a major gold-bearing area, and it would be particularly regrettable if the region were unable to take advantage of the important role that gold will continue to play in the world economy and of the high prices that the metal commands. It is also possible to envisage the exploitation of mineral resources, even in modest quantities, to meet local needs (e.g. natural phosphates for direct use in agricultural production, deposits of peat or lignite).

Energy

During the 1970s great hopes were placed on solar energy, which is abundant in the Sahel. Some thought that the sun would provide the region with a cheap and inexhaustible source of energy, and thereby accelerate industrialization.

Those hopes have not been realized: although the cost of solar energy has fallen, it nonetheless remains far higher than that of conventional energy, and the outlook for the development of those costs makes it unlikely that solar energy will become competitive in the foreseeable future with electricity produced in large quantities by thermal or hydroelectric powerplants.

It would be unwise to count on solar energy to replace modern imported sources of energy and to favor industrial development in the region. We do not suggest that solar energy has no role to play -- witness the role it played in enabling the spread of television in rural areas. Generally, solar energy is useful for satisfying small-scale energy requirements in areas that are not covered by national grids (i.e. most rural areas and a major part of peri-urban areas). In those regions, solar energy allows for improved lighting, refrigeration, mechanical water pumping (in certain cases), etc. and can thereby greatly improve living conditions. The "qualitative" impact of solar energy is far superior to its "quantitative" impact (the influence of that form of energy on trade balances, which remains almost insignificant).

Manufacturing Industries

The outlook for worldwide trends in manufacturing industries highlights the opportunities that will arise for Southern countries in both conventional and hi-tech industries. Can the Sahel take advantage of any of these opportunities?

At least two factors weigh against the likelihood of such a possibility:

a) High production costs, which prevent the region from being competitive on international markets. The latest example of this dilemma was provided by the Industries Chimiques Sénégalaise chemical corporation, which was set up to produce phosphoric acid from Senegalese phosphates, and which accumulated debts in excess of the company's capital stock within two years.

High production costs are not simply due to an unsatisfactory ratio between labor costs and productivity, but to the <u>overall cost structure,</u> comprising:

-- excessive costs imposed by an over-inflated public sector on national economies as a whole; and

-- imbalances introduced by the urban bias, i.e, abnormally high cost of labor and abnormally low cost of capital, due to the effects of foreign aid.

Production costs in Third-World countries that are undergoing rapid industrialization, especially in South East Asia, are significantly lower than those in the Sahel. Further, the currencies of those countries are often undervalued (they are certainly not overvalued), and it is obvious that those two factors are not unrelated.

The trend scenario will exclude the possibility of a major devaluation of Sahelian currencies, which is not consistent with the basic hypothesis of the stability of the forces at work within Sahelian societies. Under those conditions, it is difficult to see how the cost structure that was set up in the colonial era and reinforced by twenty-five years of independent government policy-making could disappear overnight with the wave of a magic wand. The only way to change that structure is through a persistent effort aimed at reducing industrial production costs, introducing competition, and abolishing protection at all levels. However, that hypothesis appears highly unlikely under the trend scenario.

b) <u>The shortage of skilled labor.</u> In chapter 14 we saw that there was a degree of truth to the suggestion that new technologies could be easily used by everyone. It is a fact that the majority of jobs created in the United States since 1973, including those in Silicon Valley, are largely unskilled. But we also saw the limits of that hypothesis and the fact that successful implementation of any technology, whether conventional or advanced, requires a skilled, sometimes highly skilled, workforce that is adaptable, and that possesses relevant knowhow, etc.

The Sahel is considerably handicapped in that sector when compared to long-established industrialized countries and to newly-industrialized countries, where the dissemination and level of education are superior, and where the culture is better suited to ensuring that the tasks involved in industrial production are carried out efficiently. That handicap seems unlikely to disappear within the next twenty-five years.

It is important to mention favorable as well as unfavorable factors, e.g, the ascension of education, and the loosening of restrictions linked to membership of traditional societies. However, it seems unlikely that the overall situation will improve to the extent that the Sahel gains a crucial advantage on a particular industrial market, against a background of fierce international competition.

Let us therefore suppose that, under the trend scenario:

-- <u>There will be no development of exports from Sahelian industries</u> to world markets;

-- <u>Development of the industries that supply domestic markets will be slow;</u> those industries will be protected against international competition, and growth will be hampered by:

  i) inadequate expansion of solvent demand,

ii) <u>increasing competition from the informal sector</u> where cost structures are much more favorable. [Such competition is the source of an increasing number of complaints from formal industries (especially those with foreign interests), which accuse the informal sector of unfair trading].

One result of this hypothesis is that the number of industrial jobs created in cities will be far lower than the number of city dwellers on the labor market.

The informal sector

The conclusion that the development of modern industry will create only a limited number of jobs, combined with the fact that job creation in the public sector will also be limited due to inadequate resources, and allied to a persistent and heavy rural exodus, leads directly to a contradiction that can only be overcome by hypothesizing a very high rate of growth in the informal sector, which creates jobs in Sahelian cities.

That hypothesis is not unreasonable considering the probable development of values and mentalities, and the gradual destructuring of traditional society, which should encourage a higher level of individual initiative than in the past.

In the same way as those who consider that the agricultural revolution in Northern countries is yet to come, it is feasible to suggest that the development of the informal sector in Sahelian cities has not yet occurred.

That development presents two major problems:

a) The productivity of labor in the informal sector has so far been low, mainly because of the lack of productive investment in that sector.

By contrast with the formal sector, <u>the cost of capital is very high and the cost of labor very low for informal companies</u> (which pay for factors of production at their real value and not at artificial prices); that cost ratio <u>necessarily leads to low productivity.</u>

However, for a given level of capital, low productivity is also due to insufficient labor skills at both the technical and managerial levels. Productivity would increase if the informal sector were allowed greater access to cumulative savings and if the workforce were able to receive further training. Those conditions are almost impossible to fulfill within the informal sector as it stands, and informal enterprises would be obliged to leave the system and to become "legitimate" -- which the vast majority of entrepreneurs have no desire to do. In particular, the "formalization" of those enterprises would entail high production costs and would jeopardize profitability. Let us suppose that, under the trend scenario, the current situation will not change and that <u>the informal sector will remain an area of low productivity.</u>

There is a further reason why informal entrepreneurs are reluctant to invest for increased productivity: the majority of those entrepreneurs complain of the difficulty of expanding their markets. This problem is principally caused by what could be called "intra-urban bias", i.e, the highly uneven distribution of income among different social categories of urban dwellers.

The pressure exerted by Western countries and their associated international organizations in an attempt to encourage Sahelian countries to reduce their balance of payments deficits and thereby reduce domestic demand appears to increase intra-urban bias and to have a negative effect on the incomes of poorer city dwellers, who are the "preferential customers" of the informal sector.

b) The informal sector produces goods and services, and is an effective system for redistributing the incomes of the modern sector of the urban economy. However, almost none of the goods and services produced can be exported. The contribution of the informal sector to the Sahelian balance of payments is negligible, and will most probably remain so.

The trend scenario for industry is characterized by a slow rate of industrialization and a phenomenal growth of the informal sector, which will remain an area of low productivity.

Chapter 20

THE TREND SCENARIO: COHERENT, PROBABLE AND LEADING TO TENSION

The earlier chapters of this study set the scene and provided a background for the roles to be played by the various actors in the coming twenty-five years. This is what we have called the trend scenario. However, will these different sections fit together to form a coherent whole? Will not the increasing number of contradictions create unbearable tension among the different actors? And won't those actors push the action towards another scenario?

A coherent scenario

We shall attempt to bring together the crucial elements discussed in different chapters of the study:

-- Values are developing rapidly and turbulently, but there is a growing fascination with the West and with Western consumer societies. However, the mentalities, the conception of the relationship among people and between people and their environment will remain marked, at least in part, by Sahelian tradition;

-- Power is not slipping away from the current political class, which is ensuring its progeny and which is governing through mixed regimes that are both military and civilian at the same time. Those regimes are attentive to the demands of the urban dwellers who come under their sphere of influence (urban bias has not been eliminated), and make particular efforts to defuse protests from underprivileged population groups in peri-urban areas;

-- New power groups are emerging in rural areas, and some are playing a major role at the local level by encouraging and organizing initiatives among rural population groups; however, those power groups will be unable to play a significant role at the national level;

-- Population growth remains strong, fertility is high, and although mortality rates may possibly be rising slowly, they are no longer declining;

-- The rural exodus remains significant; the evolution in values has vindicated the trend, which is being strongly encouraged by the stagnation of rural economies;

-- Traditional agriculture is starting to be transformed under the impetus of ecological problems and due to the activities of the new rural elites that are emerging with the support of NGOs. The arrival of new technologies may favor this embryonic transformation, which is less damaging to the environment but nonetheless remains as extensive as in the past;

-- That transformation is not aimed at winning back urban markets, which are mainly supplied by cereals sold off at low prices by Western countries, nor at recapturing world markets, where prices are generally depressed and where the Sahel is poorly positioned;

-- Food habits are slowly becoming diversified, and a new type of agriculture is developing around urban markets for products that are less threatened by imported cereals (e.g, fruit, vegetables, produce from small-scale livestock activities). "Rich" farmers and urban entrepreneurs play an important role in that type of agriculture;

-- Nomadic livestock activities are gradually disappearing, and new forms of livestock activities are having difficulty becoming successfully established in Sahelian regions;

-- Despite the changes that are occurring in agricultural techniques, land resources are continuing to deteriorate; although in certain areas that deterioration has ceased or even been reversed, it subsists in other regions; moreover, deforestation continues;

-- In spite of those changes, the rural world remains for the most part extremely introverted; incomes remain low and are partly generated by non-agricultural activities;

-- The Sahel is undergoing a process of relatively slow de-industrialization due to a lack of solvent and sufficiently sizeable domestic markets, and to a lack of competitiveness in the international marketplace. The region does not capitalize on the opportunities offered by the development of technologies and markets;

-- The propensity to import consumer goods remains high because of the process of de-industrialization and the development of Sahelian values; those imports, when cumulated with imports of food products, explain why trade-balance deficits are tending to increase;

-- The informal urban economy is currently expanding at a phenomenal rate and is creating the jobs necessary to respond to urban growth; it remains, however, an area of low productivity. The informal urban sector plays a key role in redistributing the incomes from the modern public and non-governmental sectors, but those involved generally enjoy only modest revenues;

-- The State -- dominated by an entourage interested in protecting its standard of living -- is increasingly unable to supply a satisfactory level of public service, and is especially unable to maintain the quality of the education and health services. Further, rural and peri- urban dwellers are less interested in obtaining an education that does not allow them access to the privileged class;

-- The State has little impact on the economy, a major part of which depends on the informal, urban and rural networks; the State is able to subsist only because of more foreign aid, which is increasingly being diverted from financing economic development to compensating for structural deficits.

This scenario structure does not appear to contain any major inconsistencies, provided that:

-- <u>An increasing volume of external financial resources</u> is earmarked for financing the excess in public and private consumption over domestic production. This means that, despite the failure of structural adjustment programs and numerous development projects, Western countries continue to send aid to the Sahel, increase their aid to that region, and accept that the Sahelian debt will increase;

-- Those same Western countries <u>make a further effort</u> to assist Sahelian countries, especially in the form of food aid, during the dry periods that will inevitably occur in the future.

The trend scenario is one of rising dependence. Is it possible to suggest an estimate of that growing dependence and of the volume of foreign aid that will have to be sent to the Sahel in various forms in order to fulfill the first of the above conditions?

First, what indicators could be selected for that estimate? Neither the volume of official development aid, which does not take into account the level of indebtedness to sources other than donors, nor the increase in debt, which does not integrate public and private grants, is a satisfactory indicator.

What international finance experts call the current account balance indicates net foreign borrowing requirements over and above foreign grants and investments ("unrequited transfers"). In 1970, the current accounts of the Sahelian countries were almost balanced. The 1984 current account balance showed a deficit of US$ 700 million.

Therefore, in less than fifteen years, <u>the dependence of the region has increased from US$ 200 million to more than US$ 1.6 billior</u>. In constant terms, dependence has been multiplied by a factor of three. It seems impossible that dependence will continue to increase at that rate. An over-simplified hypothesis suggests that rising dependence is essentially due to urban population groups, or rather to a certain fraction of those groups.

If it is accepted that dependence will develop in line with the population, the volume of financial resources that the Sahel will need in 2010 exceeds US$ 7 billion. Today, such a growth rate seems highly unlikely: the volume of financial resources needed will be similar to the total amount of official development assistance currently supplied to sub-Saharan Africa.

A more probable outcome is that dependence will grow less quickly, come what may. On the other hand, is it possible to dismiss the hypothesis that dependence will increase significantly and that, by 2010, it will be necessary to make available between three and four billion of today's dollars (if not more) to ensure the region's survival? Probably not.

A probable scenario

Is there a chance that the above condition, which is vital to the materialization of the trend scenario, will be met? Will Western countries be prepared to commit such large volumes of financial resources? Those are the basic questions that must be asked in connection with the trend scenario. Although it is difficult to provide definite answers, a number of factors weigh in favor of a positive response.

The first of those factors is that it has become difficult, and <u>will become increasingly so, to reduce aid to the Sahel severely.</u> The dependence of the region has today become such that a sharp reduction in the level of aid would provoke a social crisis in the Sahel that would not be easily accepted by public opinion in the West; this will be increasingly true in the future. Western public opinion would very quickly be alerted by the media to the dramatic consequences of that crisis, and would be even more sensitive to the problem since those consequences would most affect the poorest sections of the community. In turn, those consequences would bring about a situation of far-reaching political instability, i.e, a destabilization of the region, which, without necessarily being considered as catastrophic, would nonetheless be judged regrettable by Western governments, who would prefer to avoid such a train of events. This is highlighted by fears that Eastern countries would become strongly established in the Sahel, thereby supplanting the Western presence.

The growing backwardness of the Sahel (and several other African countries) in relation to the rest of the world, including developing countries, will constitute an additional argument for persuading public opinion to put pressure on governments to take action in this direction and for enabling individuals to supply charity to the most deprived inhabitants of the planet, thereby salving their consciences.

The second factor is that <u>aid to the Sahel, including food aid, is insignificant in global terms.</u> It may prove necessary to supply the Sahel with more than 3 million tons of cereals in normal years and perhaps 5 or 6 million tons in dry years by the beginning of the 21st century, and to supply that aid free of charge (either in the direct form of food aid or indirectly as commercial imports, which will be reflected in an increased but continuously rescheduled foreign debt). But if this eventuality occurs, it will be no hardship for the increasingly efficient farming sectors of Northern countries to provide those cereals. The West would also be able to meet the financial commitments, even if they reach the levels discussed in the preceding paragraph.

It is probable that those financial commitments will be partially reflected in an increase in the Sahelian debt; that increase will be exponential, since the Sahelian States do not have the capacity to repay the debt. Even under that hypothesis it is likely that the Sahelian debt will remain relatively low in world terms and will never reach the proportions of the Brazilian or Mexican debts.

Consequently, the most convenient solution would be to maintain the status quo until a major crisis develops.

One can reflect that donors will have to accept that their aid is persistently ineffective; that realization will be temporarily attenuated, as in the past, by occasional successes (which may even become more numerous with experience). As in the past, new structural adjustment plans, new development plans, or new and cleverly named formulas will appear at regular intervals, all of which will claim to provide the definitive solution to the problems of the Sahel. Further, Sahelian governments will adapt their policies and take the necessary measures -- at least superficially -- to partially satisfy the demands of the small number of donors that lay store by efficiency.

This does not exclude the possibility that pressure will be brought on the Sahelians to reduce dependence and lower domestic demand; and that the intensity of that pressure will vary according to the international climate and the degree of stringency of the Western governments in power at the time. It is therefore reasonable to expect <u>almost constant deflationist pressure.</u> This also means that, although investment aid will not disappear, it will be progressively scaled down in favor of balance-of-payments aid.

Although the problems of external balance may find solutions that, without always being totally satisfactory, at least prevent disaster, what may be said of internal problems? Will not those problems assume major proportions and make it necessary to leave the trend scenario relatively rapidly?

A scenario of accumulating tensions

The scenario that we have outlined is coherent, but it is also a scenario of accumulating tensions. A situation where the crisis reaches its height, and a relatively sudden change releases accumulated tensions and brings about a new balance within Sahelian societies will eventually become inevitable.

The growth in public aid provided by Western countries to the States, the minor policy adjustments made by Sahelian governments, the development of the informal urban sector, the initiatives taken in the rural sector and NGO support for those initiatives, and the beginnings of a transformation of the agricultural sector will all act as palliatives to stave off an intolerable accumulation of tensions and to prevent the crisis from coming to an immediate head.

But it is difficult to envisage anything other than an increase in the tensions that arise between the increasingly strong desire -- highlighted by the spread of the media -- to attain a Western-style consumer society, and the fact that the majority of urban and rural dwellers are unable to gain access to such a society. Strong pressure to lower domestic demand will increase those tensions still further.

Other tensions that are almost certain to increase are those between privileged urban dwellers and residents in peri-urban areas, and between urban and rural dwellers, since urban and intra-urban bias will increase.

It is also difficult to envisage anything other than an increase in the tensions between dynamic groups in rural and urban societies, and the State, which is increasingly perceived as burdensome rather than supportive.

However, those tensions may increase only gradually and we can suppose that foreign aid will not be apportioned in niggardly fashion for the reasons we mentioned earlier, and that Sahelian governments will be sufficiently sagacious to introduce measures in an effort to prevent tensions rising to danger level. If those postulates are accepted, then no major crisis will disrupt Sahelian societies over the coming quarter-century and the trend scenario will materialize.

Limited adaptation that does not solve fundamental problems

Sahelian societies have for centuries adapted to changes in the outside environment; those adaptations have not occurred without crises but the societies have always managed for the most part to retain their originality. They adapted to the rise and fall of the slave trade, to colonization, and later to decolonization.

This course of events suggests that the societies chose to respond to successive changes by limited adaptation. Today, those societies are responding to the invasion of Western values and the desire for a consumer society by limited changes in the urban and rural production systems, and by using foreign aid to finance the purchase of consumer goods they do not produce. They are responding to the deterioration of natural resources by the initiatives of village associations, which represent the beginnings of adaptation.

The trend scenario is based on the hypothesis that this strategy of limited adaptation will continue and that the action of donors will facilitate limited adaptation without giving rise to situations that would be catastrophic for the region. Thus the trend scenario suggested by the Futures Study is not the apocalyptic scenario that some pessimistic experts describe.

Since the scenario is not apocalyptic it is therefore probable.

The trend scenario is plausible and even probable since it is not an extrapolation-of-trends scenario (which would quickly become intolerable because of the catastrophic situations it would engender) but a limited-adaptation scenario that does not lead to an apocalypse, at least in the coming quarter-century.

However, if foreign dependence is allowed to increase, and no preparations are made to put an end to it, such a scenario does not solve the fundamental problems of the region.

Chapter 21

LESS FAVORABLE SCENARIOS

The trend scenario that we have constructed above clearly has a great many disadvantages, and we will discuss those disadvantages further in the next chapter. The scenario might be deemed unacceptable, but is it the worst scenario that can be envisaged today? Definitely not. Certain hypotheses that can be retained are probably less probable than those discussed above but lead to less favorable situations for the majority of Sahelians.

No attempt will be made here to systematically discuss all the interacting hypotheses that might lead to less favorable scenarios, but we will merely give a few typical examples of scenarios of this type.

The accentuated-drought scenario

We have seen that when climatic trends are extrapolated over a long period, it is difficult to draw the distinction between the continuity hypothesis (which we considered the most probable in the trend scenario) and the change-in-trend hypothesis. We cannot ignore the possibility of a growing break with trends over the coming quarter-century as a result of feedback effects that are little known today, the influence of deforestation of coastal areas, for example. Average rainfall could decline, and several acute droughts, more pronounced than the early 1980s drought, would occur.

The most probable hypothesis is that the Sahelian countries will not yet have managed to control their environment over the coming quarter-century and that droughts will hit these societies, which are still vulnerable and which are no more prepared to deal with the situation except by resorting to massive food aid than they were during earlier droughts. These droughts lead to a flight to the cities on an unprecedented scale. But as early warning systems are better organized, and even redundant (aside from AGRHYMET, each donor has its own!), and as the West has finally managed to better organize the distribution of food aid and the concentration of the Sahelian population in the cities simplifies the distribution of foodstuffs, a demographic catastrophe is averted.

The reduction in average rainfall levels forces rural activities to move further south, and populations groups relocate. This is a possibility in countries with areas in the Sudanese zone, which are still relatively sparsely populated. However, the large-scale relocation of population groups produces major problems, conflicts arise between migrants and indigenous population groups, and the new-found dynamism that had begun to be expressed within the social groups that are forced to migrate is subjected to a brutal test. Similarly, the dynamism of the indigenous societies is forced to find expression under new conditions brought about by the massive influx of migrants.

The situation is more dramatic in the countries of the Sudanese zone with fewer resources. Despite the African tradition of hospitality whereby large numbers of foreign migrants are welcomed, neighboring countries that have had their own problems are reticent, if not hostile, to the new arrivals. That attitude reinforces migration to the cities of the Sahel.

Under the pressure of public opinion, which has been made more aware of the problems of the region through the media, Western governments increase aid disbursements. This is essentially subsistence aid. The dependence of the Sahel becomes even greater than under the trend scenario (at least temporarily), and, despite this increase in aid, living conditions are more difficult both in the rural areas that have been upset by climatic phenomena, and in the peri-urban areas, which are becoming increasingly overpopulated.

It is unlikely that the increase in aid will last indefinitely, and sooner or later the region will enjoy conditions that will make it possible for another scenario, involving reductions in foreign aid, to materialize.

The Aids-explosion scenario

We saw in chapter 17 that in view of the data that is available today, it is impossible to rule out the hypothesis that Aids will increase exponentially and lead to a demographic catastrophe before this increase has been checked.

However, without a demographic catastrophe occurring, a major increase in the disease would most probably have considerable socio-economic effects:

— Markedly higher health care expenditure than at present: we saw under the trend scenario that Sahelian governments are experiencing difficulties in maintaining the quality of the health services; this increased burden could be maintained only by allocating to health care part of the foreign aid the countries receive, and levels of foreign aid would thus have to rise;

— Consequences, which are difficult to evaluate at the present time, on mentalities, social relations within the Sahel and between Sahelians and the rest of the world. If Aids spread faster in Africa than in the rest of the world, there would be grounds to fear the creation of a type of "ghetto".

The reduced foreign aid scenario

A significant, lasting reduction in aid from the Western countries was considered improbable under the trend scenario. This would be even more unlikely under the accentuated-drought scenario and under the Aids-explosion scenario. But it is far from inconceivable, and could be brought about by a number of factors:

-- Persistent stagnation or recession in the OECD countries, which would lead those countries to respond to public opinion worried about standards of living in the West by reviewing the amount of aid sent, even to the poorest countries, even if this aid only represents a tiny part of the national income, and if a reduction in aid would have practically no effect on standards of living;

-- Increased racist feeling and/or the development of campaigns denouncing the total inefficiency of aid to countries that are making no significant progress would reinforce pressure to reduce levels of aid in the event of stagnation of OECD economies, and even more so if those economies were to move into recession;

-- A major East-West crisis, even without generalized armed conflict, diminish commitments of aid to the countries of the South, including the poorest countries.

A substantial reduction in volumes of aid would inevitably lead to an acute crisis in those countries that had become heavily dependent on that aid, and a sharp reduction in the standard of living of the privileged members of the community, which would attempt to pass on to the less privileged.

The deterioration of the public services (education, health care, transportation and communications infrastructure, etc.) that was mentioned in the trend scenario would increase substantially. The lack of foreign exchange would oblige the countries of the Sahel to reduce imports, particularly the food imports that feed peri-urban population groups. The price of these imported foodstuffs would increase sharply, and that increase would probably make it possible to win back urban markets and would bring <u>a certain degree of re-linkaging of Sahelian economies.</u>

It should be pointed out, however, that this re-linkaging would only be achieved to the detriment of living conditions (an increase in the mortality rate -- perhaps even a sharp increase -- could be expected, as the result of a deterioration of health and hygiene conditions and of high food prices). Further, this re-linkaging would <u>inevitably involve a social crisis and political upheavals.</u>

Scenarios that bring into question the current role of the State

This heading covers all the scenarios under which the Western-style conception of the State would be profoundly brought into question, for various reasons:

-- The rise to power of an Islamic fundamentalist movement;

-- Secessionist movements leading to civil war;

-- Conflict between army factions;

-- Military intervention from outside;

-- The inability of the State to ensure the operation of the public services and/or the security of the population.

The extreme situation (which is not far from reality in Chad) would involve the utter collapse of the State.

It is probable that, under any of the hypotheses mentioned here, foreign aid would be reduced, that the Sahelian countries would return to the situation produced under the preceding scenario and that the situation would be further aggravated by the dismantling of the State.

*
* *

It should be pointed out that the scenarios envisaged above are not mutually independent. A severe, prolonged drought would have consequences on the power base and perhaps also on the concept of the State. A very substantial reduction in volumes of aid would have the same effect.

Naturally, in any case, Sahelian societies would not fail to react to these new situations. It is probable that the "limited" adaptation that would occur under the trend scenario would take on wider proportions.

A "new" State could be born, but it is unclear at present what form that new State would take. What is certain, however, is that the coming period would be markedly more difficult for the vast majority of the Sahelian population.

Chapter 22

CONCLUSION: IS THE PRESENT TRENDS SCENARIO ACCEPTABLE?

As long as major upheavals and fundamental doubts can be avoided, the trend scenario has a high chance of occurring if the Sahelians make some minor social changes and if Western countries continue to provide reasonable support. Does this mean that there are no disadvantages in the trend scenario and that it is acceptable?

Definitely not. <u>The trend scenario is first and foremost a scenario of stagnation, or even of falling standards of living for most of the Sahelian population for the next quarter-century.</u> If that stagnation was the price that had to be paid by one generation to develop an original social plan that responded to the deep-seated aspirations of the majority of the Sahelians, and to prepare a better future for future generations, then it could be deemed acceptable. But this is not the case.

Further, the trend scenario "maximizes" the restrictions on the Sahelians and even on the West, and sets the stage for a more difficult future, at least for the next generation of Sahelians. We now turn to a discussion of these two unacceptable consequences of the trend scenario.

Increased restrictions

Increased dependence on foreign aid, which would be inherent in the trend scenario, involves not only a more or less alarming amount of dollars that Sahelian governments would have to request from the international community. The fact that the Sahel is obliged to seek aid not only for investments, which are generally made just once and become profitable over time, but also for the day-to-day operations of Sahelian societies, creates restrictions that should not be underestimated.

<u>Restrictions on Sahelian governments.</u> During recent years, certain governments have been virtually placed under supervision and have had no choice but to accept the structural adjustment program -- and the daily restrictions that implied -- that was proposed to them. There is little chance of a lasting change in this tendency, and yet structural deficits are increasing. Sahelian governments could develop "anti-supervision" strategies

that would be more or less clearly defined and that would have varying degrees of effectiveness. The room for maneuver of the governments would in any case be significantly reduced, since they would be subject to other restrictions imposed in more subtle ways by donor agencies that had learned from their experience.

<u>Restrictions on Sahelian societies.</u> When dependence on the outside world has exceeded a certain limit and has become permanent, it is difficult for a society to implement its own autonomous plan. Dependence probably makes it difficult for a society to carry out any sort of plan at all. Since Toynbee, it has often been said that every civilization is a response to a challenge. Accepting dependence, however, is not responding to a challenge but mere resignation. It would be relevant here to give a fuller version of the quotation from Tidiane Diakité that introduced this second part of our study: "An assisted society is a society that has lost its soul as soon as that assistance does not bring about an effort for the individual to achieve something himself."

<u>Restrictions for Western countries.</u> Provided aid is investment aid, it can vary, or even stop, from one year to the next. Such action would undoubtedly have disadvantages for the recipient countries, but the fact that investments stop or diminish is not necessarily crucial. When aid is subsistence aid, and when that aid has to become permanent, the situation changes. The Western countries will be increasingly caught in a rut and will assume increasing moral responsibility. Stopping aid or severely cutting it back would have social and political consequences that would make many Western leaders think twice. Western leaders will hesitate even more when they recognize that the media are always ready to show public opinion the drastic consequences of reduced aid on the most underprivileged sectors of Sahelian society.

A difficult future

<u>The decline of the Welfare State</u>

Since independence, Sahelian leaders have been eager to develop the social services and to set up a welfare state that they can afford, or at least to start to bridge the gap that separates them from the industrialized countries in this respect. They have succeeded in this endeavor to varying degrees and in recent years they have had considerable difficulty in ensuring that the social infrastructure they have created can continue operating.

Under the trend scenario, these difficulties are going to increase. Because the economies of the Sahel are stagnating, the governments will be able to generate only limited resources to finance the social sector. It is unlikely that official aid agencies, which are receiving increasing demand from elsewhere, will substantially increase their efforts in this area. Only foreign NGOs will be able to help palliate the shortcomings of ODA and the Sahelian governments.

This means that the health services, the education system and perhaps other services (even perhaps the civil security forces) will suffer the consequences, and that situation will have an effect on the long-term future of the region. This also means that the day-to-day lives of a large sector of the population will become more difficult.

The degradation of the natural environment

Even if it were possible or probable for this trend to change, it is very unlikely that it could be reversed all over the Sahel, mainly because, in spite of the determination of the villagers, the material resources necessary will not be available and because it will be impossible to change the systems of production (agricultural, pastoral, forestry) quickly enough. This means that <u>the coming generation of Sahelians will hand on to the next one, which will be twice as large, a legacy of natural resources that is reduced from that which it received itself.</u> This will be particularly true if the coming period is drier than the current period. This means that several generations will not have managed their natural resources rationally, but will to some degree have squandered them.

Rising tensions

We will not belabor the deepening rift between the aspirations of most Sahelians and the realities of the situation, or the growing tensions within Sahelian societies. All that can be said is that these factors contribute to a future that will not be easy.

One of the conclusions of the retrospective view was that Sahelian societies were disjointed or disarticulated and that this state of affairs was an immediate result of the failure to sustain development. The trend scenario is one of persistent disintegration.

Which way out?

There is at least one certainty about the <u>trend scerario: it cannot continue indefinitely,</u> nor can it continue for very long. It is probably viable for the next twenty-five years, provided certain adjustments are made. However, neither an increase in the region's dependence on the outside world, nor the deterioration of the natural resources that are handed on to the rising numbers of future generations, nor the rise of internal tensions can be extrapolated for very long.

We will not make any indication here of what could happen to resolve a situation that is becoming intolerable. Perhaps a miracle will happen. But, as everybody knows, the basic characteristic of a miracle is its very improbability. Violent revolutions may take place. A demographic catastrophe might occur, or populations might migrate en masse.

While the trend scenario is not apocalyptic for the next quarter-century, it carries within it the potential for future disaster.

Failing a miracle or a major catastrophe, is there a door through which the Sahel could leave the trend scenario during the next 25 years, to follow a more desirable scenario and thereby prepare a more acceptable future? Part III of this study aims to examine this question.

PART III

LOOKING AT POSSIBILITIES FOR THE FUTURE

> There is no fatality from which we cannot escape. Man is responsible for History; he is not subject to its rule. Within every society lies the potential for other societies.
>
> G. Balandier

INTRODUCTION TO LOOKING AT POSSIBILITIES FOR THE FUTURE

The trend scenario and the other unfavorable scenarios examined above can all be described as "structuralist". They rely on an implicit theory that history is the product of structural logic, and that "society's processes take place above the heads of the men and women that make up that scciety" (Adorno).

However, it is now generally recognized that the history of human societies is not merely the product of logic, but that the unexpected plays an important role in shaping society, and that individuals -- or at least certain groups of individuals -- do have the means to knowingly divert the course of history. It is also recognized that not everything will be possible in the future, and the trend scenario is thus of use. It can be compared with a metal structure whose base is firmly fixed in the present: the further from the base we are, and the greater the pressure applied, the more the metal structure will bend. But the structure will only bend within given limits, and nobody can hope to bend it in all directions.

The aim of the third part and conclusion of this study will thus be to examine how the trend scenario can be bent, where pressure should be applied to produce the desired effect, and who can apply that pressure. Before exploring the field of possible futures, however, some indication should be given as to what should be regarded as desirable.

As was mentioned in the introduction, the team that carried out the prospective study did not consider itself to be in a position to state what it felt to be a desirable future for the Sahel. That can only be determined by the millions of Sahelians who will be involved in building the future of their region. However, for the purposes of this study, <u>a given scenario is judged preferable to the trend scenario if it responds to the following three criteria:</u>

-- Quantities of goods and services available to a given population group will grow faster than the population itself, thereby enabling the population group to implement a social plan of its own choosing;

-- Dependence on the outside world will decrease, thereby increasing the the local population's freedom to choose its future;

-- The future will not be compromised by the deterioration of the environment.

Part III of this report thus does not propose a scenario in the sense that a scenario has been defined above (i.e, as a logical sequence of credible events, that can be used as a "model" for the development of Sahelian societies), but simply illustrates that desirable scenarios do exist, without attempting to describe that scenario in detail. The pages that follow, therefore, do not give an inventory of the region's resources upon which more favorable scenarios could be constructed.

Part III of this study thus concentrates on the mechanisms of development and on the obstacles that stand in the way of development, rather than pointing to the form that development could take. We thus point to the elements that could change, either inside or outside the Sahelian system, and that could thereby lead to a way out of the trend scenario towards one or other of the desirable scenarios.

Chapter 23

POSSIBLE SCENARIOS

Let us re-examine the basic conclusion of Part II: in the trend scenario, the Sahel survives as well as can be expected, but without growth in real terms, and suffers both a heavy increase in its dependence on the outside world and relatively rapid erosion of its natural resources.

If one of the possible scenarios is to appear more desirable in the way "more desirable" has been defined above, the influence of the outside world is a crucial factor. We are thus going to use that factor as a means of classifying desirable scenarios.

There are only three ways of reducing dependence on the outside world:

-- Giving priority to reductions in imports: we will refer to these scenarios as "auto-centered scenarios";

-- Giving priority to increases in exports, which will lead to scenarios based on integration in the world market system;

-- Reducing imports and increasing exports at the same time: these scenarios will be referred to as "mixed scenarios".

A brief overview is given below of the essential characteristics of these three families of scenarios, and indications will be made as to the conditions that must be fulfilled for these scenarios to materialize.

Auto-centered development scenarios

Understandably, when dependence was growing, many positive points were attributed to auto-centered development, since it also provided a means to increase economic independence. However, the issue remained at the conceptual level and nothing was done in practical terms to favor this type of development. One extreme example of this is provided by the de-linking scenario -- breaking off with the West -- recommended by certain theorists. The objective of food self-sufficiency adopted by the CILSS as part of the Lagos Plan of Action, while far from being an extreme stance, would also lead to scenarios classified as "auto-centered".

Are scenarios of this type desirable and under what conditions could they materialize? In an attempt to provide answers to these questions, we are going to break down the imports of the countries of the Sahel into four main categories, and then examine the extent to which each of these types of imports can be reduced, and how.

Food products

Without seeking total food self-sufficiency, which is clearly utopian in view of the current situation in the Sahel, imports of food products could be considerably reduced. But for that to come about, food habits would need to change substantially in urban areas, and even in certain rural areas: consumers would have to give up wheat, which is difficult to produce in sufficient quantities in the Sahel (at least in the medium term) and other food products imported from the West. In view of current world market prices, such a reduction in imports can only be brought about by large-scale devaluation of local currencies, by heavy import taxes, or strict quota regulations.

Agriculture must thus concentrate on food production. Imported fertilizers cannot be used and large-scale mechanization can be ruled out. Intensification of agriculture must be brought about by wider use of animal-drawn farming techniques, organic fertilizers, local natural phosphates, and, in the longer term, perhaps even by direct nitrogen fixation. The population is due to double over the next quarter-century, and yield per hectare must thus increase; experts claim that such an increase is feasible. The specific productivity of the agricultural worker must thus increase also. According to the demographic hypotheses that have been adopted (for overall population growth and growth of the urban population), and assuming that food dependency remains constant, each agricultural worker will have to feed 4 consumers in 2010 compared with 3 consumers in 1985.

Since imports cannot be reduced to zero, and in view of the fact that neither the mining sector nor the manufacturing sector is in a position to generate the currency needed to finance incompressible imports, agriculture and other primary sectors (livestock and fisheries) must also export and can only export if they are competitive. In other words, in a world where technical progress is not about to stop, productivity in these activities must increase.

It would undoubtedly be possible to increase productivity in food-crop or export-crop production and to maintain environmental equilibrium without relying on imported fertilizers, but the investment in human resources required would probably be enormous.

Energy

It would be difficult to bring about sharp decreases in energy imports unless the lifestyles of urban population groups, which consume the majority of imported energy, undergo a radical change. (In the medium term, there is no economically viable way of replacing imported petroleum products in the transportation sector. A large proportion of the energy that Sahelian countries import is for transportation requirements). Moderate reductions can be made by optimizing use of local energy resources (fossil fuels such as peat, lignite, etc, or renewable energy sources such as hydroelectricity, solar energy and biomass) and by adopting a policy for the rational use of energy. In the medium term, the implementation of these policies, combined with the fact that world-market energy prices should remain moderate, the cost of imported energy should become tolerable. In the longer term, further increases in imported energy prices are likely and serious restrictions will probably become necessary as a result.

This state of affairs will have two consequences:

-- Imported fuel cannot be replaced by wood in the households sector; agriculture must provide not only food and most of the currency earnings needed to finance imports, but also part of the region's energy requirements;

-- Energy-intensive activities cannot be promoted, and certain modern industries will thus not be able to develop.

Consumer goods

As with energy, a sharp decrease in imports of manufactured consumer goods cannot take place unless urban lifestyles change. Reduced imports will stimulate local production of manufactured goods to a certain extent, but most of the opportunities for replacing imports with locally produced manufactured goods have already been taken in the Sahel, and no major developments can be expected in this respect. Local manufacturing concerns have a long way to go before they can claim to replace all imports of consumer goods, and, because of the difficulties encountered in importing capital equipment and energy, development should be centered around industries with low capital intensity, which would create jobs for the urban population.

Capital equipment

It is impossible to reduce the volume of capital equipment that is imported to ensure operation of the industrial facilities of the countries of the Sahel -- even in industries with low capital intensity, transportation infrastructures, social equipment, etc.

Conclusions on auto-centered development scenarios

If these scenarios were to materialize, <u>major changes would have to occur in Sahelian societies.</u> First, less importance would need to be attached to Western values, while Islamic or ancestral values would take on a greater role in the overall system of values of the Sahelians. If such changes took place, Western consumer goods would become less attractive.

A radical change would also have to take place in the relationship between the price of imported products and the price of local products, and thus in the distribution of national income between different social groups. It is hard to imagine the ruling classes and their urban clientele accepting a change of this kind today, which would seem particularly unfavorable in the short and medium term. Scenarios of this type would be more likely to materialize if Islamic fundamentalists or other radical groups came to power.

These scenarios would probably <u>only bring slow growth.</u> W. Arthur Lewis (Winner of the Nobel Prize for Economics) has demonstrated that once developing countries have set up industries to replace imports, the driving force behind growth is increased exports rather than greater reliance on the domestic economy. Certain of these scenarios would probably not even be desirable in the terms defined above, because they would bring about a fairly lengthy slump in the availability of goods and services. However, more than any others, auto-centered scenarios would make it possible for Sahelian societies to develop in a way that would at least in part be unconnected from world trends.

A regional cooperation scenario

One alternative solution would involve what could be termed a "regional auto-centered development scenario", which has occasionally been envisaged for the whole of West Africa, including Nigeria. Clearly, a wider resource base and a regional market covering a greater area than the Sahel alone should allow for faster growth, all other things being equal. But in view of the difficulties encountered by the ECOWAS, which is still a long way from becoming operational, and of the trends observed in Nigeria, which is probably not ready to become the driving force of a regional scenario of this type, the regional auto-centered development scenario is unlikely to materialize.

Further, considerable prudence should be exercised when making an appraisal of the outlooks for regional cooperation. Many Sahelians see the partitioning of the region (West and Central Africa) as the source of their current misfortunes. However, it must be remembered that the partitioning of the region has now been tempered by informal trade practices that ignore national frontiers, customs barriers and monetary areas, or that take advantage of these artifices. In the short and medium term, a West African common market would probably not have the positive effects that many observers would expect. Merely bringing together disjointed economies will not necessarily re-coordinate them, and bringing together moderately large, stagnating markets will not necessarily lead to the wide market that is needed to favor self-sustained economic growth. There are clearly other prerequisites. If all the conditions are created, then regional cooperation will clearly accelerate growth, at least in a number of countries in the area involved. If and when it becomes possible, regional cooperation will favor the most dynamic countries, and those with the best human and material resources, but probably not all the countries in the region.

Scenarios based on integration in the world market system

The scenarios proposed by the World Bank ("Berg" report and subsequent reports) could be used to illustrate this category of scenarios.

What can the Sahel hope to export? In principle, it can hope to export those products for which it has a comparative advantage. But in a world where agricultural and industrial production techniques are changing very rapidly, and where certain markets are disrupted by the intervention of major economic powers, the notion of comparative advantage is not always easy to grasp. For example, should the agricultural subsidies that the industrialized countries allocate to their farmers be taken into account as a permanent feature when estimating the comparative advantage of the Sahelian countries?

Mining and mineral products

We have seen that the world context is particularly unfavorable to opening new mines before the end of the century. Further, no systematic exploration of the Sahelian subsoil has been carried out for the last ten years, and aside from Niger's uranium fields, no major reserves have been identified that would become economically viable if the world-market situation improved. The myth of Eldorado is not completely dead in the Sahel, and certain Sahelians are convinced that untold "riches" are lying dormant beneath their feet. It would, however, be very dangerous to count on those riches.

Manufactured goods

The distinction should be drawn between conventional manufactured goods and new manufactured goods that rely on the advanced technologies that have emerged and will continue to emerge over the next quarter-century. The Sahel has little chance of moving into advanced technology manufacturing. On the other hand, however, we have seen (chapter 19) that a number of conventional industries, which are stagnating in the countries of the North, could continue to develop in the countries of the South, and, where applicable, make use of new technologies. Can the Sahel take advantage of some of these openings?

Whatever happens, the Sahel could not hope to move into these openings with production costs at their current levels. A major reduction in costs -- with or without adjustments of monetary parities -- would be essential before exports of manufactured goods could increase. In particular, the concept of a guaranteed minimum wage should be abandoned.

Agricultural products

Sahelian products should be competitive with comparable products from other Third World countries (and in particular from Latin American and South-East Asian countries, which have very aggressive trade policies) and from industrialized countries that have not abandoned oleaginous crop and cotton production.

Because of foreseeable technical progress (as we saw in chapter 18), real prices of these products will continue to fall (irrespective of dumping, which the countries of the North will be relatively likely to practice in order to move their surpluses), productivity in the Sahelian countries will have to continue to increase. If it does not, monetary parities will suffer the consequences.

In the short and medium term, the most substantial increase in exports from the Sahel will probably come from agricultural products.

Conclusions on scenarios based on integration in the world market system

The Sahel has so far failed to adopt a genuine integration policy vis-à-vis the world market. In fact, it would be more accurate to say that the Sahel has become integrated in the world market system only insofar as foreign food products, sold at prices that take into account agricultural subsidies by the industrialized countries, have spread throughout the Sahel. By contrast, the Sahel has not promoted integration in that it has not acquired the means of development that would be needed to bring about a substantial increase in exports, particularly exports of manufactured goods.

Over the next ten or fifteen years at least, there are grounds to expect that <u>the situation will be markedly less favorable to exports</u> to international markets than it was in the 1950s and 1960s, and even in the first part of the 1970s. During that period, several developing countries benefited from relatively favorable terms of exchange to acquire the capital goods that were needed for their countries' economies to take off. Mineral and agricultural raw materials prices have now reached their lowest recorded levels since the beginning of the century, and there are no signs of a durable upturn. Mechanisms of the "Stabex" type will be powerless in the face of situations brought about by structural and not circumstantial factors. Competition in manufactured-goods markets is liable to be even fiercer and the new arrivals on these markets will have to make especial efforts to impose their presence.

Advisors that encourage Sahelian governments to adopt energetic policies to further integration in the world market system tend to be rather discreet on this aspect of the question. Nevertheless, even in unfavorable situations, it is always possible to move into world markets, as has been demonstrated by certain South-East Asian countries. The basic issue is one of competitiveness, and thus relies on adjusting production costs and exchange rates to remain in line with world prices. However, the nation benefits considerably less from its exports in such cases.

Scenarios of this type cannot materialize unless substantial policy changes are introduced in order to ensure competitiveness of in products. In particular, exchange rate adjustment will lead to changes in the distribution of revenues among different social groups, which is scarcely conceivable without a change in the balance of power.

These scenarios can thus only materialize if greater priority is attached to export crops, without food crop production necessarily stagnating. In particular, adjustment of monetary parities, which would be necessary to stimulate exports, would make it more attractive to purchase local food products.

Mixed scenarios

In view of the drawbacks of both types of scenarios that we have examined here, mixed scenarios are likely to be more attractive. Mixed strategies aim to increase exports without depending too much on disorganized international agricultural-product markets, and at the same time to reduce imports, while retaining sufficient room for maneuver to import the capital equipment that is essential for the modernization of the economy.

The balance between the two objectives in a mixed scenario will depend on each country's resources, advantages and handicaps. These mixed strategies are probably the only strategies that the Sahel could reasonably be expected to adopt in the next quarter-century.

On the one hand, although greater reliance on the domestic economy will reduce dependence on the outside world, it is probably not the best way of ensuring economic growth. The same is true of food self-sufficiency, an objective that is clearly out of reach of a region so open to Western influence and that is in any case undesirable in the current international context.

On the other hand, purely and simply seeking integration in the world market system and deregulating trade (as is readily recommended by certain industrialized countries, which do not, however, apply such remedies to their own economies), is probably not the answer for the Sahel, which would be better advised to increase protectionist measures and reduce its dependence on specific sectors.

Questions of which strategy to choose are crucial to the futures study insofar as they provide an alternative to the trend scenario and orient the region towards one scenario rather than another. Thus, these questions will be re-examined in the broader context of a study of the conditions that must coincide for the region to move away from the trend scenario towards one or other of the desirable scenarios that we have examined above.

Finally, it should be stressed that the comments made concerning the potential and limitations of <u>regional cooperation strategies</u> are also applicable to mixed scenarios.

Can these scenarios materialize?

Scenarios that are more desirable than the trend scenario thus do exist. Under what conditions can those scenarios materialize? Analyses that have been made, and structural analyses in particular, have produced clear evidence of the complex interaction that exists between different external and internal variables. There is thus no simple answer to this question.

No suitable response can be given at one level: for example, it would be insufficient to simply recommend the transfer of new technologies to the Sahel, or to suggest that the region's governments change their economic policies, or to call for the replacement of corrupt officials with more honest ones, or to claim that all that is needed is a new international economic order...

The overall situation that was used to develop the trend scenario and all the other scenarios has three major components: culture, civilization and, between the two, social structures and economic operators that either do or do not harmonize culture and civilization. Environmental factors (climate, the rest of the world or the immediate surroundings) must not be overlooked, since they have an influence on all these components.

Sahelian actors (governments, rural communities, city-dwellers) clearly have a key role to play in this process of harmonization. Only they can direct their region towards a different scenario that is more in line with the new values. In particular, actors that have recently arrived on the stage and that can disrupt the established situation and bring a new balance, have an even more essential role to play.

In the first instance, without adopting a position on what different actors should be doing, we are going to examine how the roles of the principal groups of actors mentioned above (governments, rural communities, city-dwellers) could progressively change to orient the action taken towards more desirable scenarios.

It is not clear whether this change in roles could take place spontaneously. Secondly, an examination will be made of the conditions that would have to coincide for this change in roles and changes in the social structure to take place.

If these changes in roles and structures did take place, policies would automatically change also. Policy changes brought about by the actors themselves, but above all by governments, will not only have an influence on the scenarios that will materialize, but will also ultimately affect the roles of the actors. Thirdly, therefore, we will examine the policies that could be adopted in practice.

External assistance, particularly from donors, should not be overlooked here, since it is crucial to the trend scenario and would have an important role in the more desirable scenarios. Fourthly, therefore, an examination will be made of how external assistance could interfere with changes that take place inside the system.

Lastly, mention must be made of potential changes that would have only a very long-term effect -- particularly changes in attitudes, which could occur as a result of changes in the education system (including infant education), or as a consequence of wider dissemination of information on demographic problems. Such changes are hardly likely to have an impact before 2010, but efforts could be made in this direction by the generation that is active between 1985 and 2010 in order to prepare a better future for the following generation.

All these aspects -- new roles for Sahelian actors, conditions required for the changes to take place, new policies that are adopted as a result, the influence of the outside world -- are part of a system, and scenarios other than the trend scenario can only materialize through interaction between the different aspects. The reasons for this interaction and the points of access to the system will be discussed in the conclusion to this report.

Chapter 24

THE ROLE OF THE GOVERNMENT AND THE NON-GOVERNMENTAL SECTOR
IN BUILDING A BETTER FUTURE

This chapter examines how the roles of the different actors in Sahelian society could change. In the first instance, the distinction should be drawn between two main groups of actors: the public sector and the non-governmental sector. For the purposes of this examination, actors in the non-governmental sector can be defined as all those individuals and organizations that operate outside the domain of the government and parastatal sectors.

A new balance between the government and the non-governmental sector

After independence, the new governments of the Sahel did not have a genuine choice to make, because at that time only the public sector was in a position to act as the driving force in building a modern society in the Sahel.

After two or three centuries of anarchy, marked by the progressive deterioration of the social fabric and by power struggles in which rural population groups suffered consistently, and after three-quarters of a century of colonial rule, the non-governmental sector was in no position to play that role. During the preceding period, rural communities had above all been involved in protecting themselves from the demands of the colonial rulers by adopting the "covert non-cooperation" strategy, and those communities were not ready to take firm initiatives. Traders had played an important role in pre-colonial days, but now found themselves assuming a marginal role in society. The only sector of the population that could be described as dynamic and in full emergence -- although still limited -- included the government employees and politicians of the new States that replaced colonial rule.

Attempts have been made to pinpoint the reasons for which governments for some time managed -- with varying degrees of success -- to provide the driving force behind the development of Sahelian societies, but the governments' efforts to create self-sustained development in the Sahel ultimately failed.

Times have now changed. As we have already stressed, numerous members of rural communities seem to be passively watching the end of their world approach, and deploring trends that they can do nothing to alter. Nevertheless, individual and collective initiative does exist in rural areas as well as in the cities, and that initiative has had very positive results. And yet the very existence of initiative was inconceivable at the beginning of the 1960s. The non-governmental sector has now generated a certain intrinsic dynamism that is more intense than a quarter-century ago and, in view of the probable changes in the system of values, this dynamism is likely to become even more intense in the future.

What can be said of the relationships between the Sahelian State and this re-dynamized non-governmental sector? As a descendant of the colonial rulers and not an extension of the non-governmental sector, the State was considered at birth to be partly divorced from the non-governmental sector, and was felt to have limited powers over it. Efforts to build the nation and develop the economies have accentuated the separation of State and non-governmental sector rather than forge new links, and, in the words of G. Hyden, the State is now "suspended in mid-air, above society", incapable of acting on the systems of exchange that operate within that society, and often even unaware of the ways in which those systems actually operate.

The past has provided considerable evidence of the fact that the Sahelian State has an influence over rural and urban societies, but the past has also shown that the State has failed to dynamize the development of these societies.

In this respect, it is interesting to point out that during "the thirty glorious years" (les trente glorieuses (1945-1975) so called by Fourastié because of the unprecedented economic growth that took place during that period) of post-war boom, Western governments succeeded in catalyzing the development of the societies over which they had a hold and which had their own intrinsic dynamism. (Indeed, Western governments perhaps formed certain illusions as to the relative importance of the State and the dynamism of the society). For the last twenty or thirty years, the countries of South-East Asia have undergone phenomenal development: the State has been directly involved in this development but has also played an indirect role by encouraging and channeling the huge volume of spontaneous initiatives emanating from the non-governmental sector. (The two governments that take the most active role in economic life (Malaysia and Indonesia) do so to compete with nationals of Chinese origin, whose level of entrepreneurship is deemed excessive). Yet Sahelian governments, despite their determination to modernize their countries' economies, have not been able to catalyze the same development, probably because they have had much less of a hold over their societies, and because those societies are far from intrinsically dynamic.

Whatever scenario the future holds in store, <u>it seems inevitable that the new-found dynamism of the non-governmental sector and the widening gulf that exists between the State and the non-governmental sector will bring changes in the respective roles of the State and the non-governmental sector.</u> These changes can occur, however, to varying degrees. If only slight changes take place, we will remain within the trend scenario. If the changes are more substantial, we will manage to break with the trend scenario. The possibilities of change in the distribution of roles will be examined below.

There is a saying that has become fashionable in the Sahel over the last few years: "Less government equals better government" ("Moins d'Etat, mieux d'Etat"). In view of the outlooks mentioned above, what can this saying mean?

Local communities in rural areas

In times gone by, the village was governed by the village chief, the land agent, the council of elders of leading families, and each individual or body of individuals had a specific role to play in the management of community affairs. Times have changed too quickly for these institutions to have developed into bodies equivalent to the authorities that have played and still play a crucial role in Western life at the local level. In the West, local government -- and not central government -- has developed primary education, recruiting primary school teachers and providing the resources they require to exercise their profession.

Colonial rulers, followed by the governors-general of the newly-independent countries, siphoned off part of the local power in the Sahel. Old institutions perish. Today, however, villages are organizing themselves spontaneously, forming inter-village bodies for various purposes, and finding with surprising speed the funds needed to sink a well, install a pump, set up a cereals bank, and so on. New local authorities are emerging, and the importance of these authorities and the limits of their power have been discussed above (chapter 15).

Local authorities could play a greater role in at least three areas:

Social services

As we have seen, the trend scenario involves a risk that the State will become incapable of maintaining social services at the levels that have been reached in recent years. Even in a more favorable scenario, one should not harbor too many illusions as to the ability of the State in this respect, since the State will have many other priorities. To hand back responsibility to rural communities, to avoid choosing social services that are a priority only for those making the choice, and to ensure that the services continue to operate correctly, responsibility should be placed on the shoulders of the local authorities.

Mention is sometimes made of the risk of incompetent management of the social services, and that risk is probably very real. But would it not be even more serious to leave the choice of new investments and the responsibility for managing those investments to central government employees who may be competent but tend to be poorly informed on the realities of the local situation?

Environmental protection

Villages used to apply strict rules in an effort to protect the environment, but with the destructuring of traditional society these rules have more or less disappeared. Another set of rules should now be developed, taking into account demographic and economic conditions, which have now changed radically. Central government and donors have tended to be ineffective in conceiving and implementing environmental protection and rehabilitation operations, and inordinate amounts of money have been wasted on this type of project. Local authorities have recently proved that they can effectively plan and maintain their living space if they receive suitable assistance from local or foreign NGOs.

Local authorities could be responsible for management of the natural heritage (land, forestry and water resources), even if central government and donors were obliged to provide technical assistance where necessary.

Drought control and water resource management

A number of lessons can be learned from the acute droughts of the 1970s and 1980s: in general, population groups managed to subsist on emergency aid, but that aid was not used in such a way as to allow village communities to resume production after the period of drought, nor did it provide villages with the expertise they needed to manage water resources better and thus deal with future droughts in a more expedient manner. India has had considerable experience with this type of situation and has implemented decentralized policies to deal with them: each community in the areas frequently exposed to drought has a set plan of action to fight drought, aimed to re-establish the means of production at the end of the dry period and to make investments to reduce the village's vulnerability to poor rainfall. When droughts do occur, each local authority launches its plan, and emergency aid is used to pay the wages of the rural inhabitants that participate in that plan, thereby providing the income they need to ensure the survival of their families.

It should be possible to transpose strategies of this type to the Sahelian situation, and it should be feasible for local authorities to implement similar plans of action to fight drought and improve management of water resources, even if technical assistance would be required.

The possibility of <u>restructuring farming systems</u> would clearly depend on the non-governmental sector in rural areas, and if farming systems have not yet changed, it is because the non-governmental sector has so far found many more attractive alternatives to intensification of agriculture (e.g, flight to the cities, wood gathering). Here again, the natural reaction would be to create economic conditions that would make intensification of agriculture attractive. And that brings us back to the role of the State.

Let us assume for the time being that favorable conditions exist. A number of functions that the State has attempted to perform -- with little success -- could be fulfilled by non-governmental initiative (supply of inputs, purchase and maintenance of communal equipment, sales and primary processing of products, etc).

In this way, tasks could be redistributed so that the non-governmental sector would take on new responsibilities and would play a much more major role. The State would assume a lesser role in those areas, but would continue to play a vital part in shaping the context within which the non-governmental sector could consummate its dynamism.

Communities in urban areas

The associative movement that is gaining momentum in rural areas also exists in the cities: tontines, which mobilize savings for a more or less specific purpose, or neighborhood associations, for example. The movement is, however, considerably less pronounced in the cities than it is in rural areas.

Where urban communities demonstrate their initiative most is in creating formal (or more often informal) enterprises that provide a framework for those who have recently arrived in the cities or even for established city-dwellers to demonstrate unexpectedly high levels of initiative and ingenuity. The drought and the "crisis" of the last few years have given this sector new impetus despite the limited markets open to it.

The dynamism of urban communities also manifests itself in rural areas. Spontaneous moves to return to the land are probably fairly rare, but they do exist. There is already a well-established tradition of city-dwellers creating new plantations or irrigated perimeters for market gardening, which they work at the same time as they continue their activities in the public or non-governmental sector in the city. What has changed is that these practices are now increasing -- no doubt as a result of the difficult economic context -- and, although little is yet known about their global significance, diversification into small-scale livestock activities, fattening and even larger-scale agriculture is now taking place.

This interference of urban society with rural society is an important development for rural population groups, and in certain cases friction is likely to occur. However, recent experience of agricultural development in the West, where city-dwellers have played an important role in the spread of new techniques to rural areas, has shown that interference can considerably encourage changes in rural production systems.

Finally, mention should be made of another recent phenomenon, the consequences of which are difficult to gauge: the large-scale arrival of young graduates who are unable to find work in the modern public or non-governmental sector. New companies have until now largely been set up by individuals with a moderate level of education, but with this recent inflow of unemployed graduates, the situation is very likely to change.

In the post-independence period, governments felt responsible for the industrialization of their countries, but achieved only a moderate level of success, and their efforts to promote private enterprise were not always particularly convincing. In the same way as in rural areas, a new breakdown of responsibilities may now be taking shape in the cities, where the State would ultimately play a more minor role but would nevertheless retain the vital function of defining the rules of play.

The role of the State

It is fashionable today to denigrate the role that the State has assumed in the countries of the Sahel, and indeed it is true that the results achieved are fairly unimpressive. We have said that the State is "suspended in mid-air" and has little hold on society at large. It has become commonplace to criticize the policies that have been adopted, to demonstrate that those policies are ill-suited to the objectives they are intended to achieve, and to point to poor allocation of the national economy's scarce resources and to the inefficiency the State has demonstrated in all its industrial, agricultural or commercial undertakings.

It can be added that civil servants working for government agencies or for State companies are also part of traditional structures and networks that obey logic that has nothing to do with the public good in the sense that Western societies perceive that notion. That logic can still have more importance than a concept as abstract as the public good. Thus, it can be said that the founding principles of the colonial governments, which were then passed down to the new independent governments, have gradually been eroded. Many administrative procedures have progressively lost their meaning or have begun to serve a purpose for which they were not initially intended.

The Sahelian State may be suspended in mid-air, but it is also, in the words of R. Sandbrook, staunchly "patrimonialist": power and resources are not only used for the public good, but also for the benefit of a minority.

In view of the above, there is little doubt that <u>the problems of government in the Sahel are not all caused by the lack of competence of government employees</u> (on the contrary, government employees are probably becoming increasingly technically competent), <u>but are caused by much more fundamental factors</u> stemming from the origins of governments' power and from the basic differences between governments and the societies they are intended to govern. There are thus grounds to believe that experts that recommend institutional reform, increased management capacity, etc, have not fully appreciated the current predicament of the State in the countries of the Sahel.

The State nonetheless exists. States have a role to play in the Sahel, as they do in every other society. Indeed, in view of the non-governmental sector's persistent weak points -- which clearly cannot be expected to disappear overnight -- the role of the State could be more important in the Sahel than it is elsewhere. Listed below are five functions that it would appear essential for the State -- rather than the non-governmental sector -- to perform. The list should not be considered exhaustive:

-- <u>Ensuring the security of individuals and property.</u>

   Public security is clearly a prerequisite for any expression of the dynamism of the non-governmental sector.

-- <u>Creating a framework within which the dynamism of the non-governmental sector can express itself.</u>

   This framework covers all the rules of play, i.e, the legislative, economic, financial and fiscal context within which individuals, companies and local communities must act.

-- **Creating and maintaining the infrastructures needed for the expression of this dynamism.**

These infrastructures cover transportation and telecommunications infrastructures as well as the social services, which cannot be set up or operated by any other authority than central government.

-- **Assuming responsibility for scientific and technical research.**

We have already seen that unless Sahelian governments assume responsibility for specific research into the problems encountered in the Sahel, there is a strong possibility that the international research community (public-sector and non-governmental sector) will accept only limited involvement.

-- **Taking economic initiative that the non-governmental sector, in its current state of development, cannot take.**

De-linking the State from economic life is a desirable objective. However, the non-governmental sector cannot -- for want of financial resources and technical skills -- do everything in the Sahelian economy, and various opportunities cannot be capitalized upon unless the State acts as a driving force, either alone or jointly with private concerns in the same country or from abroad.

Complete de-linking of the State, as is recommended by liberal economists, is not compatible with the current situation of Sahelian societies. In South-East Asia, where the dynamism of the non-governmental sector has for some time been considerably greater than it is today in the Sahel, the State has assumed a major entrepreneurial role over the last few decades. While it would be unfair to claim that the entire Asian adventure has been plain sailing, it is undeniable that the non-governmental sector as a whole has benefited from the entrepreneurial role assumed by the State. In the Sahel as elsewhere, privatization has its limits.

The State also has a role to play in research, documentation and dissemination of economic information (e.g. information on export opportunities), although nowhere in the Sahel has a government yet demonstrated its commitment to assume that role.

*

* *

Despite the size of the public sector, these five essential roles are only being fulfilled very partially by current Sahelian governments, and this lack of performance should temper calls for "less government".

In view of the size of the public sector, therefore, which it is now difficult for national economies to support, in view of the fundamental problems faced by contemporary Sahelian governments and in view of the growing dynamism of the non-governmental sector, what may have begun as moves towards "less government" could ultimately lead to genuinely "better government".

Chapter 25

PREREQUISITES FOR ROLE CHANGES

Redistributing roles between the State and the non-governmental sector in the way outlined above would most probably allow the non-governmental sector to express its dynamism more effectively and thus to develop, and, at the same time, would allow the dynamism of government employees to concentrate less on empty tasks and thus participate more positively in social change. Social groups could thus interact in new ways, the discontinuity of Sahelian societies would be attenuated and suitable conditions for genuine development would be created.

It is of course not sufficient to state that roles should be redistributed and new forms of interaction between social groups should be introduced. Changes have to actually take place, and that is quite another problem. As we have said, even with the trend scenario, such changes will not take place spontaneously.

What conditions must exist to encourage people to move towards introducing the changes that are desirable? In attempting to answer this question, we will refer to certain measures that "must be taken". In expressing ourselves in this way, we do not intend to lay down moral obligations, or to suggest that a given social category should follow set patterns of behavior. Such moralistic stances, in any case, would have no chance of bringing the changes that are recommended. Our sole intention is to point to the fact that changes will not be possible unless certain prerequisites are fulfilled.

Awareness of the implications

The attitude of most Sahelians is characterized by what has been termed "quasi-ontological optimism" (P. Pradervand: "un optimisme presqu'ontologique"). That attitude is undoubtedly a major strong point in the region's capacity to build a better future, but it can also be a handicap in that it can lead people to ignore the real problems by preferring not to see them. (The colonial rulers recognized this aspect of African optimism in general and Sahelian optimism in particular, referring to it as "obliviousness").

By contrast, certain observers are now deeply pessimistic about the region's future, and it is that pessimism that is at the root of their desire to unilaterally pull out of the Sahel, if they are involved there, or to withdraw their support if they are involved in outside assistance.

One essential prerequisite for change and evolution towards a different scenario is for all those who are implicated in the future of the region (whether or not they are government employees, members of the ruling elite or more modest actors on the economic stage) to be informed about the real situation in the Sahel and about its outlooks. They must all come to recognize what the future holds in store (trend scenario), and to accept that it is possible to change that future.

The situation and outlooks of the Sahel are recognized with varying degrees of clarity. Certain parties accept the situation with resignation and see present trends as inevitable, while others are aware that it is possible to divert the course of events. Clearly, all those who have taken initiatives in rural areas and in the cities are in this second category.

With the drought of the 1970s and 1980s and the hardship that ensued, combined with moves to open the Sahel to the outside world, resignation has decreased somewhat. But this is far from the general rule in the Sahel today, even among the ruling elite, which is always ready to blame external factors for the failures that have occurred.

Everybody must be aware of the difficulties faced by Sahelian societies. These difficulties are not only due to drought and the world economic order, but also to the conception of development itself and to the way social groups have interacted so far.

The privileged minority must realize that its standard of living will ultimately be affected. In the trend scenario, the living standards of the privileged minority will fall sooner or later: the longer the scenario can be propped up by limited changes, the longer it will take for these living standards to be affected. But the privileged few will inevitably be affected during crisis situations, and the consequences of such situations might be drastic and lasting. On the other hand, in scenarios that are preferable to the trend scenario, even if a fall in living standards seems just as inevitable, the effect will be considerably less drastic and will be relatively short-lived -- no longer than is necessary for sustained economic growth to bring about an increase in national income without increasing dependence on the outside world.

Clearly, if the Sahelian elites are unconvinced that their situation needs to deteriorate before it can improve, and if they are awaiting some miracle solution -- such as the return of the rains, the discovery of oil, a fivefold increase in world groundnut prices or in international aid, or even further progress in computer science or biotechnologies -- rather than internal changes within their societies, there is a strong possibility that the trend scenario, or some close equivalent, will continue to follow its course for many years to come.

And if the Sahelian elites are not convinced themselves, then how can they be expected to disseminate information about the region's outlooks to members of the community that do not have the same access to information? And if the elites do not disseminate the information, who will?

Be that as it may, it is clearly not sufficient for the actors to be informed. They must also modify their behavior.

Democratization and national consensus

A second prerequisite for change and gradual evolution towards a different scenario is the demise of a seemingly die-hard myth whereby social interaction in the Sahel can take place without conflict. In the Sahel as elsewhere, social interaction is by its very nature a conflictual phenomenon. Similarly, the restructuring of Sahelian societies and the redistribution of roles can only come as the result of settled conflicts.

In Sahelian societies, as in all other societies, there can and must be a wide consensus on the major national objectives: building national unity, developing a national identity (with varying degrees of Panafricanism), economic development, etc. But it is unrealistic to expect full consensus, where the entire nation is unanimously in favor of all objectives, and it would be a serious mistake to believe that traditional community values that are specific to Africa in general and to the Sahel in particular can form the basis of socio-economic development that is totally free of domestic conflict. Calls for unanimity and the emphasis laid on the community values of traditional society in fact veil the basically restrictive nature of that society and the gerontocracy of the families with the most influence therein.

The unanimity of the single party (Prof. Adamolekun of Nigeria: "the myth of the grand consensus") or the need for a monolithic national ideology (by whatever name), which almost all political leaders have defended officially or unofficially since 1960 in the name of efficiency (as if politics was a game in which there were no winners and no losers, and all the political rivalry was a necessary evil in the process of development), hide the fact that society is dominated by a small minority of power politicians and their immediate entourages.

<u>This obsession with unanimity</u> refuses to admit that each group of actors in society has its own interests, that it is quite legitimate for each group to organize itself in order to defend those interests, and that social interaction will necessarily involve compromises and will ultimately allow society to become less unacceptable. The aim of unanimity has played a part in stultifying the social structure and <u>is partly responsible for the destructuring of Sahelian societies.</u>

Conflicts can be constructive if institutional mechanisms exist to guarantee that the rules by which they are settled are respected by everybody involved. In this way, what could be termed conflictual dynamism -- a social <u>modus operandi</u> whereby conflicts can find expression and through which rational solutions can be found to those conflicts -- can be considered a prerequisite for any change in roles.

Two conclusions can be drawn from this examination of the Sahelian situation:

-- <u>Unless a minimum consensus is achieved at the national level,</u> social interaction is impossible, and conflicts will lead to the breakdown of society. This does not seem to be the case throughout the Sahel of the 1980s, and there is evidence that the "specter of secession" has not entirely died out.

This minimum national consensus is thus <u>an absolute prerequisite</u> for change. While it is true that certain human societies are managing to develop in their own right and are unaffected by the forces that draw communities towards the hub of the social wheel, it is highly improbable that Sahelian communities are capable of laying the foundations of lasting development and of resolving the difficult problems they are facing without there being a minimum level of consensus at the national level.

-- Changes cannot take place smoothly and equitably unless <u>democracy is promoted</u> in the Sahel. We should not necessarily limit ourselves to the way democracy is expressed in the West, and it is even highly improbable -- in view of the differences in culture and social structures that exist within the Sahel -- that democratization can take place in the same way throughout the region.

The problem faced by Sahelian societies is to find how to establish a new balance between the different social groups, not only between the privileged minority and the emerging authorities, but also between emerging authorities in the cities and emerging authorities in rural areas.

Common interests undoubtedly exist, but different groups are also bound to have conflicting interests. The rules of traditional Sahelian societies left some room for the expression of the interests of different groups, and empowered chiefs to resolve conflicts, yet limited their power at the same time and provided safeguards against arbitrary decision-making. As we have said, these rules are now null and void. Sahelian societies must now progressively devise new rules that promote cohesion between the different social categories and that encourage unity within each social group. New rules are needed to settle conflicts in such a way as everybody concerned will accept the solutions proposed. The rules of Western democracies, which were developed under totally different circumstances (e.g. as a result of the struggle of the communes against the monarchy or the struggle of the middle classes against the aristocracy) can help the Sahel in certain instances. But the rules of Western democracies must not be considered a panacea that can be applied unadulterated to Sahelian societies.

Chapter 26

ROLE CHANGES AND POLICY CHANGES

Changes in the roles of Sahelian actors are linked to changes in economic policy options. Neither can take place independently and interaction exists in both directions: roles influence policies and vice-versa.

The aim of this examination of possible futures for the Sahel is not to propose new policies: Sahelians are not short of advisors, and certain observers even claim that they have too many... The present study will merely attempt to examine a few major policy options, which involve the very structures of economic life and which are necessarily linked to a new distribution of the roles among Sahelian actors, and will examine the potential consequences of those policies on moves to favor other scenarios.

These policy options can be divided into two categories: options concerning the internal organization of socio-economic interaction (referred to as the rural and urban frameworks of economic activity), and options concerning relationships between the Sahelian economy and the world economy.

The rural framework

One striking fact is the almost total absence of an institutional framework within which the new-found dynamism of the rural world can express itself. Traditional Sahelian society was strictly organized both in terms of distribution of power within the village community and in terms of distribution of natural resources (land, water, wood). This organization still exists, but the degree to which it is operational and the efficiency with which it operates varies considerably from area to area. However, the organization is no longer suited to present-day conditions:

-- Natural resources are deteriorating as a result of demographic pressure;

-- The production system requires investments and thus a suitable framework for farmers to finance those investments;

-- New social needs (water, energy, health care, education, communications), which are emerging particularly rapidly as a result of changes in values.

No new formal structure has yet taken over from the defunct traditional structures.

Certain rural communities are palliating the lack of framework by setting up associations to take responsibility for the fight against environmental deterioration. Others are setting up cooperatives to act as guarantors for the purchase of farm machinery. Elsewhere, informal arrangements are made to locate funds and help purchase communal pumps, mobilize energy resources or build schools.

If the role of the non-governmental sector in rural areas is to grow in practical terms, calls to "hand back responsibility to the rural communities", which are very popular in the Sahel at the present time, but which have no tangible basis, are perhaps insufficient. The creation of rural communities (those set up in Senegal only very partially meet new requirements), with a clear legal status and with responsibility over land tenure and natural-resource management (water, forestry, soil), that are capable of managing a budget and organizing communal services, that have borrowing power, the ability to provide guarantees, receive donations, etc. would not only provide a means of expression for the dynamism that already exists, but could also encourage new initiatives and allow that dynamism to grow in the future.

Communities of this kind, with an executive body and a supervisory assembly, could at the same time act as the bodies through which democracy could be promoted throughout the region. While it is clear that a legal status is not enough to bring about real facts, and that no formal body will be in a position to promote dynamism where no dynamism already exists, the scheme would at least give those communities that are ready to take on responsibility more chance of assuming that responsibility.

Rural communities of this type clearly cannot provide responses to all needs and it would also be useful -- still in an aim to strengthen the role of the non-governmental sector in rural areas -- to have legal frameworks that allow rural population to form associations for specific objectives not involving the entire village community. In particular, the importance of land tenure legislation should not be underestimated, and a number of key problems in village land (and grazing land) management must be solved: collective or private land tenure, land subject to seizure (as in Britain) or not subject to seizure (as has long been the case in France, where the development of agricultural credit has suffered as a result).

Communities cannot exist and develop without a minimum of organization of human relationships and organization of the ways members of the community act upon their environment. The non-governmental sector needs a framework that is not outdated, but that is suited to the type of problems that private enterprise must face.

The urban framework

The framework within which community dynamism is expressed raises a totally different issue in the cities. Virtually no traditional framework exists. The scant framework that has survived was conceived in the Western mold, was implemented in the colonial era, and has developed along the same lines since independence.

The legal framework of economic activity is that of the limited liability company, which was imported from the West and imposes a complete set of formal rules: articles of association, management and control bodies, accounting statues, etc.

The financial framework is that of the banking system created in the West, with its system of credit and loan facilities based on borrowers' collateral and backed by companies with complete knowledge of the assessment roll and property registration.

The fiscal framework was introduced under colonial rule and has not basically changed since that period. It is largely based on taxation of foreign trade (as was already practiced by the emperors of Ghana, Mali and Songhai) and on Western-style direct taxes (personal income tax and corporate tax), which are not always effectively collected.

The social framework is that of the countries of the West: labor laws and civil security legislation are directly copied from Western models.

All the above is fundamentally alien to Sahelian culture, which has its own rules to govern human relations, where personal guarantees replace collateral, etc.

It is perhaps not surprising, therefore, that a large proportion -- even the majority -- of city life takes place outside this alien framework, in what is known as the informal sector. When one considers that this imported framework also helps push up production costs in the formal sector, and that involvement in the formal sector automatically involves compliance with fiscal and labor laws, while the informal sector is largely exempt from these restrictions, one can better understand that the dynamism of communities in the cities is expressed in the informal sector rather than in the formal sector.

The development of the informal sector is not in itself a bad thing. But as has been stressed above (chapter 19), this development compounds low levels of productivity and in no way helps overcome the obstacles to increased foreign trade.

Governments have so far largely overlooked the informal sector, and have not attempted either to organize it or to supervise it. Praiseworthy as it may appear (albeit involuntary), this policy seems to have little chance of lasting, for the informal sector is now increasingly considered to be parasitic, or even to be in unfair competition with the formal sector. If the dynamism of city-dwellers is to find expression and become stronger, it must be given the possibility of developing within the informal sector. Informal activities must be rehabilitated -- in the sense that their good name must be re-established -- and they must be given <u>a framework that brings</u> a minimum of <u>"formalization"</u>, so that the future of such activities can be assured and that they can ultimately continue to develop overtly.

Productivity will not increase significantly unless the amount of capital invested in companies increases first. (Capital investment in informal companies is currently very low). Technical and management training are also essential prerequisites for increased productivity, but none of these conditions can be fulfilled in the current atmosphere of insecurity and with the current lack of framework.

In the same way as land tenure laws are fundamental to the promotion of capital investment and higher productivity in the agricultural sector, the legal framework within which companies pursue their economic activity in the cities is of considerable importance in the accumulation of capital and the growth of productivity.

Reviewing the frameworks of economic activity in the cities might also provide an opportunity to begin to "deformalize" the formal sector, which many observers consider stultified by too many regulations and too much bureaucracy.

Labor laws, for example, may be taken for granted as guarantors of social justice, but that justice is applicable only to a small proportion of the population -- the informal sector is totally unaffected by notions of guaranteed minimum wage, equal opportunities, legal working hours, etc, -- and the state of Sahelian economies is such that no legislature is in a position to provide such guarantees. Few of the newly industrialized countries of South-East Asia have any legislation of this kind, and the social justice enjoyed today in the countries of the Sahel would disappear in a cloud of smoke if outside assistance was reduced drastically. Should the Sahel merely wait for this reduction to take place, or should steps be taken now to review labor laws and thus prepare for the future, so that it will ultimately be easier for the countries of the Sahel to exist without outside assistance?

Instead of today's two-part structure where there is a clear distinction between formal and informal sectors, a more flexible structure, where the differences between the two sectors would become progressively less pronounced, would make it possible for the dynamism of the urban non-governmental sector to express itself more effectively.

It should be stressed that extreme caution must be exercised when attempting to put the suggestions made here into practice. Attempts to lessen the differences between the formal and informal sectors, or to "formalize" the informal sector by heavy-handedly channeling informal initiative into stricter frameworks, would clearly be doomed to failure, since the companies involved would simply disappear as soon as possible, only to reappear, similarly informally, elsewhere.

Food policies

In view of the role that food policies currently play in the Sahel, their importance in shaping interaction among the three main groups of Sahelian actors (the State, rural communities and city-dwellers), and in view of the crucial part they play in the relationships Sahelian governments enjoy with donors, it would be difficult to examine the future options of the region without taking into account the main food-policy options that are open.

Initially, Sahelian governments attempted to control cereals markets, to eliminate the non-governmental sector's share of the cereals trade or to reduce that share to the minimum, and to systematically fix prices in favor of urban consumers. When these policies failed, and in response to pressure from donors, governments changed directions, partly liberalizing the markets and fixing official prices that were more favorable to producers.

These new food policies were conceived during periods of drought and deficit and have not withstood the test of two successive years of good harvests. Farmers increased their cereals production without introducing more intensive farming systems, and, helped by the favorable climatic conditions, their harvests were abundant. Furthermore, world-market cereals prices reached an all-time low. Despite the taxation imposed by certain Sahelian governments, imported cereals (which urban consumers have come to prefer) have arrived in increasing quantities. At the same time, growing amounts of food aid were requested from the West and granted to the countries of the Sahel. With a cereals glut on Sahelian markets, public-sector purchasing bodies and official stock organizations could not afford to buy the surpluses and prices plummeted.

Today we are faced with a paradox: countries are continuing to import food and to request food aid, while their farmers cannot sell local cereals at an acceptable price. Falling prices can but compound the introversion of the rural world in line with the trend scenario. Falling prices herald shortages in the future, when climatic conditions worsen.

<u>Two decades of official prices have demonstrated that this type of policy is ill-suited to current conditions in the Sahel, at whatever level those prices are fixed.</u> Fluctuations in crop levels are too great and traditional cereals still play too important a role in the Sahelian diet for a price policy relying on fixed, guaranteed prices to be practicable by governments that have no financial resources. In any case, such a policy can only lead to introversion of the rural world, because either the official price is too low and thus discourages the producer to produce, or, if it is higher, because the State cannot guarantee it, and that in turn discourages producers.

What type of food policy could be adopted in a scenario where the different social groups would interact in a more cohesive fashion?

Several possibilities are open:

-- <u>Reduction of fluctuations in levels of production,</u> which are so great that the market is very difficult to manage. These fluctuations could be evened out by developing cereals production in the areas with the best rainfall records and by developing varieties that are less sensitive to climatic variations. Such action can only be taken very gradually.

-- <u>Reduction of the importance of cereals and diversification of diet.</u> Although cereals for a long time played the role in European countries that they still play today in the Sahel, Europe has not been much more successful in managing its markets, and the least privileged sectors of European communities have experienced a succession of drastic shortages, and producers, who are almost always in debt, have suffered from disastrous gluts, where they have been obliged to sell grain to pay their debts. What is different in the Sahel is that farmers no longer benefit -- as their European counterparts did for centuries -- from high prices in bad years, partly because the market is worldwide and partly because of food aid. And yet they still suffer from falling prices when climatic conditions are better.

Incidentally, guaranteed cereals prices for producers and for consumers contribute (provided that the guarantees are effective) to the rigidity of the system, and thus discourage rather than encourage diversification of the diet. Diversification of production and of the products offered to urban consumers by processing more would seem a vital first step in applying a policy to re-articulate the economies of the region.

-- <u>Control over imports of food products,</u> either by quota arrangements or by taxation, or by adjustment of exchange rates (combined with control over imports of food aid). In view of the fact that it is difficult to monitor trade within Africa, such a policy could probably only be effectively implemented at the regional level.

Only controls of this kind would allow prices of local food products delivered to producers to vary, yet remain high enough to constitute an incentive, at the same time as allowing consumer prices for local products to remain competitive with those of imported products. Only this kind of control would make it possible for part of the urban markets to be progressively won back by rural communities (and by urban entrepreneurs encouraged to become more involved in food production), which is a prerequisite for restructuring.

-- <u>Give free rein to market forces without protectionist measures.</u> Governments manifestly do not have the wherewithal to intervene effectively on food-product markets, nor will they have in the future. Even if intervention by cereals boards, for example, can regulate markets, the scope of such action will be very limited and probably the only solution is to let supply and demand determine prices beneath a solid protectionist umbrella that isolates the Sahel from the disorders of world markets.

Without going into further detail on food policies, we can conclude very briefly by saying that the longer farmers can basically only offer traditional cereals to city-dwellers, who are increasingly keen on buying more "modern" food products (and the longer these modern food products are available at attractive prices), the more difficult it will be to restructure the economies of the Sahel. In these conditions, it is difficult to see how dependence can decline, and how the region can find a lasting alternative to the trend scenario.

The relationships between Sahelian markets and international markets

This problem of controlling the inflow of food products, which is crucial to the restructuring of Sahelian societies, leads us to another issue, which we have encountered in several other fields: the interface between Sahelian economies and the world economy.

Today, imported food products are available in the heart of the Sahel at lower prices than local products. Sahelian industries are largely incapable of exporting and must be protected against competition from the outside by customs duties, which are sometimes particularly high. Clearly, there is a problem at the interface between Sahelian markets and the world market system.

International competitiveness depends on:

-- Levels of wages and incomes: generally very low in rural areas, but less low on average (without being particularly high) in industry; it is scarcely possible to lower them in the short term, at least in nominal terms;

-- Productivity of labor: still very low throughout the economy and which must increase, but can only increase very gradually;

-- The exchange rate: in view of the levels of wages and productivity, the exchange rate is the only parameter that can be changed quickly in order to increase the competitiveness of Sahelian products on international markets and reduce the competitiveness of foreign products on Sahelian markets.

The governments that have introduced high customs duties on certain industrial products that are considered as "luxury items" now recognize that Sahelian currencies are overpriced. In fact, a small minority of operators make arrangements not to pay these duties, thereby generating further opportunities to bribe public employees.

The dependence of Sahelian countries, and thus also their food dependence, now appears to be due to exchange rates, and it is conceivable that the only possible alternatives to the trend scenario will involve adjustment of those rates.

But should the exchange rates themselves be adjusted? Should currencies be devalued indirectly by imposing taxes on imports and, where possible, by subsidizing exports? Debate on these issues very quickly becomes heated, especially as the vast majority of Sahelian countries are in the franc zone, and none of those countries can unilaterally decide to change the parity of its currency without leaving the zone.

Exchange-rate adjustment

We have frequently stressed the advantages of belonging to the franc area (convertibility and exchange-rate stability, for example). In chapter 14 above, mention was made of the advantages for Sahelian countries in terms of trade with other countries in the region, whose currency is inconvertible and poorly managed. These advantages are evident and should not be underestimated.

Nevertheless, the question of monetary parity is a different problem. No law has permanently fixed parity between the CFA franc and the French franc. Indeed, parity was 1 CFA franc: 1.7 FF until 1947. Since then, the economies of France and the Sahel have not developed along the same lines. If changing parity is a prerequisite for finding a way out of the trend scenario, the issue must be examined carefully and rationally.

It is important to study the question of parity carefully, since the issue is complicated by the fact that currencies are not overpriced to the same degree throughout the WAMU, and differential adjustment would pose extraordinarily difficult problems. Further, devaluation does not always produce the desired effect (particularly in developing countries, where countless failures have occurred). Unbridled inflation can very quickly counter the positive effects of monetary adjustment on economic development.

Careful examination is also needed because most of the Third World countries that have experienced sustained development over recent years (e.g, in South-East Asia) also have underpriced currencies. And the role of the CFA franc in the West African underground economy and the resulting advantages for Sahelian countries could well not last forever (see chapter 14).

Export subsidies and protection of the domestic market

The wave of economic liberalism that is currently spreading through the world is hardly favorable to the alternative solution involving exchange-rate adjustment. Senegal's new industrial policy as proposed (not to say imposed) by the international organizations involves significant reductions -- if not complete removal -- of protection for the country's industry.

Over the last few decades, all the newly industrialized countries have protected their domestic markets and chosen specific fields in which to develop their export trade, and in many instances have provided financial incentives to promote that development. By contrast, experiences of liberalization (even when currencies are devalued) have not always been particularly successful. In view of the handicaps from which the Sahelian countries are currently suffering (cost effectiveness of labor, unsuitable exchange rates, etc), excessive liberalization of foreign trade would be damaging to the agricultural sector and would most probably lead to a sharp recession in the industrial sector, which is already particularly poorly developed, without necessarily creating suitable conditions for increased competitiveness in the future.

If exchange-rate adjustment must be rejected because of the insurmountable obstacles that would be encountered, or because of the major disadvantages that a change in parity would involve, the alternative solution of protecting the domestic agricultural and industrial markets and providing export incentives in specific fields (incentives financed by import taxes) should be examined, and should form one of the cornerstones of new food policies and new industrial policies.

Chapter 27

FOREIGN AID

Official development assistance

Official development assistance can be examined from two standpoints:

-- By its very existence, official development assistance has been instrumental in allowing the Sahel to choose the wrong path -- that of increased dependence. It is undoubtedly for that reason that the Conference of African Churches launched an appeal in 1973 for a "moratorium on aid", for fear that an accumulation of inadequately prepared projects would ultimately undermine the will of the African people to rely first and foremost on themselves. The appeal was largely ignored. In the same train of thought, certain African intellectuals are questioning the true scope of aid and are wondering whether aid actually acts as an obstacle to development (e.g.i. the recent declarations of Mahdi Elmandjra, President of the international association Futuribles).

Considered from this standpoint, the West has given too much aid to the Sahel.

-- On the other hand, in view of the increasing indebtedness of Sahelian countries, it is equally valid to consider that the aid provided by the international community is inadequate and that Western countries should in fact supply more aid to the region in the form of increased debt allowances, which are difficult to refund. However, this increased aid alone will not lead to the development of countries in crisis, and further increases will doubtless prove necessary to ensure real development.

Considered from this standpoint, the West has not given enough aid to the Sahel.

This dichotomy <u>highlights the interaction between aid and Sahelian societies,</u> i.e, aid allows those societies to choose a certain course of action, and, in return, the development of Sahelian societies along the lines they have chosen has an effect on the provision of aid.

How can this interaction be influential in the future?

As we have seen, increased aid is a vital component of the trend scenario. The basic role of such an increase is to allow the Sahel to continue to live beyond its means (as defined by its economy). Further, one hypothesis suggests that a sharp decrease in the level of that aid would lead to an acute crisis. It is possible to construct other hypotheses on trends in official development assistance and to question which of those hypotheses would lead the Sahel towards more favorable scenarios. Should aid be increased beyond the limits that would exist in the trend scenario? Should the type of aid be changed? This general line of inquiry in fact comprises two separate questions: is aid a crucial factor in moving towards a more favorable scenario, and, if so, how can aid fulfill that crucial role?

Is aid a crucial factor?

More than twenty-five years' experience in the Sahel has demonstrated that as long as the socio-economic conditions for development are absent, <u>aid, at least in its current form, is powerless to modify deeply rooted social trends</u> and to bring about development. <u>On the contrary, Sahelian societies have themselves used and re-oriented outside assistance to bring about the development that is explicitly or implicitly sought</u> by the Sahelian actors who have negotiated that aid. Hence the appearance and the increase of food aid in an effort to compensate for the deficiencies of the productive sector. Hence the appearance and increase of different forms of balance-of-payment assistance to cope with the excess of demand over domestic production. Hence the ever-increasing amounts of aid to the public and parastatal sectors, channeled through numerous "development" projects that in fact encourage the development of the corresponding administrative bodies rather than the development of productive activities per se.

The "conditionality" of aid, which began in the early 1960s, has hardly modified this state of affairs. Certain donors quickly abandoned attempts to impose real conditionality (direct or "inverted"), while others never actually put it into practice in an effort to preserve their "clientele" or to obtain commercial advantages. Although the few donors that made their action contingent on reform of the public sector, or on the liberalization of certain policies, etc, have occasionally been successful, socio-economic trends in the Sahel have never effectively been brought into question.

The situation is unlikely to change in the future. First, it appears improbable that the international community will come to an agreement on real conditionality, and even if such an agreement were reached, it is difficult to envisage Sahelian societies really accepting an outside diktat. To think that such acceptance is possible is to underestimate the capacity of these societies to react. In the light of the failure of development over the past twenty-five years and the increasing feeling among donors that aid is useless in its current form, there is considerable temptation to indulge in covert "recolonization". The fact that certain governments have been assigned a secondary role demonstrates that the temptation to recolonize is more than simply a threat. This is the epitome of the type of false solution that would not bring a lasting solution to any of the problems of the Sahel and that would inevitably lead to "covert non-cooperation" strategies, which would be at least as effective as those adopted during the colonial era.

<u>Aid can be no more than a response to the demands of Sahelian societies.</u> It can be no more than a stepping stone to the execution of the plans of these societies (even if, by its very existence, aid modifies those plans). Contrary to what was commonly accepted a few years ago, development cannot be procured by oil revenues or aid.

Thus, if one accepts the basic hypothesis of the trend scenario -- namely the permanent nature of the mechanisms currently at work in the region -- it appears unlikely that foreign aid alone can help the region move towards more favorable scenarios.

One frequently recurring idea is that of a "Marshall Plan" for the Sahel, or a "big push", which consists of massive additional assistance to provide Sahelian economies with the impulse that has been lacking until now. This idea is not as new as it may appear, since it is in line with the school of thought that has inspired aid since colonial times. The FIDES, which was set up in French territories after the Second World War, and the international assistance programs that have developed since that time, are both rooted in the same concept: that assistance will trigger economic growth. This idea considers that the economy, or what we called civilization in chapter 12, is an independent system that is not connected to culture and to social structures. It appears probable that those who subscribe to this idea have more or less explicitly waited for an initial transformation of the economy to have an effect on culture and social structures and prepare the way for subsequent self-sustained development. The wait has so far been in vain. It is possible -- though most unlikely -- that the situation is about to change.

By contrast, it is now probable that a massive increase in assistance in the form in which it has been distributed over the past decades would further increase the importance of the role played by the non-productive public sector in Sahelian societies. The burden of maintaining or renovating infrastructure would also increase, without having the desired effect on the development of production in the agricultural and industrial sectors. Under these same hypotheses, it is feasible that outside assistance will have some influence on the future of the Sahel, but that influence will remain limited.

<u>But if real development begins as a result of the intrinsic dynamism of these societies, as a result of change in roles and policies, and as a result of a change in culture and social structures,</u> or if suitable conditions for that development at least exist, <u>foreign aid is very likely to have considerable latitude to participate in real development.</u> Because, even if development cannot be bought and is the product of internal social change, it nonetheless requires capital and technology.

<u>Capital</u> is especially important. The majority of development assistance has until now been used to construct a modern society based on the Western model, and in particular to construct social infrastructure, transportation infrastructure, industries, etc. This modern society involves only a fraction of the population and today has insufficient links with the rest of Sahelian society to take root. While there is no question of completely eliminating this form of assistance, it should be totally reconsidered before it can contribute to the restructuring of Sahelian economies.

On the other hand, capital inputs that can be used to transform rural production systems, to restore the ecological balance and to develop small-scale industrial companies (formal or informal) are undoubtedly needed to back up investments made by the Sahelians themselves. Henceforth, <u>foreign assistance could become more useful and more effective by being used to complement the intrinsic dynamism of Sahelian societies,</u> rather than by attempting, with varying degrees of success, to superimpose Western-style development on Sahelian societies that doubtless hope to become Western consumer societies but that are not yet ready to introduce the corresponding production processes.

This end can be achieved only by radically transforming assistance and abandoning preconceived notions that follow the development models of Western countries. Abandoning these set patterns will be a difficult task.

<u>Technologies</u> are another vital component of development. The marked development of higher education since the beginning of the 1960s has provided the Sahel with considerable human resources for research into those new technologies that are appropriate to the natural, economic and social conditions of the region. A number of institutions have been created, within which Sahelian researchers work in close cooperation with their non-Sahelian counterparts. However, many of these institutions are so isolated from the international research community that they are only moderately effective. Outside assistance can play a major role in creating research programs that are more effective and more appropriate to the development plans that will emerge from the evolution of Sahelian societies.

Private aid

The comments made about official development assistance also apply to private aid:

-- There is too much aid. There are so many NGOs (eighty foreign NGOs including two Japanese organizations in Mali alone) that they compete against each other, that a surfeit of aid is inevitable. The NGOs contribute to the development of an "assisted" mentality among rural population groups, which obtain the social services they need (and even services they do not request) without effort. When NGOs transfer so many funds to village associations that these associations are unable to manage them effectively, and when these funds are provided before the associations have shown themselves willing to depend primarily on themselves, it is clear that there is too much aid.

-- There is insufficient aid when one considers the lack of resources of certain villages, the infant mortality rate, and the extent of illiteracy, on the one hand, and the enormous problems faced by rural population groups in preserving the natural environment, in ensuring adequate water supply and in changing production systems, on the other.

Private aid suffers especially from the determination of each donor to impose its own development projects; this involves rejecting projects that do not conform to the donor's way of thinking or even abandoning ongoing projects that have taken a direction that is deemed unsuitable. The example can be cited of an NGO that had successfully begun to implement a project to develop productivity of cereals crops in a province of Burkina Faso, but then abandoned the project when it discovered that it created "rich" farmers, a concept that ran contrary to the NGO's ethic.

In the same way that official development assistance has allowed Sahelian societies to opt for false development and increased dependence over the last quarter-century, <u>the current proliferation of private aid may well have a negative effect</u> on the new-found dynamism of the rural non-governmental sector, despite the good intentions that evidently lie behind such aid. Aid might again direct this dynamism towards increasing dependence. <u>Private aid can play an extremely useful role</u> by proposing the most efficient techniques and by training people to use them, by helping village associations to organize themselves, and by providing capital for projects and programs that are under way. Like official development assistance, <u>private aid can effectively sustain change</u> and can probably do so more effectively than official development assistance.

Private aid can be applied in a more decentralized manner that corresponds better to real needs and that enjoys greater independence from central government interference, thereby increasing the effect of large numbers of projects and initiatives that it is difficult for official development assistance to reach. But that involves the difficult task of abandoning preconceived development models.

Finally, it should be pointed out that private aid, which until now has concentrated primarily on rural areas, has vast and hitherto unexplored potential to promote activity in peri-urban areas and to increase productivity in the informal sector. There is no doubt that involvement in this field is fraught with difficulties. Few NGOs have tangible experience (other than in social action) in urban areas, and few of those NGOs have even considered what action they could take to increase productivity in urban and peri-urban areas. However, for the future of the region, the dynamics of urban change are as important as the dynamics of change in rural areas.

Chapter 28

PREPARING THE FUTURE FOR THE NEXT GENERATION

The formal education system

Education systems have several functions, including passing on culture from one generation to another and transmitting the technical knowhow that will shape civilization in the sense we have given above.

The formal education system in the Sahel -- primary schools, high schools and universities -- was set up in colonial times. The system was designed to meet the needs of a colonial world and was copied from the Western model and grafted onto Sahelian societies. For the most part, the system has remained intact and has undergone only superficial reforms since independence. The technical knowhow and the system of values conveyed are mainly those of Western societies. True Sahelian values -- those which form the building blocks of the personality of each and every individual -- are put across by an "informal " education system involving the family and the village or neighborhood community.

The formal education system has contributed to the changes in values that have taken place by disseminating the values of the West, and is coherent with a Western model of society. However, that formal system may not be relevant to the plans for society that are implicit in the desirable scenarios, which necessarily include the transformation of rural and peri-urban production systems.

Through the values it disseminates and the knowledge it purveys, the formal education system contributes to the rural exodus and to the growth of the public sector. The knowledge that is passed on to younger generations is hardly appropriate to a civilization that undoubtedly does require engineers, doctors and economists but that also needs to transform the system of production on which it is based.

Further, the system is costly and accounts for a large part of government expenditures, while in general the school-age population is still far from able to take advantage of it. Sahelian governments <u>will be unable to extend the current system</u> to the whole of a particular age group in the foreseeable future.

The results achieved by the current system are mediocre, particularly because that system has been imposed on Sahelian society. The use of European languages from the beginning of schooling, while the children are unable to speak them at home, is merely the most visible aspect of an exogenous system.

In industrialized societies, the education system is at the same time a product of the society and a driving force behind social development and economic growth. It is precisely because the education system is a product of the society that it is capable of spurring social development.

The Sahel must find an education system that is not alien to Sahelian societies and that is not totally exogenous to them, but that becomes the locomotive for social development. Further, Sahelian societies must be able to afford the cost of such an education system. However, radical reform of the education system will not take place overnight: a long time will be required to design the system, to train teachers to accept a different concept of education, and to educate new age groups under that concept. The effects of such a reform will thus not be felt for at least one generation, but this is no reason not to consider reforms in the coming years.

Meanwhile, there is little doubt that action can be taken to improve the way the formal sector operates. One point in particular should be mentioned here: <u>adult literacy training.</u> So-called functional literacy training organized since the 1960s for a long time achieved disappointing results. Perhaps because the critical mass for literacy training initiatives has been reached in certain villages, and doubtless also because conditions have changed and these villages are now showing new dynamism, such initiatives now seem to be producing more tangible results (although no figures are available on the extent of literacy training operations undertaken by NGOs or on the results achieved). Literacy programs accompanied with the transmission of basic knowledge provide a powerful means of increasing the efficiency of village associations and increasing productivity by making the introduction of new techniques possible. This approach is also virtually a prerequisite for democratic government in rural communities, and as such should be accorded much higher priority.

Literacy training of peri-urban population groups is more neglected, perhaps because these groups have easier access to the school system. But levels of illiteracy are still very high, even among those individuals who have been to school, but have only achieved limited levels of learning, which is practically never applied and very quickly becomes unusable. However, the need for literacy training and basic knowledge is as necessary for increased productivity in the informal sector as it is in rural areas. Adult literacy in the informal sector should thus be given greater priority.

The informal education system

Despite the efforts that have been made, approximately 60 per cent of children do not go through the formal school system. And many of those who have been through the system have already received informal primary education in a social context that has often been described as restrictive for adults and laxist for the very young. Even if this contrast between initial laxism and subsequent restrictiveness has become less pronounced with the destructuring of traditional society, it has not completely disappeared.

The specific features of primary education in Sahelian societies clearly have an effect on attitudes. The lack of restrictions in infancy, almost permanent physical contact with the mother during the first months, the shock of weaning and the sudden transition into adult society shape conceptions of the outside world and relationships with other people in different ways in different cultures. Some researchers have stressed the importance that these specific features could have on the individual's world view and in particular on the conception of time and the facility to anticipate, the ability to organize knowledge in order to take action, etc. The way in which roles are distributed within the family unit (nuclear or extended), and in particular the role of the mother, the father (or father figure) probably also have an importance in personality formation.

Chapter 15 above examined the theory that the destructuring of traditional society and the fact that values are changing should favor the development of entrepreneurship. But are there not also cultural factors that stand in the way of development of production systems in rural areas as well as in the cities? For example, is the very low level of investment in rural production systems and in the informal sector simply the result of a lack of funds, or is it also the manifestation of a cultural characteristic that has been encountered in the Sahel for centuries? Sahelian societies have always had a tendency not to accumulate capital (see chapter 1): is this the consequence of a different attitude to time from that observed in European or Asian societies? And could this different attitude to time be the cause of behavior patterns that make it more difficult to apply organization methods that have been developed by and for European societies?

Management methods employed by public-sector organizations, which have been tried and tested in Western countries, have turned out to be poorly suited to contemporary Sahelian culture. Should a specific approach to management be sought for the Sahel (in the same way as Japanese management has developed differently from European and American management), or should culture evolve? Or both?

It should be pointed out here that the fields we are discussing have been very little explored to date. What links exist between informal education and development, between informal education and the ability to use modern technologies, achieve genuine integration of those technologies in the country's activities, and gain control over the environment? Should action be taken on informal education methods, and if so, what type of action? There are no straightforward answers to this type of question. Can the formal education system act on the personality traits imparted during informal primary education, and how? Straightforward answers to this type of question are even harder to find.

In the Sahel as elsewhere, women have a key role in transmitting culture from one generation to the next and in determining the way in which attitudes are forged during infancy.

As Algerian educationalist Cheikh ben Badis said at the beginning of the century: "Educate a boy, and you are educating an individual. Educate a girl and you are educating a nation." This statement is undeniably true, but "educating a girl" again raises the issue mentioned above -- how well is the formal education system matched to the future needs of Sahelian societies".

Population policy

The Sahel as a region is both underpopulated and overpopulated. It is underpopulated because none of the countries of the Sahel can offer sufficient markets to ensure the economic viability of mass-production industry and because the expenditure incurred through construction and maintenance of infrastructure such as transportation systems is a heavy burden on national economies. The Sahel is overpopulated because, as we have seen, today's unprecedented levels of population are causing major ecological problems, and production systems have not developed to meet the needs of this growing population without damaging the environment.

While the size of the population is clearly at the root of many problems, it is the rapid rate of growth of that population that is probably most alarming. Sahelian societies have been manifestly incapable of making the investments needed to cope with a population that doubles within the space of a generation, and of developing production systems sufficiently quickly to maintain the ecological balance.

In the future, the development of industrial technology will make smaller industrial facilities economically viable, thereby reducing the need for extensive markets. It is quite feasible that the rate of environmental deterioration will fall in the future, but this will not happen without considerable human investment. The fact that the population doubles every twenty-five years is going to cause untold problems, not only in re-establishing the ecological balance but also in terms of economic and social infrastructures, and these problems will have to be faced even if a more favorable scenario than the trend scenario materializes.

In the subsequent quarter-century (2010-2035), the ecological problems caused by another doubling of the population will be enormous, and, while these problems may not be insurmountable, the cost of finding solutions to them will be extremely high.

It will probably be necessary to reduce the rate at which populations are growing before sustained economic growth can be achieved for a long period. However, as we saw in chapter 17, before the advantages of lower fertility rates have been clearly appreciated, and before birth-control measures (traditional or from outside) are applied, there is little chance that the population will actually fall. Be that as it may, by systematically disseminating information to population groups, it is possible to increase awareness of the advantages of lower fertility rates.

FINAL CONCLUSIONS

CONDITIONS FOR FINDING A WAY OUT OF THE TREND SCENARIO

> The way out is through the door.
> Why do people want to find other
> ways of leaving?
>
>   Confucius

Chapter 29

CONDITIONS FOR FINDING A WAY OUT OF THE TREND SCENARIO

Where is the way out?

The way out is through the door. OK, but where is the door?

In the proposals mentioned above, we have used expressions such as "the Sahel must" or "Sahelian governments or donors should...". It would be very naive to imagine that all that is needed for the Sahel to find a way out of the trend scenario and move towards a better future is to apply all or some of these proposals. These proposals are not magic formulas that will automatically open the door to a bright future for the region. In fact, the proposals are inextricably intertwined. This can be demonstrated by two examples.

It has become fashionable to say that the "urban bias" (whereby economic policies systematically favor city-dwellers) must be eliminated, and the analysis made here will not contradict that appraisal. The urban bias is clearly one of the causes of what we have called the destructuring of Sahelian societies. But it would be naive to think that Sahelian politicians can eliminate that bias through legislation. Because they do not have to take the reactions of their electorate into account to the same extent, they may appear to have greater liberty than many of their Western counterparts to apply the policies that they feel to be the best for their countries. In fact, things are considerably more complicated, and politicians are constantly trapped in a web of restriction that limits their room for maneuver. It is true that the outstandingly charismatic politician will manage to break free of this web of restrictions and manage to convince his fellow citizens -- and fellow politicians -- to accept the directions that they would not spontaneously have welcomed. But in the Sahel as elsewhere, outstandingly charismatic politicians are few and far between.

Similarly, it is not uncommon for observers to deplore donors for not attaching more priority to projects aiming to intensify cereals production and re-establish the ecological balance, which are widely recognized as being vital to the future of the region. Decision-makers in donor organizations are most probably just as aware as everybody else of these priorities, but they are also aware of the difficulties that are encountered in conceiving and implementing effective projects in this field. They know about the failures of the past and are well aware of the uncertainties that beset projects of this type. They too are caught in a web of restrictions formed by the demands of Sahelian governments and their own inability to implement projects, as well as public opinion and pressure groups in Western countries, and the attitudes of decision-makers in other donor agencies. They are also dependent on the decisions that have been made in the past, the options that their agency has already taken, the projects that are already under way and that are considered worthwhile continuing, etc.

Can donors decide to give more priority to cereals production and apply that decision more easily than Sahelian governments can legislate against the urban bias? Judging by the experience of the last ten years or so, this is far from certain. Reforestation projects provide a typical example of this fact. Between 1975 and 1980 donors realized how serious the problem of deforestation is in the Sahel. They reacted to this realization by "decreeing" to increase financing for projects aimed to alleviate the problem, and by the early 1980s allocations of aid to this type of project began to rise. Allocations subsequently fell to a very low level. Was this because the deforestation problem had been resolved or had become less worrisome? Certainly not. Nevertheless, such decrees were clearly not sufficient to ensure that more aid was allocated over a long period of time.

In view of the above, the way out of the trend scenario would appear to be labyrinthine. Each prerequisite for finding an alternative solution is dependent on several other conditions, and vice-versa. But is there no way of finding the way out of this labyrinth?

There is a need to come back to the notion of a system, and to look at the ways in which a system can be changed from within.

The actors and the system

Everything is connected, and no single actor can hope to act effectively on his own. Sahelian governments and donors are part of the system.

Isolating the Sahelian system and considering it as subject to a number of outside influences (as we have in parts II and III of this study) is a working arrangement that has proved useful in developing scenarios. But in examining conditions for finding a way out of the trend scenario, the examples given above demonstrate that it would perhaps be more meaningful to widen our concept of the system and take into account the whole of the Sahel plus the donors. (The limits of this corpus are more blurred: which organizations should be considered as donors? Should Western governments be included, for example?). Donors and Sahelian countries now have so many relationships of all types that it would not be unreasonable to consider them together as a single system.

From this viewpoint, all the actors that we have taken into account are in the system. Those that are the least implicated in the system are probably the Sahelian farmers, or at least a large proportion of them. The farmer who produces enough to feed his family and who has one or more children working in the informal sector in the city and who receives regular financial assistance from them depends very little on the system. G. Hyden has said that he is "non-captured" and that this position at the edge of the system is not compatible with development.

If all the actors are in the system, does this mean that they are all dependent on the logic of the relationships between different parts of the system and that voluntary change is thus impossible?

All the actors are dependent on the logic of the system to which they belong, and are caught up in the web of restrictions that was mentioned above. None of the actors can escape from the system, but certain actors are more involved than others. Certain groups of actors are completely set in their ways, while certain other groups have more autonomy. In any system, the development of certain subsystems can upset the overall system to such a degree that its logic is altered. In all societies, action taken by minorities can lead to a change in social structures.

In the broad definition of the Sahelian system given above, which groups can play a role in finding a way out of the trend scenario? There are grounds to think that the groups that can play the most important role are those groups that are involved in other systems of logic, without being completely divorced from the Sahelian system: intellectuals, expatriate Sahelians returning to their home countries, young people who are strongly influenced by the media, and donors and NGOs, which are only partially involved in the system. Four "driving groups" can thus be proposed:

-- Donor agencies, which are involved in the system but clearly have a separate status, and whose action is fundamental to the materialization of the trend scenario;

-- What can be termed Sahelian intellectual elites, whether they are in positions of responsibility in the government or civil service, or are in a position to directly or indirectly influence future society or major policy leanings;

-- What can be termed emerging Sahelian actors, whose role and status is currently changing: expatriates who have experienced other cultures and who then return home; women, who are beginning to play a new role; young people; and all those individuals or associations that take initiatives at the village level or in the informal sector;

-- Foreign NGOs, and all those non-Sahelian actors that wish to contribute to finding a solution to the region's problems, and that enjoy very considerable autonomy to do so.

The emerging Sahelian actors clearly play a special role. It is this group of actors that will lead the Sahel towards a better future, and it is this group that is liable to progressively exert an influence over the traditional "non-captured" farmers, whose numbers are in any case bound to fall.

<u>What can the other driving groups do to support</u> the emerging actors or at least give them a chance of succeeding? The present study of possible futures for the Sahel will attempt to provide a tentative response to this question, which will not propose concrete solutions, but will suggest topics for further consideration.

Topics for consideration by donors

Increasing levels of aid are indispensable if life is to continue at all in the Sahel under the trend scenario. More aid will probably also be needed -- although to a lesser extent -- under more desirable scenarios. Further, it has been said that if a development plan comes to the surface from within Sahelian societies, aid will have a vast field of action and could accompany that development. Two essential questions will then inevitably arise.

<u>Structural adjustment aid and development aid</u>

Demand exceeds supply because of high levels of dependence, and structural adjustment programs thus aim to reduce demand. Excess demand can also be reduced by increasing supply, and that is the aim of development programs. It is not clear whether these two objectives are compatible. To quote R. Cassen on the efficacy of aid, "it is worrying to see the lack of consistency between adjustment programs and long-term development requirements". The inevitable deflationary aspects of a policy aimed to reduce demand are clearly not favorable to economic expansion. In an industrialized country, well conducted structural adjustment can lead to increased productivity and thereby prepare the way for subsequent expansion. In contemporary Sahelian societies, there is a risk that the same adjustment would lead to greater introversion of the different social groups, and would scarcely prepare the way for the restructuring of the economy that is necessary.

However, it would also be justifiable to argue that the countries "are absorbing their domestic resources in unproductive expenditure to the detriment of growth" (J. de Larosière) and that structural adjustment programs would eliminate such unproductive expenditure and therefore "[would not] create an obstacle to growth, but would be a condition for growth" (ibid.).

Since the dependence of the Sahelian countries is not about to disappear, there is a risk that this question of compatibility between reductions in demand and increases in supply, or between structural adjustment and development, will become a permanent problem. Donor agencies will be faced with a problem of how to maintain pressure on Sahelian governments to reduce dependence on the outside world, at the same time as mitigating that pressure so as not to compromise chances of development. This study does not intend to propose solutions, but there is no doubt that the problem is serious enough to merit more in-depth examination.

Aid to the public sector and aid to the non-governmental sector

Until now, a large proportion of official development assistance has been allocated to Sahelian governments, and even when it has been intended to reach the non-governmental sector via the government's offices, it has by no means always reached its targets and even less been used efficiently. State structures that are "suspended in mid-air" and the autonomy of rural communities create conditions that are unfavorable to the transmission of aid to groups such as the most underprivileged sectors of society that donor agencies naively seek to reach by sending aid to governments. This situation is not likely to change overnight.

Will the redistribution of the roles of the State and the non-governmental sector necessarily involve changes in official development assistance? Can that assistance reach the non-governmental sector more directly and thereby support the initiatives taken by the most dynamic groups, and if so, how? Should a greater proportion of that assistance pass through the offices of NGOs, which are more likely to act efficiently? Donors will inevitably have to find answers to these complex questions. To answer these questions, moves must be made to change the way in which action is traditionally taken, and, as we have said, preconceived notions of development must be abandoned.

In general, aid and the role it plays has so far been considered in a fairly narrow economic context, and discussion has concentrated on the volume of aid that is allocated and how that aid is distributed, the conception and appraisal of development projects, methods of implementing structural adjustment programs, etc. These past few years, Western countries have implicitly or explicitly delegated consideration of the main orientations of aid to the international organizations, and those organizations, by their very nature, are only able to consider institutional aspects of the problems, while political and socio-cultural aspects are necessarily swept to one side. The present study, as was stated in the introduction, is an attempt to place aid in a more global context. But in view of the complexity of the issues and the amount of interference that occurs within the Sahelian system, it might be more meaningful to go even further and to systematically re-position aid in this complex picture.

Lastly, and for the record more than anything else, we should again point to the <u>links between aid and international trade,</u> since Western countries' trade policies, as we said in chapter 18, tend to have the opposite effect to that of aid. But this problem can clearly not be examined within the strict confines of the Sahel.

Topics for consideration by Sahelian elites

Aid can accompany the development plans of Sahelian societies. But how much progress have these plans made? A large proportion of the Sahelian elites undoubtedly plan implicitly to live according to a Western model, and yet there is no chance that the society as a whole will follow suit in the foreseeable future. What plan can be proposed? Although a few attempts have been made to consider this topic, plans are still unclear, or else revolve around illusory subjects such as food self-sufficiency that can no longer really be considered to play a driving role. Whatever level of self-sufficiency is achieved, dire poverty is never exalting.

Even if it is impossible to formulate a development plan, the dynamism of Sahelian society can be relied upon to progressively build up initiative. The least the State can be expected to do is to allow this private-sector dynamism to express itself to the full. It is within the government's power either to stifle that dynamism or to allow it full expression, or even to encourage it or to direct it along the same lines as a given plan, if such a plan exists.

Sahelian elites, and all those that play a role in orienting national policies, could consider the crucial questions that were mentioned in chapter 26:

-- What framework should be given to rural dynamism?

a) What legal structures allow rural communities to exercise responsibility over land and natural resources?
b) What tasks (education, health care, etc.) should be transferred to the local authorities?
c) How can democracy be promoted at the local level?
d) Which food policies should be adopted?

-- What framework should be given to urban dynamism? What structures should companies be offered? How can the informal sector be formalized and the formal sector informalized? Which industrial policy should be adopted?

Another topic for consideration is the long-term future that should be prepared. What type of formal and informal <u>education</u> will be needed tomorrow? Which <u>population policy</u> should be adopted? At a time when most Western countries are considering how to adapt their education systems in line with technological and social change, Sahelians (perhaps even more than the West) should also be thinking about how to adapt their more or less imported education systems to face the problems of tomorrow. (Particular mention should be made of the U.S. report, "A Nation at Risk" and the recent French report "Education and Society Tomorrow. From Research to Real Questions".)

Finally, an interface between Sahelian markets and international markets that does not discourage urban dynamism is also a key topic for consideration, but care should be taken not to deal with this topic in complete isolation from the situation of Western countries.

Topics for consideration by Western countries and by the Sahelian elites

Trade -- and thus the interface between the Sahel and the rest of the world -- is a vital issue for two reasons: first, so that Sahelian dynamism in rural areas as well as in the cities is not stifled by abusive invasion of domestic markets and so that it can find greater expression on international markets; and secondly, so that dependence will decline.

The Sahel plays too minor a role in the world for it to be claimed that the region asserts more than minimal influence on world markets and on the policies adopted by the major powers. Further, international prices will inevitably fluctuate in the future because of future technological changes.

It will thus be impossible to dodge the issues of interface, exchange rate, and particularly CFA franc parity. If it is recognized that the current parity level is now an obstacle to development, it would probably be pointless to expect deflationary policies to have forced down relative price levels in the Sahel sufficiently to have brought an end to overpricing of currencies. The level of deflation needed would cause a serious crisis and would bleed Sahelian economies dry. That means that a careful study must be made of the best way of reducing this monetary handicap -- generalized protectionism (or at least product-specific protectionism) or else parity changes -- and that study can only be made in association with the monetary authorities of the franc area.

Structural analysis has demonstrated that France acts as an important driving force in the Sahel. After having been the principal colonial power in the region, France twenty-five years later still plays a very special role through the influence its culture exerts over the Sahelian elites, through the volume of aid it provides and through the monetary connections it maintains with five Sahelian countries. As much as, or perhaps even more than in the immediate post-independence period, France still has a specific role to play. That role is accepted to varying degrees by the Sahelians, who are as ready to shower abuse on the former colonial power as to criticize it for abandoning its former subjects. This intellectual influence should give France a very special place in the discussion suggested above, not least because of its involvement in monetary issues. Be that as it may, France must first be prepared to accept its responsibility in assuming its role in these discussions.

Topics for consideration by NGOs

Foreign NGOs have a role to play alongside Sahelian dynamism -- a role that can be particularly important, and that NGOs can assume more effectively than official donor agencies. Consideration should be given to the following points:
   -- How should NGOs distribute their efforts in the future between purely social assistance and assistance aiming to change the production system in rural areas (including restoration of ecological balances)?

   -- What role can NGOs assume in the cities? How can they help the informal sector increase productivity?

-- What role can NGOs play in organizing farming communities? How can they support organization at the village level and how can they help federations of village associations in order to promote cooperation?

Conclusion: no magic formula, but enough hope to mobilize efforts

Readers expecting this futures study to propose a magic formula for redressing the situation in the Sahel will be disappointed. An overview has simply been given of the factors upon which the future of the region will depend. Through insufficient knowledge, certain of these factors have merely been mentioned, and certain other factors will doubtless have been overlooked. Nevertheless, this brief and incomplete overview will hopefully have made it possible for the reader to appreciate the enormous complexity of the Sahelian system.

When this complexity is taken into consideration, it is easier to understand that simple formulas are not sufficient, and it is easier to see the poor conception of certain of the policies that have been recommended and adopted. _The Sahelian system,_ like all other systems, _is defined by its internal relationships. These relationships have so far changed very little, while the changes that are already under way and that are about to occur (new values, a changing world, population explosion) call for a more profound transformation of the way in which these relationships are structured._ No investment plan, however well conceived, can resolve the region's current problems, since investment will not alter this internal structure. Action taken on a specific part of the system -- cereals prices yesterday, tomorrow perhaps exchange rates -- creates a disturbance that will very soon be absorbed by the system, which is very resilient, and will not ultimately change the internal structure of that system. Structural adjustment programs themselves, despite their name, do not really affect the structures of Sahelian societies. They modify the distribution of wealth, and may help create conditions for subsequent changes in the internal structure, although this is far from certain.

The possible futures of Sahelian societies can be summarized, in an extremely simplified manner, as follows:

-- Either the structure of the system will not really change at all, but will adapt to a greater or lesser degree in order to avoid catastrophes, and in this case, what we have called the trend scenario will materialize, causing economic stagnation and progressively increasing the region's dependence on the outside world;

-- Or sudden changes in external influences (worsening climatic conditions, a sudden reduction in levels of aid), or in internal influences, will bring into question current conceptions of the State, and will bring sudden changes to the structure of the system, probably under drastic conditions, and will delay any possibility of genuine development;

-- Or else action taken by what we have called driving forces (including donors) will make it possible to progressively change the structure of the system and to find a way out of the trend scenario, averting catastrophes and triggering genuine development that will ultimately make it possible to reduce dependence on the outside world and to implement a specifically Sahelian social plan.

The door leading to this structural transformation is undoubtedly a narrow one. But everything points to the fact that a door exists, and that Sahelians, under the influence of the most dynamic among them and helped by those that wish to help them, can find that door and go through. And the strongest reason to hope that this transformation will occur in the next twenty-five years, as we have said on various occasions, is the new-found dynamism of Sahelian societies.

When the father of the great Soundiata, founder of the Mali empire whose golden years are recounted by all the griots, came to find the diviner of Niani, worried to see his son persistently falling behind the children of his age group, the blind diviner assured him that the seed had germinated. This study of the futures of the Sahel has voluntarily remained blind to a vision of the Sahel which, by remaining too limited because of current difficulties, leads to utter pessimism and thus succeeds in building nothing. Without having the gift of clairvoyance of the diviner of Niani, the authors of this study have tried to see far into the future, even if that vision is imprecise. The seed is germinating, and Sahelian societies -- after all the trials and tribulations they have experienced -- are finding a new dynamism that provides grounds for hope and optimism. Without the life within the seed, no harvest would ever be reaped.

But all Sahelians know that between the moment that the seed germinates and the time the harvest is brought in, much has to be done. The crops must be watered, the land must be weeded, the predators must be chased away... and maybe fertilizers and pesticides and new farm machinery must be brought from far-off lands. But, as the diviner of Niani added, man is impatient.

ANNEXES

Annexe 1

SUMMARY OF PROCEEDINGS
OF THE 7TH CLUB DU SAHEL MEETING

held at N'Djamena, 26-27 January, 1988

Agenda Item on the Futures Study

A brief presentation was made of the Futures Study conducted by the Secretariats of the CILSS and the Club du Sahel following a resolution taken at the Brussels meeting of the Club du Sahel. The participants in the ensuing debate unanimously recognized the innovative nature and the great significance of the study. Several participants expressed regret that there had been insufficient time to study the report before the meeting, and that in-depth discussion of the various topics covered was thus difficult. Several Ministers also regretted the fact that a meeting of Sahelian experts had not been convened beforehand in order to examine the various topics and to make observations.

Despite these reservations, the presentation of the Study gave rise to a valuable exchange of views on the approach adopted by the report, and on its conclusions. Certain participants found that the Study laid too much emphasis on retrospective analysis, since certain Sahelian societies are today subjected to influences that have virtually nothing to do with earlier historical factors; certain points in the historical analysis were contested, while at the same time it was recognized that, during the Sahel's history, the region had experienced numerous shocks, and that those shocks were partly responsible for the current state of affairs.

Other participants would have preferred that greater emphasis be laid on the importance for donors to shoulder part of the responsibility for formulating and implementing policies. Individual criticism was made of a number of specific points in the study: structural adjustment policies, the deterioration of the terms of trade, the schism between governments and population groups, a regional market incorporating more than just the Sahel, etc.

The objective of the Futures Study was clarified: to initiate a form of consideration that differed from customary reflection in that it was based on the examination of a broader range of aspects of Sahelian societies and made a more thorough exploration of the past and the future. It would be unrealistic to expect to reach full consensus on the results of such an undertaking, since the evolution of a society cannot be viewed from a single standpoint. Indeed, in order to achieve its aim, a study of this type is bound to be provocative and will inevitably cause offense to certain parties.

The participants agreed that the study was a starting point for fuller consideration. The meeting recommended that in the first instance a committee of CILSS experts should be mandated to make a detailed examination of the different themes covered by the Futures Study and to submit its conclusions to a meeting of Ministers.

Annexe 2

**REGIONAL MEETING OF EXPERTS FROM CILSS MEMBER COUNTRIES
ON THE FUTURES STUDY**

Bobo-Dioulasso, 7-9 June, 1988

After examining the "Futures Study", the Council of Ministers of the CILSS suggested that Sahelian experts analyze this Study and make recommendations as to the further action that should be taken.

In response to this suggestion, the Executive Secretariat of the CILSS organized a meeting in Bobo-Dioulasso from June 7-9, 1988.

Conclusions and Recommendations

Participants considered that the "Futures Study: 1985-2010" provided a good framework for analysis and a suitable reference document for Sahelians involved in prospective examination of the region.

The Study could thus be very widely disseminated in an effort to provide a basis for consideration of the long-term future of Sahelian countries.

Further studies should nevertheless be conducted or the important issues that were not developed in sufficient detail by the Study, particularly the informal sector, the future of the franc zone, the adaptation of technologies, and the conditions that would be required for closer regional integration.

In conclusion, the following propositions were approved:

1) Prospective studies should be conducted by individual Sahelian governments in order to provide inspiration for development strategies;

2) Consideration should be given to a few aspects of the future that are shared by the countries of the Sahel;

3) Not only should the production of information be encouraged, but moves should be made to promote the dissemination and circulation of that information among the different actors in Sahelian society (decision-makers, researchers, journalists, associations, etc.) both within each Sahelian country and between the different countries.

Prospective Reflection and Long-Term Development Strategy

The Futures Study provides a methodological model and a good framework for analysis, which should be used by the governments of the Sahel in their efforts to foster reflection on the long-term future, and which will ultimately make it possible to find a way out of the present-trends scenario.

This reflection could be conducted in each country by a study group made up of senior civil servants, researchers, academics and representatives of the private and parastatal sectors in rural and urban areas.

The study groups would aim to give global consideration to society within its international and natural environment, in an effort to submit to their respective governments several scenarios that portray plausible views of the long-term future (one generation).

The social project selected by the government would point the way to the medium-term strategic choices that should be made in the country's economic and social development plan.

In this respect, there is a <u>need at the regional level to encourage the development of a reference methodology for the national prospective studies that are to be conducted.</u>

Prospective Reflection on Aspects of the Future Shared by the Sahelian Countries

It would subsequently be useful to organize meetings of Sahelians involved in prospective examination in order to direct prospective reflection on a few aspects of the future that are shared by the countries of the Sahel.

The topics covered could include:

-- The forms of education that are best adapted to Sahelian values;

-- Protection strategy (common market);

-- Adoption or addition of new technologies;

-- The monetary and economic zone;

-- Conservation of the natural environment;

-- Trans-Sahelian infrastructures and the opening-up of the region to the outside world;

-- Development aid and optimum use of that aid, etc.

Annexe 3

BIBLIOGRAPHY

This Futures Study has drawn on a number of documents prepared by the Secretariats of the CILSS and the Club du Sahel, and by donor agencies, including the World Bank, the French Cooperation Ministry, the FAO, etc. Those documents are not cited in the bibliography, which lists only the principal works that have been consulted for the Study.

Introduction

Berger,G. (1967), Etapes de la prospective, PUF, Paris
Cazes, B. (1986), Histoire des futurs, Seghers, Paris
Godet, M. (1977), Crise de la prévision, essor de la prospective, PUF, Paris
Godet, M. (1985), Prospective et planification stratégique, Economica, Paris
Futuribles, (1983), Prospective, prévision, planification stratégique,
    November 1983 issue, Paris

CHAPTER 1 – The Sahel from Imperial Times to the Eve of Colonization

Ba, A. and DAGET, J, (1984). L'empire peul du Macina, NEA, Dakar
Baiers, S. (1980), An Economic History of Central Niger, Clarendon Press,
    Oxford
Barry, B. (1972), Le royaume du Waalo, Maspero, Paris
Coquery-Vidrovitch, C. (1985), Afrique Noire, Payot, Paris
Cuoq, J. (1984), Histoire de l'islamisation de l'Afrique de l'ouest, Genthner,
    Paris
Curtin, P. (1985), Economic Change in Pre-Colonial Africa, University of
    Wisconsin Press
Deschamps, H. (1971), Histoire générale de l'Afrique noire, PLF, Paris
Diop, M. (1971), Histoire des classes sociales en Afrique de l'ouest,
    Maspero, Paris
Hopkins, A.G. (1973), An Economic History of West Africa, Loncman, London
Ki-Zerbo, J. (1978), Histoire de l'Afrique noire, Hatier, Paris
Ly-Tall, M. (1977), L'empire du Mali, NEA, Dakar
Mauny, R. (1961), Tableau géographique de l'ouest africain au Moyen-Age,
    IFAN, Dakar
Meillassoux, C. (1986), Anthropologie de l'esclavage, PUF, Paris
Rodney, W. (1972), How Europe Underveloped Africa, Bogle, Loncon
UNESCO, (1985). Histoire générale de l'Afrique, Unesco/N.E.A.

CHAPTER 2 - The Colonial Period

Balandier, G. (1955), Sociologie actuelle de l'Afrique noire, PUF, Paris
David, P. (1980), Les Navétanes, NEA, Dakar
Labouret, H. (1941), Paysans d'Afrique occidentale, Galimard, Paris
Marchal, J.Y. (1980), Chronique d'un cercle de l'AOF, Ouahigouya 1908- 1941, ORSTOM, Paris
Nicolas, G. (1981), Dynamique de l'islam au sud du Sahara, Publications orientalistes de France, Paris
Pelissier, P. (1966), Les paysans du Sénégal, Fabrègue, Saint Yrieix
Richard-Molard, J. (1956), L'Afrique occidentale française, Berger-Levrault, Paris
Schreyger, E. (1984), L'Office du Niger au Mali, Steiner, Wiesbaden
Suret-Canale, J. (1958, 1964 and 1972). Afrique noire, Editions sociales, Paris

CHAPTER 3 - Population Trends Since 1960

EMF/WSF. The World Fertility Survey. Annual Report 1982
United Nations (1982), Les perspectives d'avenir de la population mondiale, évaluées en 1980, New York
SCET-SEDES (1984), Une image à long terme de l'Afrique au sud du Sahara, Paris

CHAPTER 4 - The Development of Agriculture Since 1960

World Bank, (1985), Politique agricole et son rapport avec la politique alimentaire dans les pays africains au sud du Sahara, IDE, World Bank, Washington
Copans, J. (1975), Sécheresses et famines du Sahel, Maspero, Paris
Coulomb, J. Serres, H. Tacher, G (1980), L'élevage en pays sahéliens, PUF, Paris
FAO (1976), Etude prospective pour le développement agricole des pays de la zone sahélienne, Rome
Giri, J. (1973), Le Sahel demain : renaissance ou catastrophe
Hart K. (1982), The Political Economy of West African Agriculture, Cambridge University Press, Cambridge
Lericollais, A. (1970), La détérioration d'un terroir : Sob en pays serer, ORSTOM, Paris
CILSS/Club du Sahel (1981), L'intensification des cultures pluviales dans les pays du Sahel,
    Paris

CHAPTER 5 - The Disruption of the Ecological Balance

World Bank (1985), La désertification dans les zones sahélienne et soudanienne de l'Afrique de l'Ouest, Groupe de travail présidé par J. GORSE, Washington
Broekhuyse, J. Th. (1985), Désertification et auto-suffisance alimentaire, Cebema, The Netherlands
Dumont, R. (1986), Pour l'Afrique, j'accuse, Plon, Paris
Giri, J. (1986), Désertification du Sahel, Etudes, Paris
Glantz, M. (1977), Desertification, Westview Press, Boulder

Glantz, M. (1983), Desertification: A Review of the Concept, Published
    in the Encyclopedia of Climatology, Hutchinson Ross Publishing Company
ORSTOM, (1983), Enjeux fonciers en Afrique noire, Karthala, Paris
Timberlake, L. (1985), Africa in Crisis, Earthscan, London

CHAPTER 6 – Industry, Services and the Informal Sector

World Bank, Rapport sur le développement dans le monde 1985, Washington
Barbier J.P. and GIRI, J. (1984), L'industrialisation des pays ACP en
    question, in Le Courrier, Brussels
Deble, I. and Hugon, Ph. (1982), Vivre et survivre dans les villes
    africaines, PUF, Paris
Revue Tiers-Monde (1986), La nouvelle industrialisation du Tiers-Monde,
    N° 107, PUF, Paris
Steel, W. and Evans, W. (1986), L'industrialisation en Afrique au sud du
    Sahara, World Bank, Washington
Van Dijk, M.P. (1966), Le secteur informel de Dakar, l'Harmattan, Paris
Van Dijk, M.P. (1986), Le secteur informel de Ouagadougou, L'Harmattan,
    Paris

CHAPTER 7 – Overall Economic Trends

Giri, J. (1986), L'Afrique en panne, Karthala, Paris
OECD, (1985), Afrique subsaharienne : de la crise au redressement, OECD, Paris
    Secrétariat du Comité monétaire de la Zone franc, Rapports annuels sur
    La Zone franc, Paris

CHAPTER 8 – The Destructuring of Rural Society

Adams, A. (1977), Le long voyage des gens du fleuve, Maspero, Paris
Copans, J. (1980), Les marabouts de l'arachide, le Sycomore, Paris
Duval, M. (1985), Un totalitarisme sans Etat, l'Harmattan, Paris
Gallais, J. (1984), Hommes du Sahel, Flammarion, Paris
Marchal, J.Y. (1983), Yatenga – La dynamique d'un espace rural
    soudano-sahlien, ORSTOM, Paris
Olivier de Sardan J.P. (1984), Les sociétés songhay-zarma, Karthala,
    Paris

CHAPTER 9 – The Increased Importance of Urban Society

Ela, J.M. (1983), La ville en Afrique noire, Karthala, Paris
Projet, (1982), L'explosion urbaine du Tiers-Monde, special issue,
    February 1982, Paris

CHAPTER 10 – Developments in the Power Base

Bates, R. (1981), Markets and States in Tropical Africa, University of
    California Press, Berkeley
Coulon, C. (1985), Les Musulmans et le pouvoir en Afrique noire,
    Karthala, Paris
Hyden, G. (1983), No Shortcuts to Progress, Heinemann, London
Kouassigan, G.A. (1985), Afrique : révolution ou diversité des possibles,
    l'Harmattan, Paris

Nagassouba, M. (1985), L'Islam au Sénégal. Demain les mollahs ?
    Karthala, Paris
Young, Crawford (1986), Africa's Colonial Legacy, in "Strategies for African
    Development", University of California Press, Berkeley

CHAPTER 12 - The Evolution of Society as a Product of Tensions

Balandier, G. (1969), Anthropologie politique, PUF, Paris
Braudel, F. (1958), Histoire et sociologie, in Traité de sociologie de
    G. Gurvitch, PUF, Paris
Ogburn, W. (1964), On Culture and Social Change, The University of
    Chicago Press, Chicago
Pham-van-Thuan, (1970), Société traditionnelle et société moderne : le cas du
    Japon de Meiji, in "Sociologie des mutations" de G. Balandier,
    Anthropos, Paris

CHAPTER 13 - The Sahelian Environment: Tomorrow's Climate

Courel, M-F. (1985), Etude de l'évolution récente des milieux sahéliens
    à partir des mesures fournies par les satellites, Thesis,
    University of Paris I
Symposium de Nouakchott sur la désertification (1974), IFAN, Dakar

CHAPTER 14 - The Sahelian Environment: Tomorrow's World

Lesourne, J. (1981), Les mille sentiers de l'avenir, Seghers, Paris
Lesourne, J. and Godet, M. (1985), La fin des habitudes, Seghers, Paris
OECD, (1979), Face aux futurs, OECD, Paris
Papon, P. (1983), Pour une prospective de la science, Seghers, Paris

CHAPTER 15 - Values and Mentalities: Sahelian Culture in the Future

Cheikh Anta Diop (1979), Nations nègres et culture, Présence africaine,
    Paris
Ki-Zerbo, J. (1985), Les identités culturelles africaines, in Genève-Afrique,
    N° 1-1985, Geneva

CHAPTER 17 - Population

Boserup, E. (1970), Evolution agraire & pression démographique,
    Flammarion, Paris
Caldwell, J.C. (1974), The Study of Fertility and Fertility Change in
    Tropical Africa, WFS, London
Cantrelle, P. (1987), La contre-offensive de la mortalité en Afrique ?,
    in Santé, médicament et développement, Liberté sans Frontières, Paris
ENDA, (1987), SIDA et Tiers-Monde, ENDA, Dakar
Locoh, T. (1984), Fécondité et famille en Afrique de l'ouest, PUF, Paris
Revue Tiers-Monde (1983), Population et développement N° 94, PUF, Paris

CHAPTER 18 - The Rural World Tomorrow

Feuillet, P. (1986), Les biotechnologies au service de l'agriculture, in
    Futuribles, September 1986, Paris

IFRI, (1986), RAMSES 1986-87, Atlas-Economica, Paris
CILSS/Club du Sahel, (1987), Colloque de Mindelo, OECD, Paris
Sasson, A. (1987), Quelles biotechnologies pour les pays en développement, UNESCO, Paris

CHAPTER 19 – The Industries of the Future

IFRI, RAMSES 83/84, Economica, Paris

CHAPTER 24 – The Role of the Government and the Non-Governmental Sector in Building a Better Future

Hyden, G. (1986), African Social Structure and Economic Development, in Strategies for African Development, University of California Press, Berkeley
Sandbrook, R. (1985), The Politics of African's Economic Stagnation, Cambridge University Press, Cambridge

CHAPTER 26 – Role Changes and Policy Changes

Michailof, S. (1984), Les apprentis sorciers du développent, Economica, Paris
Lewis, W.A. (1979), Développement économique & planification, Payot, Paris
Guillaumont, P. and S. (1984), Zone franc et développement africain, Economica, Paris
Leonard, D. (1986), Putting the Farmers in Control : Building Agricultural Institutions, in Strategies for African Development, University of California Press, Berkeley
Vinay, B. (1986), La zone franc aujourd'hui, in Marchés Tropicaux, November 28 1986, Paris

CHAPTER 28 – Preparing the Future for the Next Generation

Court, D. and Kynianjui, K. (1986), African Education: Problems in a High Growth Sector, in Strategies for African Development, University of California Press, Berkeley
Erny, P. (1978), L'enfant et son milieu en Afrique noire, Payot, Paris
Eschliman, J.P. (1982), Naître sur la terre africaine, INADES, Abdijan
Sugier, J.B. and C. (1986), Famille, rituel et développement, Saint Quentin en Tourmont F80120
Todd, E. (1984), L'enfance du monde. Structures familiales & développement, Seuil, Paris

WHERE TO OBTAIN OECD PUBLICATIONS
OÙ OBTENIR LES PUBLICATIONS DE L'OCDE

ARGENTINA - ARGENTINE
Carlos Hirsch S.R.L.,
Florida 165, 4º Piso,
(Galeria Guemes) 1333 Buenos Aires
Tel. 33.1787.2391 y 30.7122

AUSTRALIA - AUSTRALIE
D.A. Book (Aust.) Pty. Ltd.
11-13 Station Street (P.O. Box 163)
Mitcham, Vic. 3132   Tel. (03) 873 4411

AUSTRIA - AUTRICHE
OECD Publications and Information Centre,
4 Simrockstrasse,
5300 Bonn (Germany)   Tel. (0228) 21.60.45
Gerold & Co., Graben 31, Wien 1   Tel. 52.22.35

BELGIUM - BELGIQUE
Jean de Lannoy,
Avenue du Roi 202
B-1060 Bruxelles   Tel. (02) 538.51.69

CANADA
Renouf Publishing Company Ltd/
Éditions Renouf Ltée,
1294 Algoma Road, Ottawa, Ont. K1B 3W8
Tel: (613) 741-4333
Toll Free/Sans Frais:
Ontario, Quebec, Maritimes:
1-800-267-1805
Western Canada, Newfoundland:
1-800-267-1826
Stores/Magasins:
61 rue Sparks St., Ottawa, Ont. K1P 5A6
Tel: (613) 238-8985
211 rue Yonge St., Toronto, Ont. M5B 1M4
Tel: (416) 363-3171
Federal Publications Inc.,
301-303 King St. W.,
Toronto, Ont. M5V 1J5
Tel. (416)581-1552
Les Éditions la Liberté inc.,
3020 Chemin Sainte-Foy,
Sainte-Foy, P.Q. G1X 3V6,
Tel. (418)658-3763

DENMARK - DANEMARK
Munksgaard Export and Subscription Service
35, Nørre Søgade, DK-1370 København K
Tel. +45.1.12.85.70

FINLAND - FINLANDE
Akateeminen Kirjakauppa,
Keskuskatu 1, 00100 Helsinki 10   Tel. 0.12141

FRANCE
OCDE/OECD
Mail Orders/Commandes par correspondance :
2, rue André-Pascal,
75775 Paris Cedex 16
Tel. (1) 45.24.82.00
Bookshop/Librairie : 33, rue Octave-Feuillet
75016 Paris
Tel. (1) 45.24.81.67 or/ou (1) 45.24.81.81
Librairie de l'Université,
12a, rue Nazareth,
13602 Aix-en-Provence   Tel. 42.26.18.08

GERMANY - ALLEMAGNE
OECD Publications and Information Centre,
4 Simrockstrasse,
5300 Bonn   Tel. (0228) 21.60.45

GREECE - GRÈCE
Librairie Kauffmann,
28, rue du Stade, 105 64 Athens   Tel. 322.21.60

HONG KONG
Government Information Services,
Publications (Sales) Office,
Information Services Department
No. 1, Battery Path, Central

ICELAND - ISLANDE
Snæbjörn Jónsson & Co., h.f.,
Hafnarstræti 4 & 9,
P.O.B. 1131 - Reykjavik
Tel. 13133/14281/11936

INDIA - INDE
Oxford Book and Stationery Co.,
Scindia House, New Delhi 110001
Tel. 331.5896/5308
17 Park St., Calcutta 700016   Tel. 240832

INDONESIA - INDONÉSIE
Pdii-Lipi, P.O. Box 3065/JKT.Jakarta
Tel. 583467

IRELAND - IRLANDE
TDC Publishers - Library Suppliers,
12 North Frederick Street, Dublin 1
Tel. 744835-749677

ITALY - ITALIE
Libreria Commissionaria Sansoni,
Via Lamarmora 45, 50121 Firenze
Tel. 579751/584468
Via Bartolini 29, 20155 Milano   Tel. 365083
La diffusione delle pubblicazioni OCSE viene
assicurata dalle principali librerie ed anche da :
Editrice e Libreria Herder,
Piazza Montecitorio 120, 00186 Roma
Tel. 6794628
Libreria Hœpli,
Via Hœpli 5, 20121 Milano   Tel. 865446
Libreria Scientifica
Dott. Lucio de Biasio "Aeiou"
Via Meravigli 16, 20123 Milano   Tel. 807679

JAPAN - JAPON
OECD Publications and Information Centre,
Landic Akasaka Bldg., 2-3-4 Akasaka,
Minato-ku, Tokyo 107   Tel. 586.2016

KOREA - CORÉE
Kyobo Book Centre Co. Ltd.
P.O.Box: Kwang Hwa Moon 1658,
Seoul   Tel. (REP) 730.78.91

LEBANON - LIBAN
Documenta Scientifica/Redico,
Edison Building, Bliss St.,
P.O.B. 5641, Beirut   Tel. 354429-344425

**MALAYSIA/SINGAPORE -
MALAISIE/SINGAPOUR**
University of Malaya Co-operative Bookshop
Ltd.,
7 Lrg 51A/227A, Petaling Jaya
Malaysia   Tel. 7565000/7565425
Information Publications Pte Ltd
Pei-Fu Industrial Building,
24 New Industrial Road No. 02-06
Singapore 1953   Tel. 2831786, 2831798

NETHERLANDS - PAYS-BAS
SDU Uitgeverij
Christoffel Plantijnstraat 2
Postbus 20014
2500 EA's-Gravenhage   Tel. 070-789911
Voor bestellingen: Tel. 070-789880

NEW ZEALAND - NOUVELLE-ZÉLANDE
Government Printing Office Bookshops:
Auckland: Retail Bookshop, 25 Rutland Stseet,
Mail Orders, 85 Beach Road
Private Bag C.P.O.
Hamilton: Retail: Ward Street,
Mail Orders, P.O. Box 857
Wellington: Retail, Mulgrave Street, (Head
Office)
Cubacade World Trade Centre,
Mail Orders, Private Bag
Christchurch: Retail, 159 Hereford Street,
Mail Orders, Private Bag
Dunedin: Retail, Princes Street,
Mail Orders, P.O. Box 1104

NORWAY - NORVÈGE
Narvesen Info Center - NIC,
Bertrand Narvesens vei 2,
P.O.B. 6125 Etterstad, 0602 Oslo 6
Tel. (02) 67.83.10, (02) 68.40.20

PAKISTAN
Mirza Book Agency
65 Shahrah Quaid-E-Azam, Lahore 3 Tel. 66839

PHILIPPINES
I.J. Sagun Enterprises, Inc.
P.O. Box 4322 CPO Manila
Tel. 695-1946, 922-9495

PORTUGAL
Livraria Portugal,
Rua do Carmo 70-74,
1117 Lisboa Codex   Tel. 360582/3

**SINGAPORE/MALAYSIA -
SINGAPOUR/MALAISIE**
See "Malaysia/Singapor". Voir
«Malaisie/Singapour»

SPAIN - ESPAGNE
Mundi-Prensa Libros, S.A.,
Castelló 37, Apartado 1223, Madrid-28001
Tel. 431.33.99
Libreria Bosch, Ronda Universidad 11,
Barcelona 7   Tel. 317.53.08/317.53.58

SWEDEN - SUÈDE
AB CE Fritzes Kungl. Hovbokhandel,
Box 16356, S 103 27 STH,
Regeringsgatan 12,
DS Stockholm   Tel. (08) 23.89.00
Subscription Agency/Abonnements:
Wennergren-Williams AB,
Box 30004, S104 25 Stockholm Tel. (08)54.12.00

SWITZERLAND - SUISSE
OECD Publications and Information Centre,
4 Simrockstrasse,
5300 Bonn (Germany)   Tel. (0228) 21.60.45
Librairie Payot,
6 rue Grenus, 1211 Genève 11
Tel. (022) 31.89.50
United Nations Bookshop/Librairie des Nations-
Unies
Palais des Nations,
1211 - Geneva 10
Tel. 022-34-60-11 (ext. 48 72)

TAIWAN - FORMOSE
Good Faith Worldwide Int'l Co., Ltd.
9th floor, No. 118, Sec.2
Chung Hsiao E. Road
Taipei   Tel. 391.7396/391.7397

THAILAND - THAILANDE
Suksit Siam Co., Ltd., 1715 Rama IV Rd.,
Samyam Bangkok 5   Tel. 2511630
INDEX Book Promotion & Service Ltd.
59/6 Soi Lang Suan, Ploenchit Road
Patjumawan, Bangkok 10500
Tel. 250-1919, 252-1066

TURKEY - TURQUIE
Kültur Yayinlari Is-Türk Ltd. Sti.
Atatürk Bulvari No: 191/Kat. 21
Kavaklidere/Ankara   Tel. 25.07.60
Dolmabahce Cad No: 29
Besiktas/Istanbul   Tel. 160.71.88

UNITED KINGDOM - ROYAUME-UNI
H.M. Stationery Office,
Postal orders only: (01)211-5656
P.O.B. 276, London SW8 5DT
Telephone orders: (01) 622.3316, or
Personal callers:
49 High Holborn, London WC1V 6HB
Branches at: Belfast, Birmingham,
Bristol, Edinburgh, Manchester

UNITED STATES - ÉTATS-UNIS
OECD Publications and Information Centre,
2001 L Street, N.W., Suite 700,
Washington, D.C. 20036 - 4095
Tel. (202) 785.6323

VENEZUELA
Libreria del Este,
Avda F. Miranda 52, Aptdo. 60337,
Edificio Galipan, Caracas 106
Tel. 951.17.05/951.23.07/951.12.97

YUGOSLAVIA - YOUGOSLAVIE
Jugoslovenska Krjiga, Knez Mihajlova 2,
P.O.B. 36, Beograd   Tel. 621.992

Orders and inquiries from countries where
Distributors have not yet been appointed should be
sent to:
OECD, Publications Service, 2, rue André-Pascal,
75775 PARIS CEDEX 16.

Les commandes provenant de pays où l'OCDE n'a
pas encore désigné de distributeur doivent être
adressées à :
OCDE, Service des Publications, 2, rue André-
Pascal, 75775 PARIS CEDEX 16.

71784-07-1988

OECD PUBLICATIONS, 2, rue André-Pascal, 75775 PARIS CEDEX 16 - No. 44575 1988
PRINTED IN FRANCE
(44 88 01 1) ISBN 92-64-13157-4